OECD Food and Agricultural Reviews

Agricultural Policies in Argentina

AF212480

OECD
BETTER POLICIES FOR BETTER LIVES

This work is published under the responsibility of the Secretary-General of the OECD. The opinions expressed and arguments employed herein do not necessarily reflect the official views of OECD member countries.

This document, as well as any data and any map included herein, are without prejudice to the status of or sovereignty over any territory, to the delimitation of international frontiers and boundaries and to the name of any territory, city or area.

Please cite this publication as:
OECD (2019), *Agricultural Policies in Argentina*, OECD Food and Agricultural Reviews, OECD Publishing, Paris.
https://doi.org/10.1787/9789264311695-en

ISBN 978-92-64-31168-8 (print)
ISBN 978-92-64-31169-5 (pdf)

Series: OECD Food and Agricultural Reviews
ISSN 2411-426X (print)
ISSN 2411-4278 (online)

The statistical data for Israel are supplied by and under the responsibility of the relevant Israeli authorities. The use of such data by the OECD is without prejudice to the status of the Golan Heights, East Jerusalem and Israeli settlements in the West Bank under the terms of international law.

Photo credits: Cover © Meichtry E. Martin.

Corrigenda to OECD publications may be found on line at: *www.oecd.org/about/publishing/corrigenda.htm*.

© OECD 2019

You can copy, download or print OECD content for your own use, and you can include excerpts from OECD publications, databases and multimedia products in your own documents, presentations, blogs, websites and teaching materials, provided that suitable acknowledgement of OECD as source and copyright owner is given. All requests for public or commercial use and translation rights should be submitted to *rights@oecd.org*. Requests for permission to photocopy portions of this material for public or commercial use shall be addressed directly to the Copyright Clearance Center (CCC) at *info@copyright.com* or the Centre français d'exploitation du droit de copie (CFC) at *contact@cfcopies.com*.

Foreword

The *Review of Agricultural Policies in Argentina* is one in a series of reviews on national agricultural policies undertaken by the OECD Committee for Agriculture (CoAg). It has been prepared by the OECD Trade and Agriculture Directorate in collaboration with the Secretariat of Agroindustry of the Government of Argentina. The *Review* examines key trends and policy issues that have shaped the development of Argentina's agricultural sector over the last two decades and presents a quantitative evaluation of support provided through Argentina's domestic and trade policies. The *Review* classifies and measures the support provided to agriculture using the methodology that the OECD employs to monitor agricultural policies in all OECD countries and a growing number of non-member economies, including Brazil, the People's Republic of China, Colombia, Costa Rica, India, Indonesia, Kazakhstan, the Philippines, the Russian Federation, South Africa, Ukraine, and Viet Nam. The *Review* is the first step in the inclusion of Argentina in the annual OECD *Agricultural Policy Monitoring and Evaluation* report. The *Review* also features discussion of issues in the Argentine agriculture sector under the main areas of work of the CoAg, such as innovation, productivity, sustainability, risk management and value chains.

The OECD team for the *Review* comprised Jesús Antón (project lead), Dalila Cervantes-Godoy, Santiago Guerrero and Florence Bossard [who undertook the Producer Support Estimate (PSEs) analysis]. The Argentine team in the Secretary of Agroindustry comprised Simona Paulero, Maximiliano Moreno, Gerardo Petri and Santiago Bonifacio. Additionally, valuable inputs were provided by Veronica Barrenechea, Norma Dobano, Alexandro Jara Podesta, Nicolas Lucas, Gisela Margot Mair, Consolacion Otaño, Joaquin Daniel Perez Martin and Jose Posse, all from the Secretariat of Agroindustry in Argentina. The *Review* benefited from background reports from the following Argentinian experts: Esteban Barelli, Mercedes Ciampi, Miguel Fusco, Marcos Gallacher, Eduardo Trigo, and Daniel Lema, who also contributed to the PSE calculations. Anita Lari and Michèle Patterson of the OECD provided publication support.

The OECD team also received inputs and contributions from Hubertus Gay, Catherine Moreddu, Urszula Ziebinska, and Karine Souvanheuane of the OECD Trade and Agriculture Directorate. Early drafts of the Review benefited from comments by Carmel Cahill, Ken Ash, Julia Nielson, Guillaume Gruère, Franck Jesus, Vaclav Vojtech, Frank van Tongeren, Martin von Lampe (all from the Trade and Agriculture Directorate, OECD), Jens Arnold and Robert Grundke (from the Economics Department, OECD), Bert Brys (from the Centre for Tax Policy, OECD), and Richard Sigman (from the Environment Department, OECD).

The *Review* was discussed at the 171th session of the OECD CoAg in November 2018. The Argentine delegation was led by Secretary of Government of Agroindustry Luis Miguel Etchevehere. Lead discussants for the report were Ms. Louise Van Meurs, First Assistant Secretary, Department of Agriculture, Australia; Esperanza Orellana, Director General of Production and Markets, Ministry of Agriculture, Fisheries and Food, Spain;

and Rodrigo Vega, Agricultural Attaché, Mission of Chile to the European Union. A first draft of the *Review* had previously been discussed on 31 July 2018 in Buenos Aires at a roundtable chaired by Santiago del Solar Dorrego, Chief of Staff of Agroindustry, with the participation of Argentinian officials as well as experts from the government, academia and the private sector.

The OECD is grateful to the Government of Argentina and Argentinian experts for their engagement and contributions throughout the review process.

Table of contents

Foreword 3

Acronyms 11

Executive summary 15

Note 18

Chapter 1. Assessment and policy recommendations 19

1.1. A history of successful innovation against the odds 20
1.2. Policy assessment 25
1.3. Policy challenges and recommendations 29
References 36
Notes 36

Chapter 2. The context of Argentinian agriculture 37

2.1. An economy marked by the strength of the agricultural exporting sector 38
2.2. An upper-middle income country with high urban poverty 39
2.3. Dynamic grain and oilseed production but other sectors lagging 42
2.4. A changing export profile and participation in value chains 46
2.5. The farming sector is dominated by big farms in the Pampas region 50
References 52
Notes 53

Chapter 3. Agricultural policy framework and objectives 54

3.1. A history of back and forths on trade openness 55
3.2. Institutional arrangements 57
3.3. Overview of the main agricultural policy areas 61
References 64
Notes 64

Chapter 4. Benchmarking agricultural policies: PSE results 65

4.1. Introduction 66
4.2. Unlike most other countries Argentina has negative producer support 66
4.3. Most negative producer support is a reflection of highly distorting export taxes 68
4.4. Support is provided to first buyers of primary agricultural products 71
4.5. Argentina provides significant support for general services for agriculture 72
4.6. Support to the agricultural sector as a whole is still negative 73
References 78

Chapter 5. Export taxes generate distortions and negative support to the sector 79

5.1. Introduction 80
5.2. Export tax rates have been high and unpredictable 80
5.3. Export taxes have been a significant source of revenue for the federal government 83

5.4. Quantitative restrictions on exports created additional disincentives ... 85
5.5. Export restrictions distorted production without controlling food inflation ... 87
5.6. Import tariffs have played only a secondary role for agricultural commodities ... 88
5.7. Overall policy assessment and recommendations ... 89
References ... 92
Notes ... 94

Chapter 6. Innovation success and the need for modernisation ... 95

6.1. Introduction ... 96
6.2. Impressive productivity performance, but innovation duality ... 96
6.3. The rapid adoption of a new technological package for crops ... 98
6.4. The changing role of different actors in the national innovation system ... 102
6.5. The National Institute of Agricultural Technology (INTA) ... 106
6.6. Public and private investment in innovation ... 108
6.7. Knowledge flows: Extension and entrepreneurship ... 111
6.8. Intellectual Property Rights and international co-operation ... 113
6.9. Overall policy assessment and recommendations ... 114
References ... 117
Notes ... 120

Chapter 7. Sustainability of Argentina's agricultural transformation ... 121

7.1. Potential environmental impacts of the technological package for crops ... 122
7.2. Agri-environmental indicators reveal lower environmental pressures than in the OECD ... 123
7.3. Potentially mild impacts of climate change on agriculture, but higher frequency of extreme events ... 129
7.4. Agri-environmental policies ... 129
7.5. Policy assessment and recommendations ... 135
References ... 137
Notes ... 139

Chapter 8. Managing agricultural risks in a volatile environment ... 141

8.1. Introduction ... 142
8.2. Risk assessment ... 142
8.3. Farmers' strategies and retention of risks at farm level ... 144
8.4. Risk transfer and pooling through markets and private arrangements ... 147
8.5. Coping with catastrophic risks ... 152
8.6. Managing plant and animal health ... 153
8.7. Assessment and recommendations ... 154
References ... 157
Notes ... 158

Chapter 9. Value chains in Argentina: Apples and pears, and viticulture ... 159

9.1. Introduction ... 160
9.2. The apple-and-pear value chain ... 161
9.3. The viticulture value chain ... 170
9.4. Policy assessment and recommendations on value chains ... 179
References ... 182
Notes ... 183

Annex A. Main agro-industrial organisations in Argentina ... 184

Annex B. Argentina's main agricultural products 189
Annex C. OECD indicators of support to agriculture 192
Annex D. Argentina: Estimates of support to agriculture 194

Tables

Table 1.1. Contextual indicators, multiple years 20
Table 2.1. Contextual indicators of Argentina's agricultural sector 39
Table 2.2. Agriculture backward and forward linkage with value chains 50
Table 2.3. Farm structure and farm area in 2002 50
Table 3.1. Main developments in agricultural policies 55
Table 4.1. Argentina: Estimates of support to agriculture (provisional), USD million 70
Table 4.2. Market Price Support calculations in Argentina's PSEs 77
Table 5.1. Tariffs on imports by product groups 89
Table 6.1. R&D outcomes, 2006-11 115
Table 7.1. National agri-environmental performance compared to the OECD average 124
Table 7.2. Imports of pesticide active substance 126
Table 7.3. Characteristics of main agri-environmental policies in Argentina 132
Table 8.1. Main risk management strategies reported by farmers in Argentina 145
Table 8.2. Emergency resolutions by year 153
Table 9.1. Size distribution of producers and number of apple and pear producers 162
Table 9.2. Average yields 2002-12, selected countries 162
Table 9.3. Apple and pear prices along the value chain (USD/kg), 2015 165
Table 9.4. Apple and pear export firms in Argentina, 2015 166
Table 9.5. Competitiveness in apple and pear production, ranking, 2010 167
Table 9.6. SWOT analysis of the apples and pears value chain, 2018 169
Table 9.7. Vineyards and planted area, 2015 170
Table 9.8. Grapevine farms structure, 2016 170
Table 9.9. SWOT analysis of the viticulture value chain, 2018 178

Table A B.1. Main products produced in each province 191
Table A D.1. Estimates of support to agriculture, ARS million 194

Figures

Figure 1.1. Evolution of crop production 23
Figure 1.2. Argentina's agro-food trade 23
Figure 1.3. Agriculture and economy-wide R&D intensity in selected countries 24
Figure 1.4. Environmental pressures from agriculture in Argentina 24
Figure 1.5. Level and composition of Producer Support Estimate in Argentina, 1997-2017 25
Figure 2.1. Inequality in Argentina and selected Latin American countries (Gini coefficient) 40
Figure 2.2. National urban poverty rates, selected points in time 41
Figure 2.3. Evolution of hectares in selected uses, 1990-2015 42
Figure 2.4. Evolution of production of selected crops and livestock products, 1980-2016 43
Figure 2.5. Contribution of selected commodities to agricultural value of production, 2015-17 44
Figure 2.6. Total Factor Productivity of agriculture in Argentina 45
Figure 2.7. Argentina's agro-food trade: Exports, imports and trade balance 46
Figure 2.8. Share of main commodities in Argentina's agro-food exports 47

Figure 2.9. Growth in commodity production in Argentina (annual average growth rates) 48
Figure 2.10. Share of Argentina's agro-food exports by country of destination 49
Figure 3.1. Organigram of the Secretariat of Agroindustry of Argentina 58
Figure 3.2. The institutional agricultural framework of Argentina 60
Figure 4.1. Producer Support Estimate (PSE) in Argentina and selected countries, 2015-17.............. 67
Figure 4.2. Level and composition of Producer Support Estimate in Argentina, 1997-2017 68
Figure 4.3. Level and composition of budgetary transfers to producers in Argentina, 1997-2017....... 69
Figure 4.4. Consumer Support Estimate (CSE) in Argentina and selected countries, 2015-17 72
Figure 4.5. Level and composition of General Services Support Estimate (GSSE) in Argentina, 1997-2017 73
Figure 4.6. Level and composition of Total Support Estimate in Argentina, 1997-2017 74
Figure 4.7. Total Support Estimate in Argentina and selected countries, 2015-17 75
Figure 5.1. Export tax rates in Argentina 80
Figure 5.2. Level and composition of Market Price Support (MPS) in Argentina.............................. 82
Figure 5.3. Export tax escalation 82
Figure 5.4. Revenue from export taxes 83
Figure 5.5. Wheat price differentials: Export taxes vs quantitative restrictions.................................. 86
Figure 5.6. Single Commodity Transfers, Argentina and all countries, 2000-02 and 2015-17............ 86
Figure 5.7. Consumer transfers 87
Figure 6.1. Evolution of total production (in tonnes) and cultivated land (in hectares) of total oilseeds and cereals, 1900-2016 97
Figure 6.2. Adoption rate of no-tillage and soybean GMO 98
Figure 6.3. Number of new conventional and genetically modified cultivars registered at the National Register of Cultivars (RNC), 1996-2017 101
Figure 6.4. Fertiliser consumption in Argentina.. 102
Figure 6.5. The Argentinian agricultural innovation system 104
Figure 6.6. Human resources of INTA 107
Figure 6.7. Public R&D investments by socio-economic objective, 2015 109
Figure 6.8. GSSE expenditures on agricultural knowledge and innovation system 110
Figure 6.9. Agriculture and economy-wide R&D intensity in selected countries 110
Figure 7.1. Environmental pressures from agriculture are increasing in Argentina 124
Figure 7.2. Fertiliser use shows a positive trend in Argentina 125
Figure 7.3. Pesticide intensity in cropland is higher in Argentina than in other countries 126
Figure 7.4. Annual deforestation rates in Argentina are high relative to the world and the Latin American region 127
Figure 7.5. Agri-environmental policies in Argentina 131
Figure 7.6. There is room for improving current agri-environmental regulations 133
Figure 8.1. Climatic map: Precipitation and temperature, average values (1981-2010) 143
Figure 8.2. Intensity and frequency of not reaching the breakeven yield.. 146
Figure 8.3. Financial markets are hardly developed.. 148
Figure 8.4. Insurance penetration by crop 149
Figure 8.5. Volume traded in Argentinian futures markets 150
Figure 8.6. GSSE expenditures on inspection and control 154
Figure 8.7. Main agricultural risk management strategies and policies 156
Figure 9.1. Argentina's apple-and-pear value chain... 162
Figure 9.2. Grapes, wine and must production.. 171
Figure 9.3. Value chain of table wines 174
Figure 9.4. Value chain of fine wines.. 175
Figure 9.5. Argentina wine exports 176
Figure 9.6. Wine export price as a proportion of French wine export prices 177

Boxes

Box 1.1. Argentina: Agricultural production and agro-food trade indicators 23
Box 1.2. Argentina: Agricultural innovation and environmental indicators 24
Box 1.3. Economic turbulences and policy developments affecting Argentina's agricultural sector in 2018 35
Box 2.1. The agricultural outlook for Argentina: Beef is back to growth 47
Box 2.2. Official statistics in Argentina 51
Box 3.1. The Belgrano Plan 57
Box 3.2. The Special Tobacco Fund (FET) 62
Box 4.1. Calculation of PSE for Argentina 75

Follow OECD Publications on:

http://twitter.com/OECD_Pubs

http://www.facebook.com/OECDPublications

http://www.linkedin.com/groups/OECD-Publications-4645871

http://www.youtube.com/oecdilibrary

OECD Alerts http://www.oecd.org/oecddirect/

This book has...

StatLinks
A service that delivers Excel® files from the printed page!

Look for the *StatLinks* at the bottom of the tables or graphs in this book. To download the matching Excel® spreadsheet, just type the link into your Internet browser, starting with the *http://dx.doi.org* prefix, or click on the link from the e-book edition.

Acronyms

AACREA	Argentine Association of Regional Consortia for Agricultural Experimentation
AAPRESID	Argentine Association of No-till Farming
ACA	Argentine Cooperatives Association
ACSOJA	Argentine Soybean Chain Association
AFA	Argentine Federated Farmers
AFIP	Federal Public Revenue Agency
AIS	Agricultural Innovation System
AMS	Aggregate Measure of Support
ANPCYT	National Agency for the Promotion of Science and Technology
APEA	Argentine Exporting Producers Association
ARGENTRIGO	Argentine Wheat Association
ARS	Argentine peso
ASAGIR	Argentine Sunflower Association
ASTI	Agricultural Science and Technology Indicators
BCRA	Central Bank of the Argentine Republic
BN	*Banco Nación*
C	Carbon
CAME	Argentine Confederation of Medium-sized Enterprises
CASAFE	Chamber of Animal and Plant Health and Fertilisers
CEPAL	Economic Commission for Latin America and the Caribbean
CET	Common External Tariff
CETA	Consortia for Agricultural Technology Experimentation
CFA	Agriculture and Livestock Council
CFA	Federal Agricultural Council
CIAFA	Chamber of the Argentine Industry of Fertilisers and Agro-chemicals
CIF	Cost, Insurance and Freight
CIL	Dairy Industry Center
CONABIA	National Advisory Commission on Agricultural Biotechnology
CONICET	National Scientific and Technical Research Council
CONINAGRO	Argentine Rural Confederation

COPAL	Coordinator of Food Industries
CoViAr	Argentine Viticulture Corporation
CPI	Consumer Price Index
CRA	Argentine Rural Confederations
CREA	Regional Consortium for Agricultural Experiments
CSE	Consumer Support Estimate
DJVE	Sworn Statement of Sales Abroad
DP	Dissolved Phosphorus
EMBRAPA	Brazilian Agricultural Research Corporation
EM-DAT	Emergency Events Database
ENSO	*El Niño* Southern Oscillation
EUV	Export Unit Value
FAA	Argentine Farming Federation
FERTILIZAR	Fertilise Civil Association
FET	Special Tobacco Fund
FINAGRO	Fund for the Financing of the Agricultural Sector
FINEP	Brazilian Innovation Agency (Funding Authority for Studies and Projects)
FONCYT	Fund for Scientific and Technological Research
FONDAGRO	National Agro-Industry Fund
FONDEF	Fund for the Promotion of Scientific and Technological Development (Chile)
FONEDA	National Fund for the Mitigation of Agricultural Emergencies and Disasters
FONTAR	Argentine Technological Fund
GDP	Gross Domestic Product
GHG	Greenhouse Gas
GM	Genetically Modified
GM-NT	Genetically Modified, No-Till
GMO	Genetically Modified Organism
GSSE	General Services Support Estimate
GVC	Global Value Chain
IADB	Inter-American Development Bank
ICT	Information and Communication Technology
ICTSD	International Centre for Trade and Sustainable Development
INASE	National Institute of Seeds
INDEC	National Institute of Statistics and Censuses
INIDEP	National Institute of Fishing Research and Development
INIFAP	National Institute in Forestry, Agriculture and Livestock Research
INPI	National Institute of Industrial Property

INTA	National Institute of Agricultural Technology
INTI	National Institute of Industrial Technology
INV	National Wine Institute
IP	Intellectual Property
IPCVA	Institute for the Promotion of Argentine Beef
IPR	Intellectual Property Rights
LULUCF	Land use, land-use change and forestry
MAIZAR	Argentine Maize Association
MATBA	*Mercado a Término de Buenos Aires* (Buenos Aires Futures Exchange)
MERCOSUR	Southern Common Market
MFN	Most Favoured Nation
MINCYT	Ministry of Science, Technology and Productive Innovation
MPS	Market Price Support
N	Nitrogen
NAC	Nominal Assistance Coefficient
NDC	Nationally Determined Contributions
NDVI	Normalised Difference Vegetation Index
NGO	Non-Government Organisation
NPC	Nominal Protection Coefficient
NT	No-till
OECD	Organisation for Economic Co-operation and Development
ONCCA	National Office of Agricultural Trade Control
P	Phosphorus
PAC	Conservationist Agriculture Project
PBR	Plant Breeders' Rights
PEVI	Strategic Viticulture Plan
POA	Annual Operative Project
POC	Particulate Organic Carbon
POS	Point of Sale
PP	Particulate Phosphorus
PROFAM	Project for Family Strengthening and Social Capital Promotion
PROFEDER	Federal Programme for the Support of Sustainable Rural Development
PROSAP	Provincial Agricultural Services Programme
PSE	Producer Support Estimate
PTM	Program for Technological Modernization
R&D	Research and Development
RAICES	Network of Argentine Researchers and Scientists Abroad

RER	Real Exchange Rate
RIAN	National Agricultural Information Network
RNC	National Register of Cultivars
ROE	Export Operation Register
ROFEX	*Mercado a Término de Rosario* (Rosario Futures Exchange)
ROI	Import Operation Register
S	Sulphur
SAGyP	Secretariat of Agriculture, Livestock and Fisheries
SCT	Single Commodity Transfer
SENASA	National Service for Agri-Food Health and Quality
SIGLeA	Integrated System for Milk Production Management in Argentina
SIO-Granos	Unified System of Compulsory Information on Grain Trade Operations
SME	Small and Medium-sized Enterprise
SMN	National Meteorological Service
SOG	Soil Organic Carbon
SOM	Soil Organic Matter
SPS	Sanitary and Phytosanitary Measures
SRA	Argentine Rural Society
ST&I	Science, Technology and Innovation
TAD	Distance Procedures Platform
TFP	Total Factor Productivity
TiVA	Trade in Value Added
TRIPS	Agreement on Trade-Related Aspects of Intellectual Property Rights
TSE	Total Support Estimate
UPOV	International Union for the Protection of New Varieties of Plants
USDA	United States Department of Agriculture
VUCE	Single Foreign Trade Desk
WTO	World Trade Organization

Executive summary

The Argentinian agro-food sector has grown and innovated remarkably in the last three decades, driven by technological change and, over much of the period, by high international agricultural prices. An upper-middle income country, well-endowed with natural resources and human capital, Argentina has a history of macroeconomic volatility and policy instability that has contributed to its long term overall poor economic performance. Despite challenges, agriculture is the country's main exporting sector and an exception in terms of performance. Agriculture in the extended Pampas region has experienced a major structural transformation involving crops, manly cereals and soybeans, productivity growth and new on-farm practices, technologies, institutions and contractual arrangements. Land use and production have significantly changed in favour of soybeans, and exports have shifted towards China and other Asian economies. Meanwhile, other products in other regions have under-performed: agricultural goods produced outside the Pampas region such as vegetables, fruits, cotton and tobacco have experienced lower productivity growth rates.

Argentinian agricultural policies have been subject to cyclical variations in trade policies: an open economy approach in the 1990s, including the signature of WTO and MERCOSUR agreements; economic isolationism and import substitution policies, with tariffs and export taxes in 2001-15; and a renewed open economy approach following the change of government in 2015. Despite these shifts in policy, several decentralised institutions responsible for implementing agricultural policies and services have a long tradition of competence and stability. Among these, the National Institute of Agricultural Technology (INTA) provides important general services in research and extension, and the National Service for Agro-Food Health and Quality (SENASA) does so in animal and plant health. There are almost no input or output subsidies paid to producers in Argentina, nor direct payments based on area or animal numbers. Exceptions are the programmes under the Special Tobacco Fund (FET), preferential credit mainly to small producers through FINAGRO, and infrastructure programmes such as the Agricultural Provincial Services Programme (PROSAP).

Conversely, Argentina's policies have burdened the agro-food exporting sector over most of the last two decades, mainly through the use of export taxes. The producer support estimate (PSE) was negative at -14% in 2015-17 and as low as -51% in 2008. This negative value is an outlier compared to OECD countries, which usually have positive support values. Beginning in 2015, the current administration reduced export taxes for soybean and eliminated them for all other farm products, reducing the absolute value of the negative PSE. However, a new tax on all exports, agricultural and non-agricultural, was introduced in 2018.[1] Argentina's PSE is therefore likely to remain negative over the next few years. Most of Argentina's budgetary support to the sector finances general services such as the Knowledge and Innovation system and inspection services that are part of the General Services Support Estimate (GSSE). The Total Support Estimate (TSE) remains negative as spending is much smaller than the negative support created by taxing agricultural exports.

Export restrictions and taxes on soybean, sunflower, wheat, corn, beef, milk and poultry have reduced producer prices for these commodities, while export taxes have typically been lower for processed products. Although their stated intention, quantitative restriction and export licences on food products such as wheat and beef have had only a small impact in reducing food inflation. However, agricultural export taxes were effective in generating revenue for the federal government. Those revenues reached their peak during years of high food commodity prices – up to 3% of GDP in 2008. Pervasive use of export taxes is at least partly explained by the fact that they are the only federal tax whose revenue is not shared with the provincial governments.

Argentinian agriculture has gone through notable innovation in recent decades although progress was uneven across regions. While regions outside the Pampas showed low dynamism, the Pampas region has experienced a remarkable increase in the amount of arable land cultivated and in crop total factor productivity (TFP) with the adoption of new technologies such as no-tillage and genetically modified varieties, and the expansion of the production of soybeans. Innovations have also affected organisational structures with new actors such as large service contractors, sowing pools and farmers' innovation associations. Innovation was mainly led by the private sector responding to economic incentives, with general support on research and extension from INTA. However, Argentina benefited from exploiting genetic innovations under very advantageous conditions – such as no royalties on key varieties – that are unlikely to recur.

The innovative process and the expansion of the agricultural frontier has opened up new opportunities for the sector but has also increased environmental pressures. For most agri-environmental indicators these pressures are still lower than in OECD countries. However, deforestation rates are still high and a matter of concern and the use of pesticides has risen. In the context of strong export demand and reducing export taxes on the principal export commodities, legislation like the Native Forest Law (Law 26.331) has not been able to contain deforestation, and better environmental practices are needed.

Volatile macroeconomic conditions, policy instability and an underdeveloped financial sector create a difficult environment for the management of risks in Argentina. Currently, ex post disaster support under the Agricultural Emergencies Law and the plant and animal health services provided by SENASA are the only public risk management policies available. This has actually favored the development of private institutions and market initiatives such as insurance, futures and contracts. More recently, some provinces have piloted limited support to insurance.

Public policy has not addressed key production problems outside the Pampas region ('regional economies'), and public investment in agricultural infrastructure, R&D, extension and technical assistance in these areas has been limited. In particular, the apple-and-pear value chain in Argentina contains a dual structure, where fully integrated farms (usually large and medium-size) coexist with less integrated ones (mostly small-scale). Small-scale apple and pear farms suffer from low technology levels, deficient pest control, old orchards, and, in general, very limited investments at farm level. By contrast, the viticulture value chain has seen significant investment and dynamism since the 1990s. Both foreign and local investors have been attracted by deregulation in agroindustry and by the relatively low land prices and good soil quality; nonetheless, the wine sector still experiences constraints arising from limited research and development, training and extension services.

Looking ahead, Argentinian agriculture confronts several policy challenges, many of which are economy-wide: the scarcity of financial services, deficiencies in public investment in infrastructure, and the deterioration of statistical information in the period 2007-15. The overall policy approach to agriculture needs to be rebalanced towards stability and sustainability. Trade policies in the form of export restrictions have created negative price support, uncertainty and distortions that negatively affect production and investment. The agricultural innovation system needs to modernise its institutions, better monitor its results, refocus on environmental sustainability and "regional economies" and make Intellectual Property Rights (IPR) enforceable. With environmental pressures growing, producers need to take more responsibility for reducing negative externalities (Polluter-Pays-Principle PPP). Market-based risk management tools exist, but policies should focus more holistically on preparedness and prevention. Finally, public policies should facilitate innovation and adjustment in the less developed value chains and regions outside the Pampas.

The report suggests the following recommendations to improve agricultural policies in Argentina:

1. Agricultural policy could be better anchored in broad legislation, such as a specific framework law and an economy-wide reform of the tax system, gradually reversing the policy bias against the agricultural sector (negative PSE) and moving towards a more neutral, stable, predictable and targeted policy package.
2. As part of an ongoing, long-term, comprehensive tax reform, phase out export taxes on agriculture, integrate the sector into a reformed economy wide tax system, and enhance policy certainty. In the current environment it will be crucial to find the right balance between the long-term objective of phasing out export taxes and the current short term needs to raise fiscal revenues.
3. Undertake an in-depth evaluation of the negative externalities associated with different types of pesticides, their level of application and impact at specific locations and hotspots, with a view to implementing targeted measures to better manage the use of pesticides. Apply best environmental and agricultural practices, in particular on pesticide use and crop rotation.
4. Undertake an in-depth independent evaluation of the Native Forest Law to analyse its effectiveness in stemming deforestation and take the appropriate legal and budgetary decisions to strengthen its enforcement.
5. Develop a systematic method and process to measure and monitor Argentinian R&D and innovation, and to define and implement strategic priorities.
6. Undertake an in-depth evaluation of INTA with a view to an eventual re-organisation of its different lines of action: research, extension and rural development.
7. Strengthen the holistic policy approach to risk management, investing in prevention and preparedness and improving the predictability and monitoring of disaster assistance.
8. Budget permitting, support the search for new markets for wine and pears and apples and other viable products produced in the regional economies, through active policies such as agricultural promotion agencies and trade agreements beyond MERCOSUR.
9. Reform the Special Tobacco Fund (FET), eliminating output payments and targeting investment to human and physical capital.

10. Considering creating a system of technical assistance for innovation in specific regional economies' value chains and small-scale producers, building on INTA's capacities in agricultural R&D and extension services.

Note

[1] In early September 2018, while this review was being written, the government decided several policy measures in response to economic turmoil triggered by a large depreciation of the peso. Among these measures, the introduction of temporary taxes on all exports will directly affect the agricultural sector and the estimate of support (Box 1.3).

Chapter 1. Assessment and policy recommendations

Argentina's agriculture sector has gone through a notable innovation process in the last two decades. This transformation was mainly led by the private sector in a context of policies that significantly tax producers but support large public investments on general services such as research, extension and animal and plant health. The Review of Agricultural Policies in Argentina is a comprehensive analysis of the agricultural sector and its transformation, and of the role of public policies in facilitating innovation, risk management and the development of value chains, while contributing to resource sustainability. Based on the analysis in other chapters, this chapter assesses the main challenges for the sector and provides policy recommendations.

1.1. A history of successful innovation against the odds

Argentina is well-endowed with natural resources but has historically suffered from unstable policies that have hindered its economic performance

Argentina is an upper-middle income country well-endowed with natural resources and human capital, including for farming. The macroeconomic volatility that characterised Argentina's history in the last century have negatively affected long term growth, population wellbeing and income distribution. Since December 2015, the current administration has committed to promoting the agro-industrial sector as an engine of sustainable growth. It has already taken important steps to ease trade restrictions, through the elimination of most agricultural export restrictions and a gradual reduction of the export tax for soybean. In response to the economic turmoil in September 2018, the government has introduced a tax on all exports until 31 December 2020. (Box 1.3)[1].

Table 1.1. Contextual indicators, multiple years

	1995	2000	2005	2010	2016[1]	OECD 2016
Economic context						
GDP (billion USD in PPPs)	354	438	541	756	874	54 075
Population (million)	35	37	39	41	44	1 284
Land area (thousand km^2)	2 737	2 737	2 737	2 737	2 737	34 404
Agricultural area (AA) (thousand ha)	128 045	128 510	137 798	147 481	148 700	1 225 182
Population density (inhabitants/km^2)	13	14	14	15	16	37
GDP per capita (USD in PPPs)	10 130	11 810	13 818	18 334	19 934	42 104
Trade as % of GDP[2]	16	18	35	29	21	40
Agriculture in the economy						
Agriculture in GDP (%)	6	5	9	9	8	2
Agriculture share in employment (%)	1	1	1	3	2	5
Agro-food exports (% of total exports)	53	45	47	51	64	10
Agro-food imports (% of total imports)	6	6	3	3	4	9
Characteristics of the agricultural sector						
Crops in total agricultural production[3] (%)	62	58	57	58	62	n.a.
Livestock in total agricultural production[3] (%)	38	42	43	42	38	n.a.
Share of arable land in AA (%)	21	22	24	26	26	32

n.a.: not applicable.

1. Or latest year available.
2. Ratio of the sum of exports and imports to GDP.
3. The column on OECD 2016 represents total for OECD countries for the variables that measure absolute values (GDP, population, land and area) and OECD average for the rest.

Source: Authors' calculations based on (WDI, 2018[1]) and Comtrade database (UN, 2018[2]).

Despite a difficult policy context, the agricultural sector has grown, driven originally by high commodity prices and then by innovation in oilseeds and grains

Argentina is a large net exporter of agricultural products such as soybean, wheat, corn, sunflower, sorghum, rice, beef and milk. Despite public policies hampering the sector for many years, agriculture is in general well developed, with high levels of productivity. Agricultural production has grown at an annual rate of 2.8% in the last two decades, driven originally by high world grain prices and by technological innovation as prices have fallen over the past years. Inputs used in the grain sector, including land, have grown rapidly together with Total Factor Productivity (TFP) of crops. Unfavourable public policies, particularly export taxes, are likely to have pushed the private sector to innovate in order to remain competitive and benefit from Argentina's comparative advantage in international markets (Box 1.1).

Agro-food exports quadrupled in the decade 2002-11, mainly driven by growing soybean exports to Asian countries. Soybean and its derivatives (beans, oils and cake) represented almost 50% of agro-food exports in 2015-17. China was the main trade partner, accounting for 12% of all Argentinian agro-food exports. Bovine meat production has been one of the areas most damaged by policy, with the country losing its position of leader in the international meat market. Both the livestock sector and some crops other than soybean have struggled to be competitive due to low investment and low productivity growth.

New technological packages and organisational innovations have been massively adopted

The technological transformation of agriculture in the Pampas region has been outstanding in the last three decades, with a very rapid rate of adoption of new technologies. The most important technological development include: improved seeds (particularly herbicide resistant for genetically modified soybean), no-till farming, increased use of pesticides (mainly glyphosate) and crop rotations (soybean and cereals). Only four years after introduction in the late 1990s, the Soybean RR (Roundup Ready) variety was planted on 90% of the land used for soybean.

Innovation in the organisation of production has also been rapid and massive. New contract farming schemes have flourished, many farming activities have been outsourced to large service providers, and seeding pools bringing together assets from many farmers have been created. Private sector initiatives and organisations have played a leading role in innovation and increasing productivity.

The business climate is unfavourable, with distorting export taxes and access to finance is difficult

Macroeconomic and financial instability has compromised the competitiveness of the Argentinian economy, including the agro-food sector. Some economy-wide factors have significantly constrained the agricultural sector in recent times, in particular a penalising tax system, underdeveloped domestic financial markets and low investment in infrastructure such as roads. Credit from banks to non-financial institutions represents only 18% of the economy, well below the OECD levels and those of the neighbouring countries. Contract and pooling arrangements have been an alternative financial source for rolling working capital or investment in agriculture.

Furthermore, agriculture export taxes have been used recurrently to raise government revenue and reduce prices for first consumers. These taxes are established or changed directly by federal executive decrees and, unlike other taxes, their revenues are not shared with the provinces, hence their importance for the federal government.

Environmental pressures are on the rise

Argentinian soils had been deteriorating for decades in the second half of the previous century, affecting large areas of grain production in the Pampas region. The widespread adoption of no-till farming technologies in response to this trend made Argentina a world leader in the use of these soil conservation practices, with these technologies used in 95% of its grain and oilseed production (Box 1.2). However, no-till farming as a system, needs to be combined with crop rotation, adequate fertilization and other agronomic practices.

But Argentina faces growing environmental pressures associated with the expansion of the agricultural frontier into both pasture land and native forest. The use of agro-chemicals, in particular pesticides, has grown markedly and its impact on water, air quality and health needs to be monitored. The large increase in use of fertilisers has increased nutrient balances and phosphorous runoff could become problematic if the application of fertilisers is not well managed. Despite this deterioration, most agri-environmental indicators such as water and energy use and nutrient balances reveal that these pressures are lower in Argentina than in the OECD countries on average.

Climate change is expected to have only a mild impact on Argentina's agriculture. However, evidence suggests that there has been an increase in the frequency of extreme weather events such as floods. The area of agricultural land flooded reached a historical high in 2016. A new water management infrastructure is being planned and built, including through the Belgrano Plan.

Outside the Pampas region, productivity is low and value chains are poorly developed

Total agriculture production in Argentina is dominated by extensive farming and the use of mechanisation and modern technologies in the Pampas prairies. This explains the low share of the agricultural sector in employment: at 2% in 2016, it is one of the lowest in the world, and much smaller than the sector's share of the country's GDP (8%). That said, the extended agro-food and agro-industrial sector is estimated to provide 18-35% of Argentina's total employment (Regúnaga and Tejeda Rodriguez, 2015[3]).

Agricultural production in Argentina is integrated in domestic and global value chains. The links of agriculture value added with downstream domestic and foreign sectors (forward linkages) are high: 33% of all agricultural value added ends in foreign countries, as Argentinian agricultural primary exports are widely used as inputs in other countries, and 55% is incorporated into other domestic sectors. However, the links of the agricultural sector production with the value added of input providers from global value chains (backwards linkages) are weak, with only 11% coming from other countries.

Argentina's agricultural sector has a dualistic structure where highly developed supply chains like grains coexist with less developed ones (e.g. horticulture, fruits, tobacco, wine). These products grow outside the main grain production area (Pampas), mostly in the north, south and west parts of the country, and comprise what are known as 'regional economies'. These value chains have not organised themselves or benefited from the innovation associations that have emerged in the Pampas regions and the grains sector. Unlike production in the Pampas, the regional economies have not been taxed; on the contrary, some policy support has been given to specific farmers, such as tobacco producers. However, key economic and social problems in these regions have not been widely addressed by public policy, and public investment on agricultural infrastructure, R&D, extension services and technical assistance has been limited.

Box 1.1. Argentina: Agricultural production and agro-food trade indicators

Figure 1.1. Evolution of crop production

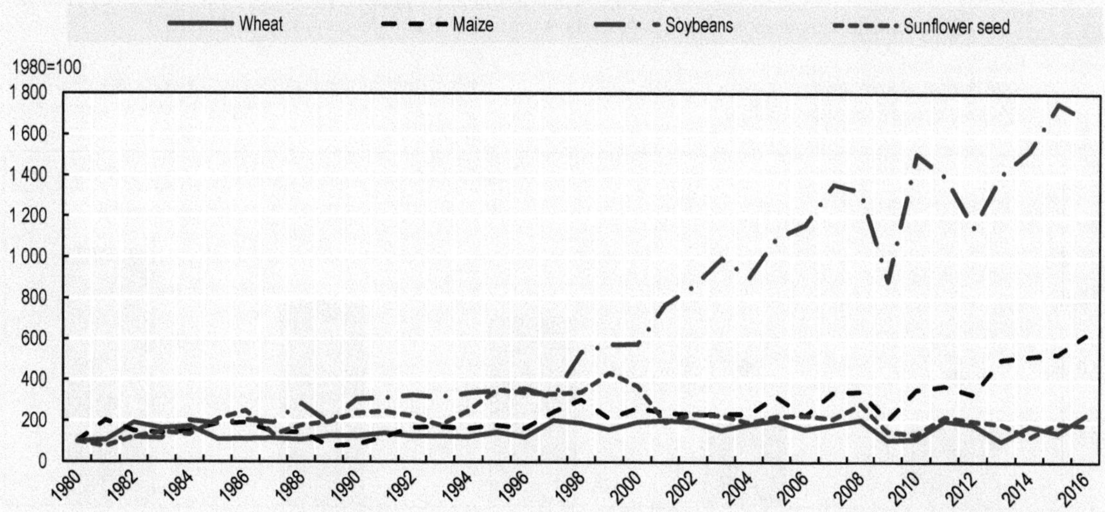

Source: FAOSTAT (FAO, 2018[4]).

StatLink https://doi.org/10.1787/888933907507

Figure 1.2. Argentina's agro-food trade

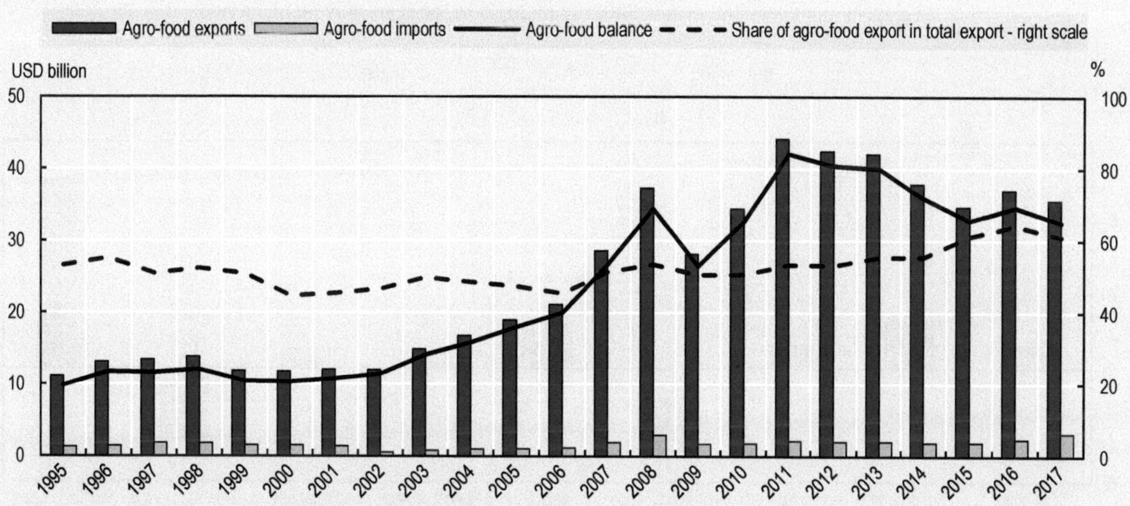

Note: Agro-food trade includes fish and fish products.
Source: Comtrade Database: (UN, 2018[2]).

StatLink https://doi.org/10.1787/888933907526

Box 1.2. Argentina: Agricultural innovation and environmental indicators

Figure 1.3. Agriculture and economy-wide R&D intensity in selected countries

Government budget appropriations or outlays for research and development (GBAORD)

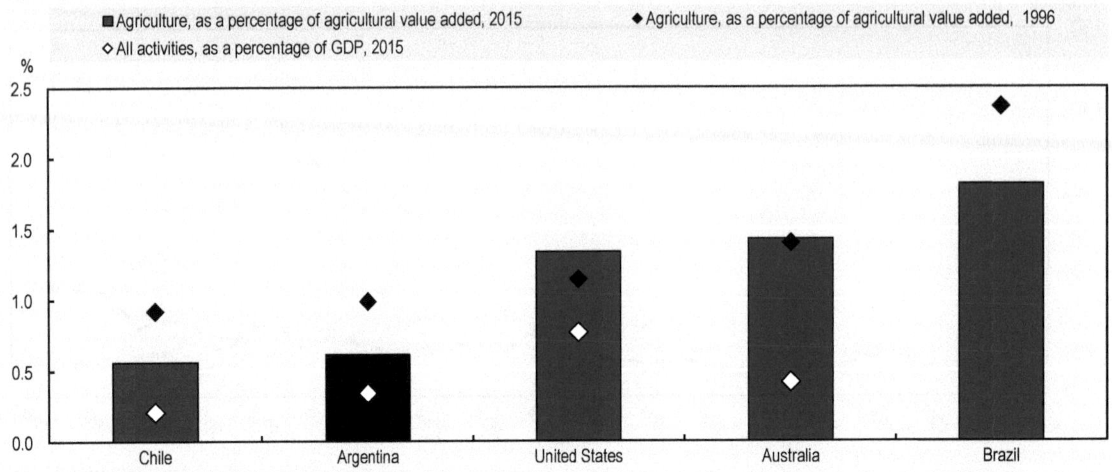

Note: 2015 and 1996 or closest available year.

Source: OECD estimates based on OECD (2018), "Research and Development Statistics" and "National Accounts", OECD Statistics (databases), http://stats.oecd.org/; For Brazil: ASTI (2018), Agricultural Science and Technology Indicators (database), https://asti.cgiar.org/data.

StatLink https://doi.org/10.1787/888933907545

Figure 1.4. Environmental pressures from agriculture in Argentina

Average annual per cent change 2002-04 to 2012-14, or nearest available period

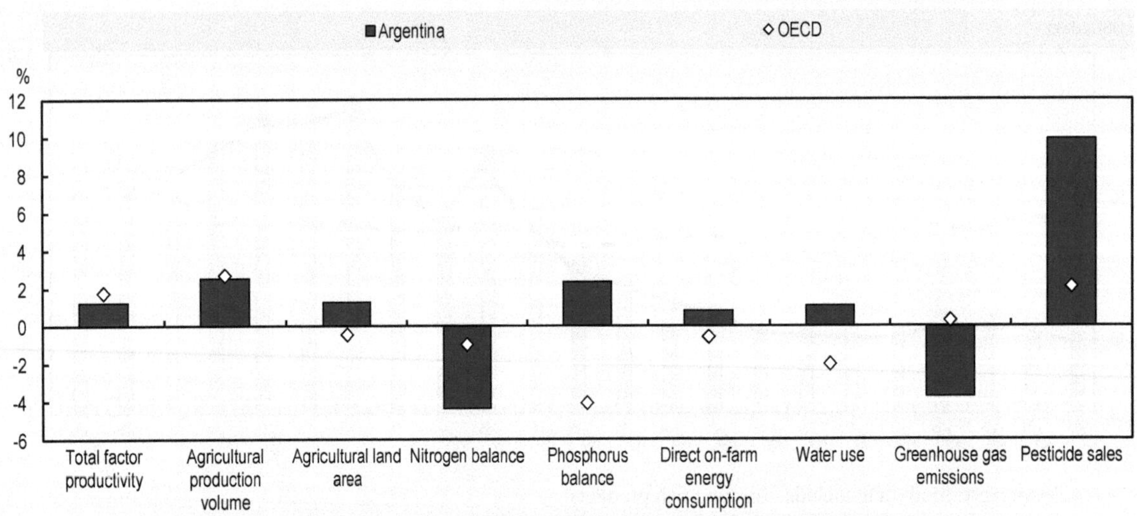

Source: OECD Agri-environmental Indicators database (2018). USDA Economic Research Service Agricultural Productivity Database for Total Factor Productivity. Pesticide sales for Argentina were retrieved from (FAO, 2018[41]) as a proxy for pesticide use.

StatLink https://doi.org/10.1787/888933907564

1.2. Policy assessment

The agricultural policy package in Argentina is biased against the sector and distorts domestic production decisions. In quantitative terms, by far its most significant components are export taxes and restrictions that have been imposed almost continuously throughout the last two decades on the most competitive parts of the sector. Agriculture has been hampered, with low producer prices reflected in very large negative support to producers (PSE). Ideally, in the context of a broad tax reform in Argentina, the sector would be subject to either economy-wide taxes on personal and corporate income, or taxes on rural assets, or taxes targeted to environmental impacts (negative externalities).

Border measures – mainly in in the form of export restrictions – distort the economy, disadvantage farmers and do not benefit final consumers

Export taxes and restrictions, Argentina's main agricultural policies for many years, have hurt the sector. This has depressed domestic producer prices and has driven the producer support estimate (PSE) to negative values of -14% in 2015-17, and as low as -51% in 2008 (Figure 1.5). As a consequence, prices received by farmers have been lower than international prices, creating negative market price support for the main crop and livestock commodities (soybeans, corn, wheat, sunflower, milk and beef).

Figure 1.5. Level and composition of Producer Support Estimate in Argentina, 1997-2017

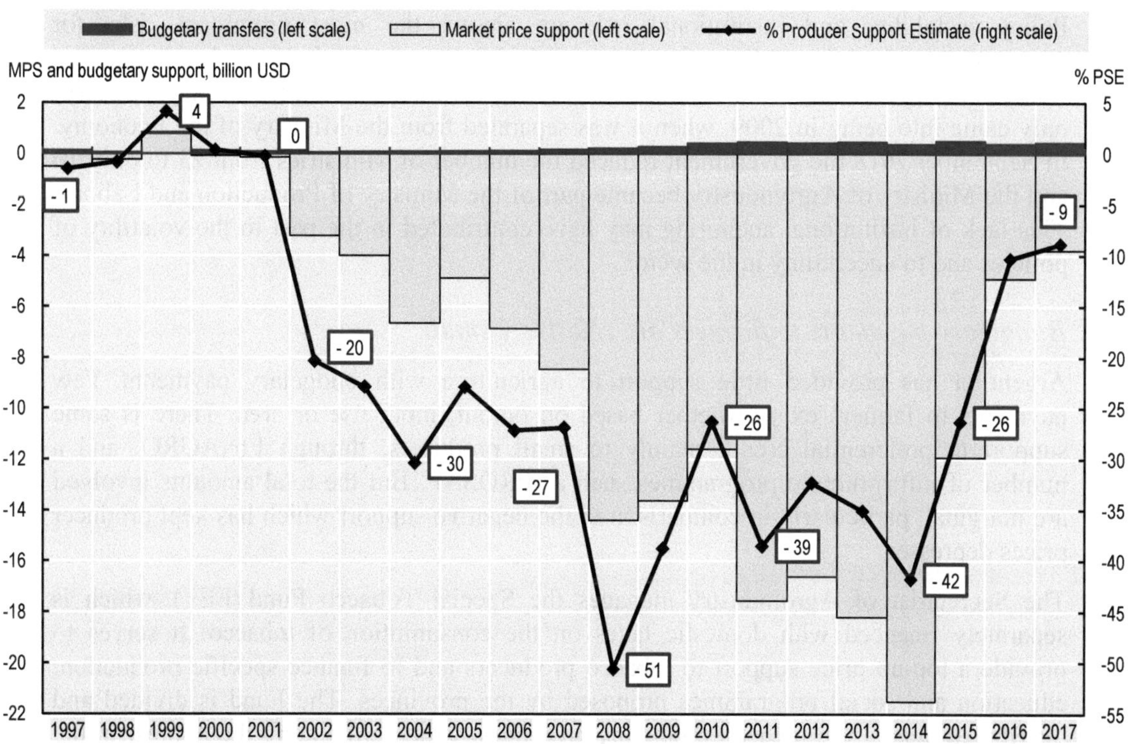

Source: (OECD, 2018), "Producer and Consumer Estimates", OECD Agriculture Statistics Database.

StatLink https://doi.org/10.1787/888933907583

For some products such as pork, a degree of positive market price support exists through tariffs and (negative) excess feed costs; for fruit and vegetables, no significant border trade measures exist, and price support is estimated at zero. Import taxes, which are relatively high in international terms, have also increased the costs of some inputs and reduced their use.

The Consumer Support Estimate (CSE) calculations show that first consumers (i.e. first buyers of primary agricultural products) ended-up being supported through export restrictions. This means that wholesalers or processors are benefiting from lower prices of food inputs such as wheat and beef. However, the evidence suggests that the impact on final consumer prices have been marginal. Export taxes are neither an effective nor sustainable manner to control food inflation (Calvo, 2014[5]).

In the historical context of unstable macroeconomic policies, the lack of a framework agriculture law may have also contributed to sectoral policy uncertainty

One of the most damaging aspects of export restrictions are their ad hoc nature, making them unpredictable and volatile. For example, in the past, export licenses for wheat and beef created considerable uncertainty, adding costs for producers and investors on top of the nominal value of export taxes. This uncertain policy environment favours the production of goods which require less investment and working capital (such as soybeans) than more capital-intensive ones (such as livestock).

Policy instability and institutional risk are among the most prominent risks for Argentinian agriculture. Policies for the sector lack any periodically revised and approved framework legislation. A separate Ministry of Agriculture (now called of Agroindustry) only came into being in 2009, when it was separated from the Ministry of the Economy. In September 2018 the government reduced the number of Ministries from 23 to only 10 and the Ministry of Agroindustry became part of the Ministry of Production and Labour. This lack of institutional anchoring may have contributed in the past to the volatility of policies and to uncertainty in the sector.

Budgetary payments to farmers are relatively small

Argentina has provided little support to agriculture with budgetary payments. Few payments to farmers exist, whether based on output, input use or area. There is some support to preferential credit, mainly to small producers, through FINAGRO, and a number of infrastructure programmes such as PROSAP. But the total amounts involved are marginal, particularly in comparison to the negative support which has kept producer prices depressed.

The Secretariat of Agroindustry manages the Special Tobacco Fund (FET), which is separately financed with domestic taxes on the consumption of tobacco. It serves to provide a top-up price support to tobacco producers and to finance specific production, education and social programmes proposed by the provinces. The Fund is divided and distributed among the tobacco producing provinces, which are among the poorest in the country, according to their level of production. Most of the fund expenditure is not well targeted to improve the competitiveness of the sector, or to facilitate the economic and social development of poor tobacco producers, including their transition to other economic activities.

Agricultural policies in the General Services Support Estimate: Focus on innovation and animal and plant health

Around 80% of the public agricultural budget is spent on general services. Argentina's agricultural research is well regarded internationally, particularly on biotechnological issues, as are its patents, for example on rice seeds. The main institution of the agricultural innovation system is the National Institute of Agricultural Technology (INTA), which also provides extension services. The other service entity which uses a large share of budgetary resources is the National Service for Agro-Food Health and Quality (SENASA), which is in charge of the animal and plant health.

Both INTA and SENASA have a good professional reputation in their respective areas. However, given their budgetary importance and their prominent role in innovation and competitiveness, their institutional organisation and their design and portfolio of activities require continuous monitoring and evaluation to maintain their focus on the provision of priority public goods.

The successful adoption of technological packages in the Pampas region was mainly driven by private initiatives

Important private innovation initiatives such as the Argentinean Association of Regional Consortia for Agricultural Experimentation (AACREA) and The Argentinean Association of No-till Agriculture (AAPRESID) have emerged over the past 30 years to meet farmers' needs and facilitate the adoption of technology and innovation. These successful initiatives have complemented the public agricultural innovation system of INTA and private research by input suppliers. The young average age of farmers in the Pampas Region and their high level of education has facilitated the adoption of innovation.

In recent decades INTA has evolved from providing research and extension services to fulfilling additional functions in the implementation of social and rural development programmes, mainly in the regional economies. These different functions are not always well defined or reflected in the structure and management of the institution; this circumstance may contribute to the difference between the innovation and production performance of the crop sector in the Pampas and that in other sectors and regions.

Argentina has private insurance, futures and contracts to manage certain risks while ex post government disaster assistance is limited

Argentina's production growth and innovation in the last decades has been very much focused on a single commodity, soybean. Driven by growing world demand, high prices and policies, this commodity has increased its share in Argentina's production and export portfolio, displacing other crops and limiting cattle breeding and milk production activities. Recent evidence suggests that this trend has been partially reversed, in particular since policy changed at the end of 2015. The agricultural sector's strong orientation towards this single crop has decreased the diversity of the national portfolio of crops and rural activities. This has increased the sector's exposure to a variety of production and market risks.

The dynamism of the farming sector in Argentina has allowed private and market initiatives such as insurance, futures and marketing contracts to develop, covering at least certain risks. Insurance penetration reaches more than 50% of all agricultural land. The government has a limited role in managing agricultural risks in Argentina, favouring the development of private strategies. For example, the relatively small funding provided to the Agricultural Emergencies Law and the disaster declaration requirements prevent disaster assistance from crowding out market instruments. More recently, some provinces have experimented with providing some support to insurance on a pilot basis.

Increasing agricultural risks associated with climate change, particularly floods, are a policy concern for the federal and the provincial governments. Limited annual funds for disaster assistance exist, and they are focused on ex post assistance rather than on preparedness and prevention. Risk exposure needs to be assessed and analysed in a comprehensive manner to contribute to more holistic risk management strategies that would respond to the broader needs and opportunities of the agro-industrial sector.

Limited access to financial services like credit is a constraint for the sector and cannot be solved by sectoral policies alone

The underdevelopment of Argentinian financial markets is not unique to the agricultural and rural sectors, but it is a major limitation to efficiently developing investment strategies and managing agricultural risk. Basic tools which are widely used in other countries – such as secure and accessible saving accounts and access to credit – are limited. Underdeveloped financial markets are a barrier for long term investment, while some credit is provided by input suppliers. The existing programmes for preferential credit provided by the Secretariat of Agroindustry are small in size and are not designed to tackle the structural deficiencies of the whole financial system.

Argentinian agriculture has a dual structure, with high productivity value chains for grain and poorly developed value chains for regional economies

Agricultural policy only imposes negative support on production in the Pampas region. The regional economies have not been similarly burdened; on the contrary, some positive support has been given to specific products such as tobacco; however, structural deficiencies in regional economies have not been addressed, with limited public investment on agricultural infrastructure, R&D, extension services and technical assistance. Rural infrastructure, roads to distant provinces and railways have deteriorated in recent years of low investment. This situation has created some relatively lagging sub-sectors in the regional economies together with more dynamic ones driven by local and foreign investment like wine, and internationally competitive leader products such as the lemons of Tucuman.

The deterioration of statistical information is a burden for both the sector and policy design

Argentina's statistics deteriorated in the period 2007-15 amid growing political pressure. In July 2011, the IMF found Argentina in breach of its minimum reporting requirements. This affects many statistics relevant for the analysis of the agro-food sector, which are currently missing or unreliable: national accounts, food inflation, rural poverty, value of production, agricultural censuses and household surveys. These information gaps affect private and public sectoral assessment, decision-making, and the capacity to implement evidence-based policy making. Since 2016, the National Institute of Statistics and Censuses (INDEC) has been working with the OECD Statistical department to improve its methodologies and information systems, which start to be visible in INDEC deliveries.

1.3. Policy challenges and recommendations

The overall policy approach to agriculture needs to rebalance the policy package towards policy stability and sustainability

The main challenge for Argentina is to re-balance its approach to agriculture. A stable policy, macroeconomic and fiscal environment is needed that avoids hampering a sector that can positively contribute to growth and development while ensuring that its development makes sustainable use of natural resources.

- **Recommendation 1: Agricultural policy could be better anchored in broad legislation, such as a specific framework law and an economy-wide reform of the tax system, gradually reversing the policy bias against the agricultural sector (negative PSE) and moving towards a more neutral, stable, predictable and targeted policy package.** Overall, budgetary support in Argentina is relatively well focused to provide general services to the sector such as on plant and animal health and inspection services, and on creating and transferring knowledge and innovation. Policies should strengthen their focus on the provision of these services while enhancing the sustainable use of natural resources.

Trade policies in the form of export restrictions have created negative price support, uncertainty and distortions

Market Price Support (MPS) policies – either negative or positive – are among the most distorting forms of support to agriculture. In the past, Argentina has used export restrictions and taxes heavily, motivated by objectives related to fiscal revenue or inflation control. During agricultural price spikes, export taxes accounted for up to 13% of all fiscal revenue in Argentina but were not effective in controlling food inflation. In this regard, the decisions taken in 2015 and 2016 to reduce export taxes for agricultural products were steps in the right direction, reducing distortions and the size of the negative market price support. However, in light of the emerging economic turmoil, in September 2018 the government introduced taxes to all exports including agricultural products, with the objective of reducing its fiscal deficit. Although, the introduction of export taxes will expire in 2020, this measure will have consequences for agriculture as a main exporting sector.

Export restrictions do not merely distort in a static sense, they also generate uncertainty because they are decided and implemented in an ad hoc discretionary manner through government decrees which have low predictability. This uncertainty creates additional distortions and disincentives for long-term investment. Furthermore, export restrictions and policy uncertainty have spill-over effects in exacerbating volatility in agricultural world markets, as during the 2008 episode of price spikes.

Decisions about export taxes have to be taken in light of the potential distortion from alternative sources of fiscal revenue, particularly when the country is under pressure to reduce its fiscal deficit. Such considerations may justify a temporary recourse to tax instruments that otherwise would not constitute an ideal or first best choice. Furthermore, tax reforms in a federal state like Argentina are politically difficult to implement due to their implications for the revenue collected by different levels of government (i.e. federal and provincial).

- **Recommendation 2: As part of an ongoing, long-term, comprehensive tax reform, phase out export taxes on agriculture, integrate the sector into a reformed economy wide tax system, and enhance policy certainty**. In the current environment it will be crucial to find the right balance between the long-term objective of phasing out export taxes and the current short term needs to raise fiscal revenues.
  - The long-term phasing-out of export taxes should be part of a more ambitious tax reform package beyond agricultural policies. The soybean exporting sector could be appropriately taxed through economy-wide tax bases such as the corporate and personal income taxes. These and other taxes should be an integral part of a long-term structural reform to generate a stable tax and macroeconomic environment that provides policy certainty and prevents erratic discretionary policy changes.
  - Given the limited capacity to collect fiscal revenues in a progressive and non-distorting manner, the political and institutional complexities of the federal system and the urgency of economic turmoil, temporary measures may be required. Uncertainty would be minimised by maintaining current policy plans as announced, using export taxes temporarily in the context of strong fiscal consolidation needs, while maintaining their announced expiration on December 2020.
  - Tax reforms will affect production incentives with implications on environmental pressures and should be accompanied by policy measures to strengthen agri-environmental sustainability.

Environmental pressures are growing, calling for strengthening the responsibility of producers in reducing negative externalities

Argentina's agriculture sector has transformed in recent years at an accelerated pace, increasing environmental pressures. Water use, nutrient balances and energy use are still relatively low compared to OECD countries, but increased deforestation and relatively high rates of pesticide use in cropland are a concern. Other potential risks are associated with loss of organic matter and phosphorous (P) fertiliser applications that may not be sufficient to compensate the P uptake from crops. Deforestation rates are higher than regional and global figures. In the 25-year period from 1990 to 2015, Argentina lost 22% of its forest mainly due to agriculture. Moreover, in the last 15 years, deforestation rates increased, contrary to regional and global trends. Greenhouse gas emissions and loss of biodiversity and water-related ecosystem services have been on the rise due to the loss of forested land. Strengthening the responsibility of producers in reducing negative externalities (Polluter-Pays-Principle PPP) is imperative.

While no-till practices are widespread, have reduced erosion rates and helped to maintain the organic matter content in soils, such practices may not contribute to the improvement of soil quality if not accompanied by crop rotation. Additionally, pesticide use is considerably larger than in OECD countries, and there are risks associated with the use of the active substance Atrazine in particular due to its persistence and capacity to contaminate drinking-water sources. Strengthening of policies and legislation targeted towards monitoring and reducing negative environmental impacts is needed, particularly as the tax burden on export commodities is reduced in the long run.

- **Recommendation 3: Undertake an in-depth evaluation of the impacts (negative externalities) associated with different types of pesticides, their level of application and impact at specific locations and hotspots, with a view to implementing targeted measures to limit harmful pesticide use. Apply best environmental and agricultural practices, in particular on pesticide use and crop rotation.**
  - It is essential to gather good information and knowledge to support efficient evidence-based policy design. The analysis should focus on identifying potential misalignments between legislation and good practices on pesticide use and its final environmental effects on water, biodiversity and health in specific locations. The results of this evaluation should be used to improve, target and update legislation and to improve environmental practices such as Integrated Pest Management.
  - Incorporate new knowledge and research in a continuous update of the best agri-environmental practices, in response to the particular challenges of new technological packages. In this respect, Argentina is well positioned in institutional terms, and the government can work in partnership with both private associations of farmers such as AAPRESID or AACREA and with the extension services of INTA. Advisory and information programmes run in collaboration between farmers' associations and government agencies can be crucial to fostering action and promoting pro-environmental practices, particularly on crop rotation and pesticide use.
- **Recommendation 4: Undertake an in-depth independent evaluation of the Native Forest Law to analyse its effectiveness in stemming deforestation, and take the appropriate legal and budgetary decisions to strengthen its enforcement.** The main focus of the analysis and the resultant reforms should address weak enforcement capacity in different provincial jurisdictions, the environmental targeting methods and procedures to identify conservation priorities, and the strength of the economic incentives to deforest under the different agricultural technological packages. Furthermore, the evaluation should estimate the budgetary allocations needed for compensation and implementation.

The Innovation system needs to modernise its institutions, monitor its results, refocus on environmental sustainability and make the IPR of seeds enforceable

The Argentinian agriculture innovation system is mainly privately driven by domestic and international economic incentives. However, the public sector has provided very valuable strategic support on specific knowledge inputs and their transmission to human capital, mainly from INTA and the whole Science, Technology and Innovation (ST&I) system. The percentage of GDP going into ST&I activities is modest but growing. Organisational innovations have provided new roles for private actors in sharing experience and facilitating the adoption of innovation. However, R&D expenditure is mainly public and more needs to be done to make the system more responsive to demand and less supply-driven. Investment levels in agricultural innovation policies are high in comparison with all agricultural support measures, with a high share in the General Support Estimate (GSSE) dedicated to agriculture knowledge and innovation system (mainly through INTA). Nonetheless, the relative research intensity of the agri-food sector has fallen in the last two decades.

- **Recommendation 5: Develop a systematic method and process to measure and monitor public Argentinian R&D and innovation, and to define and implement strategic priorities.** No good measurement is in place for investment on Agricultural Innovation Systems (AIS) in Argentina. A system needs to develop and institutionalise ways of measuring the public innovation effort and monitoring the performance of different initiatives and projects, learning from the experience of other OECD countries. Strategic priorities for the agricultural innovation system should be more clearly defined and implemented based on evidence of results and involving stakeholders at an early stage. The priorities of the public actors of the innovation system such as INTA need to evolve towards the provision of public goods and long-term investments in sustainability. These are the areas typically overlooked by the private actors in the AIS, for example the sustainable use of natural resources, the protection of the environment (soils, water, forest, and biodiversity) and the mitigation and adaptation to climate change. The AIS needs also to rebalance its priorities towards regional economies in response to the poor productivity performance outside the Pampas region. A federal subsidiarity approach to innovation policy and capacities is needed, but the specific pathways go beyond agricultural innovation policies.
- **Recommendation 6: Undertake an in-depth evaluation of INTA with the view to an eventual re-organisation of its different lines of action: research, extension and rural development.** INTA is being displaced by other public and private actors in the development of main technologies, and its portfolio is being diversified outside R&D and innovation into rural and social development. The role of INTA as the most important actor in the AIS needs to be better defined, in particular to ensure its efficiency in facilitating adoption. The next innovation is likely to come from other actors such as universities and CONICET. Building on the current ongoing assessment of INTA, it is recommended to undertake an open external analysis to evaluate and discuss the available alternatives for INTA and other institutional frames to tackle more efficiently its different policy areas: innovation, R&D and extension activities, and broader social and community development objectives. The analysis should look beyond the allocation of the budget into the optimal management and operational structures for good priority setting and human resources management of different staff profiles and activities. INTA needs to be ready to respond to the increasing demand for innovation knowledge and public goods related with climate change and environmental sustainability, which should be the focus for public investments in R&D. As the central component of public policy, INTA plays a key role in linking research to adoption.

Additionally, the ongoing work to renew the legal framework and the operational capacities of the National Institute of Seeds (INASE) provides an opportunity to strengthen the enforcement and implementation of the Intellectual Property Rights (IPRs) for seed varieties. This requires a good assessment and evaluation of the current system and of the available alternative. It is also important that an acceptable equilibrium is found among a diversity of interests such as those of small farmers, medium and large agricultural producers, domestic breeding firms, multinational firms, and public institutions. They need to be involved in the redesign of INASE to make it enforceable. In this context, the adoption of the UPOV-91 agreement on the Protection of New Varieties of Plants should be considered.

Market-based risk management tools exist, policies could also focus on improving preparedness and prevention

The Argentinian agricultural risk management system has significant strengths, in particular regarding the institutions and the organisation of the sector. Most Argentinian farms are commercial entities with an entrepreneurial approach to farming, including the assessment and management of agricultural risks. Agricultural spot and future markets are dynamic in Argentina. There are also strong public institutions providing research (INTA) and managing plant and animal health (SENASA). Information about market and weather risks is available and accessible.

Argentina already has a well-developed private market for agricultural insurance, even if restricted to few risks and commodities. This circumstance has been facilitated by policies that have not expanded beyond the catastrophic risk layer. The insurance sector still has the potential to explore the potentialities of index insurance and digital technologies to expand agricultural insurance. Building on ongoing private initiatives, index insurance can reduce the administration cost of insurance and eradicate moral hazard and adverse selection. These indexes can use meteorological, sensor and satellite information and digital technologies. If appropriate research and knowledge is developed to reduce basis risk, index insurance could be an option to increase insurance coverage and availability for more commodities and locations.

The main weaknesses of the Argentinian agricultural risk management system lie beyond the agricultural sector. Policy and macroeconomic volatility has been a significant source of risk for the sector, while the financial markets are shallow and credit is scarce. The main policy actions that could improve the management of agricultural risks in Argentina are beyond the scope of agricultural policies: raising public policy predictability, achieving macroeconomic stability and developing of the financial sector. All of these are areas in which progress is being made, but further progress would have substantial pay-offs (OECD, 2019 forthcoming[6]). Efforts to develop deeper financial markets could also facilitate the emergence of more diverse insurance and derivatives products.

- **Recommendation 7: Strengthening the holistic approach to risk management policy, investing in prevention and preparedness, and improving the predictability and monitoring of disaster assistance**. Risk management policies in Argentina are rightly focused on catastrophic risks but are too centred on ex-post assistance. More policy efforts should be concentrated on ex-ante risk management and prevention through strategies and technologies that diminish risk exposure, training on holistic risk management approaches to preparedness, adaptation to climate change and diversification. Strong private and public entities in Argentina, such as INTA, CONICET, universities, AACREA, AAPRESID, CRA, SRA, CONINAGRO and FAA (see list of acronyms), can partner and play an important role in the adoption of risk management and sustainability strategies. Information systems are crucial to develop preparedness strategies and practices, and initiatives to improve statistics such as census or surveys should consider collecting the individual characteristics of farmers and their risks. The government should improve the monitoring of disaster assistance, creating a register of beneficiaries. Innovations such as indexes from meteorological stations or satellite images could be used to trigger emergency and disaster declarations of droughts and floods, to improve efficient delivery and predictability. Finally, the fund for disaster assistance, FONEDA, should be able to work with multiyear budgets, to accumulate emergency funds during the years in which there is no high impact, and to reserve them for years with high damage.

Facilitating innovation and adjustment in the value chains and regions outside the Pampas

In comparison with those in the Pampas region, value chains in regional economies have relatively low levels of productivity and dynamism. Even if some support is provided, the key problems in these regions have not been widely addressed by public policy, and public investment on agricultural infrastructure, R&D, extension services, and technical assistance has been limited.

The apples-and-pears value chain in Argentina is a dual sector. Farms fully integrated into value chains (usually large and medium size) coexist with less integrated farms (mostly small scale). Small-scale farms of apples and pears do not adopt technology innovations, inefficiently control pests, and own old orchards with very limited investments at the farm level.

Viticulture is more dynamic and has benefited from private investments since the 1990s but lacks a long-term strategy for its value chain. For instance, quality improvement and innovation in organisations would allow increases in quality and competitiveness to be achieved. Other organisational innovations required in this sector include: building networks of knowledge and experience; compliance with appropriate standards; export specialisation; and co-ordination of the value chain between primary producers, suppliers and industry (wineries); distribution and marketing systems; R&D, training in new technologies and extension services.

- **Recommendation 8: Budget permitting, support the search for new markets for wine and pears and apples and other viable products produced in the regional economies, through active policies such as agricultural promotion agencies and trade agreements beyond MERCOSUR.** Increased participation in export markets is a necessary condition for growth for the value chains of both the apple-and-pear and viticulture industries. In Argentina, domestic demand for food can be expected to increase primarily as a function of (relatively low) population growth, and only secondarily as a result of per-capita income growth. A search for new markets is crucial for expansion. Agricultural promotion offices in emerging international markets could facilitate this.
- **Recommendation 9: Make and assessment and reform the Special Tobacco Fund (FET), eliminating output payments and targeting investment to human and physical capital.** A legacy policy, the FET needs to be refocused on facilitating the economic transformation of the tobacco producing regions, which are among the poorest in Argentina, into other productions and sectors. The first step should be to eliminate the support to the price of tobacco – a contradictory policy that stimulates supply while taxing demand. The second step should be to invest the tobacco tax revenues into infrastructure and education in the tobacco regions. These steps should be supported by the development of social policies targeted to the poor and facilitating economic adjustment.
- **Recommendation 10: Consider creating a system of technical assistance for innovation in specific regional economies' value chains and small-scale producers, building on INTA's capacities in agricultural R&D and extension services.** This innovation effort should complement efforts on other lagging areas

such as education and infrastructure that are tackled by other policies. New alternatives should be explored for organisational structures that improve the co-ordination among primary producer co-operatives, access to markets and interlinkages with the processing industry. Broad public investments in rural roads, agricultural infrastructure, storage and cold chains would help the regional economies to overcome high transaction costs. Because the future of small-scale farmers may not lie in primary agriculture, value chains and non-farm economic alternatives should be explored for a gradual re-allocation of resources.

Box 1.3. Economic turbulences and policy developments affecting Argentina's agricultural sector in 2018

After seven consecutive quarters of positive growth, the economy began to stall as the Argentinian peso came under pressure as of April 2018. Over a period of 4 months, the value of the currency vis-à-vis the US dollar was reduced to half, risk premiums and credit default swap (CDS) spreads spiked and inflation rose sharply. These events plunged the economy back into recession during 2018. The prospects of a significant deterioration in access to foreign financing led the government to seek financial support from the International Monetary Fund (IMF).

Following renewed market pressure on the Argentinian peso, the authorities front-loaded fiscal adjustment plans and committed to a balanced primary budget, which excludes interest payments, as early as 2019, with primary surpluses thereafter. This implied a substantial fiscal consolidation relative to previous plans, based on both revenue and expenditure measures.

Revenue measures include the establishment of a temporary (until December 31, 2020) export tax of up to 12% applied to all the goods and services exports, including products from agriculture (Decree 793/2018). The tax cannot exceed a maximum of ARS 4 per dollar of exports of primary agricultural goods, and ARS 3 per dollar for other products. This new tax on all exports is added on top of the previous tax applied to soybeans whose rate was reduced from 26% to 18%.

The authorities have been clear that they see export taxes as a temporary emergency revenue measure, with a clearly defined sunset clause. It is important to see them in the current context. The strong devaluation of 50% has increased competitiveness significantly and generated windfall gains to agricultural exporters. The temporary export taxes take back only a small part of the newly gained competitiveness. The new level of the exchange rate is the most competitive one that Argentina has had in years, even when deducting the effect of the temporary export taxes.

At the same time, public expenditures are being cut in several areas, including public investment, current expenditures and through an accelerated phase-out schedule for economic subsidies, mainly on energy and transport.

References

Calvo, P. (2014), *Welfare Impact of Wheat Export Restrictions in Argentina: Non-parametric Analysis on Urban Households*, UNCTAD. [5]

FAO (2018), *FAOSTAT.* [4]

OECD (2019 forthcoming), *Economic Survey of Argentina.* [6]

Regúnaga, M. and A. Tejeda Rodriguez (2015), *Argentina's agricultural policies, trade and sustainable development objectives*, International Center for Trade and Sustainable Development (ICTSD). [3]

UN (2018), *UN Comtrade database.* [2]

WDI (2018), *World Development Indicators*, World Bank, Washington, DC. [1]

Notes

[1] On the 3 September 2018, while this review was being written, the government announced several policy measures in response to an economic turmoil triggered by a large depreciation of the peso. These measures are summarised in Box 1.3 and include the introduction of taxes on all exports to reduce the fiscal deficit will directly affect the agricultural sector and the estimate of support.

Chapter 2. The context of Argentinian agriculture

Argentina is an upper-middle income country well-endowed with natural resources and human capital. Its history of macroeconomic instability and volatility in policy orientations from open markets to import substitution has led to overall poor long-term economic performance. The main exception has been the agricultural sector which, despite policy impediments, has innovated and grown over the last two decades. Driven by higher international agricultural prices, Argentinian agriculture – in particular, in the extended Pampas region – has experienced a major structural transformation in production and productivity, in on-farm practices and technologies, and in its institutions and contractual arrangements. This has been reflected in large changes in the use of land and the portfolio of commodities in favour of soybean, and in the composition and destination of exports towards Asia. However, other agricultural production lags behind – notably that in regional economies (outside of the Pampas), including tobacco, cotton and fruits and vegetables.

2.1. An economy marked by the strength of the agricultural exporting sector

The Argentinian economy has been subject to many severe fluctuations and economic crises over the last decades. One hundred years ago, income per capita was 92% of the average of the 16 richest economies, while today is only 43% (Bolt and van Zanden, 2014[1]). Argentina's low population density and abundant fertile land have contributed to its comparative advantage in agricultural commodities, exports of which were the basis of the high income per capita in the early 20th century. The tension between agricultural export growth and the development of a domestic industrial sector has been at the core of recurrent policy cycles that have been described as "stop and go" (Gerchunoff, 2016[2]).

After decades of trade openness from the end of the 19th century, Argentina suffered from the demand contraction of 1929 and began a more inward-looking cycle (OECD, 2017[3]). After World War II, import substitution policies to develop an industrial sector were deployed under a succession of military and civilian governments, until the return to democracy in the 1980s. Two episodes of hyperinflation occurred in 1975 and 1989-90, respectively. In the 1990s, the country opened again to trade with a currency pegged to the US dollar and reduced inflation; however, rising fiscal imbalances led to the 2001 debt default (Lence, 2010[4]).

In the period 2002-10, the economy grew, supported by rising commodity prices and despite the reintroduction of import restrictions and agricultural export taxes. However, growth stalled to virtually zero in the period 2009-14, with an overvalued fixed exchange rate, capital controls and trade restrictions. The new government, elected in November 2015, has taken important steps to correct various imbalances. It has done so through the abolition of capital controls and most export taxes, simplification of import procedures, and correction of the national statistics. In September 2018 a temporary tax on all exports was introduced to raise fiscal revenue.

Reflecting these decades of policy and economic volatility, trade as a percentage of GDP has also been erratic, falling from 36% in 2005 to 21% in 2016 (Table 2.1). Primary agricultural production represented 8% of the GDP in 2016, while the whole agro-industrial transformation sector was estimated to be 32% of GDP (Regúnaga and Tejeda Rodriguez, 2015[5]). Due to this high share of the agro-food sector in the economy in general and in exports in particular (64% in 2016), Argentina's fiscal and external balances are highly sensitive to developments in this sector.

Total agricultural production in Argentina is dominated by extensive farming and the use of mechanisation and modern technologies in the Pampas. This explains one of the lowest shares of the agricultural sector in employment in the world: 2% in 2016. However, the extended agro-food and agro-industrial sector is estimated to provide 18-35% of total employment (Regúnaga and Tejeda Rodriguez, 2015[5]).

Table 2.1. Contextual indicators of Argentina's agricultural sector

	1995	2000	2005	2010	2016[1]	OECD 2016
Economic context						
GDP (billion USD in PPPs)	354	438	541	756	874	54 075
Population (million)	35	37	39	41	44	1 284
Land area (thousand km^2)	2 737	2 737	2 737	2 737	2 737	34 404
Agricultural area (AA) (thousand ha)	128 045	128 510	137 798	147 481	148 700	1 225 182
Population density (inhabitants/km^2)	13	14	14	15	16	37
GDP per capita (USD in PPPs)	10 130	11 810	13 818	18 334	19 934	42 104
Trade as % of GDP[2]	16	18	35	29	21	40
Agriculture in the economy						
Agriculture in GDP (%)	6	5	9	9	8	2
Agriculture share in employment (%)	1	1	1	3	2	5
Agro-food exports (% of total exports)	53	45	47	51	64	10
Agro-food imports (% of total imports)	6	6	3	3	4	9
Characteristics of the agricultural sector						
Crop in total agricultural production[3] (%)	62	58	57	58	62	n.a.
Livestock in total agricultural production[3] (%)	38	42	43	42	38	n.a.
Share of arable land in AA (%)	21	22	24	26	26	32

n.a.: not applicable.
1. Or latest year available.
2. Ratio of the sum of exports and imports to GDP.
3. The column on OECD 2016 represents total for OECD countries for the variables that measure absolute values (GDP, population, land and area) and OECD average for the rest.
Source: Authors' calculations based on (WDI, 2018[6]) and Comtrade Database (UN, 2018[7]).

2.2. An upper-middle income country with high urban poverty

Argentina is the second largest country of Latin America, just after Brazil, at 2.78 million km^2, and the fourth most populous (after Brazil, Mexico and Colombia) with a population of 44 million people, of which 92% live in urban areas[1] (INDEC, 2010[8]; WDI, 2018[6]). Argentina is well-endowed with natural resources, including land for farming and water. The country is a federal constitutional republic and a representative democracy. The President is both the head of state and of the government. Presidential elections take place every four years, with the possibility of one re-election. Argentina is a federation of 23 provinces and the autonomous city of Buenos Aires. Provinces are further divided into 512 departments and 2 164 municipalities (INDEC, 2017[9]).

With a GDP per capita of USD 18 489 [PPP 2011] Argentina is an upper-middle income country (WDI, 2018[6]). In terms of income distribution, it has similar level of inequality as the rest of Latin America, with a Gini coefficient of 43% in 2016, and has participated in the region's decreasing trend (with the exception of Costa Rica). The country nonetheless compares unfavourably to OECD standards (31.6% in 2012).

Figure 2.1. Inequality in Argentina and selected Latin American countries (Gini coefficient)

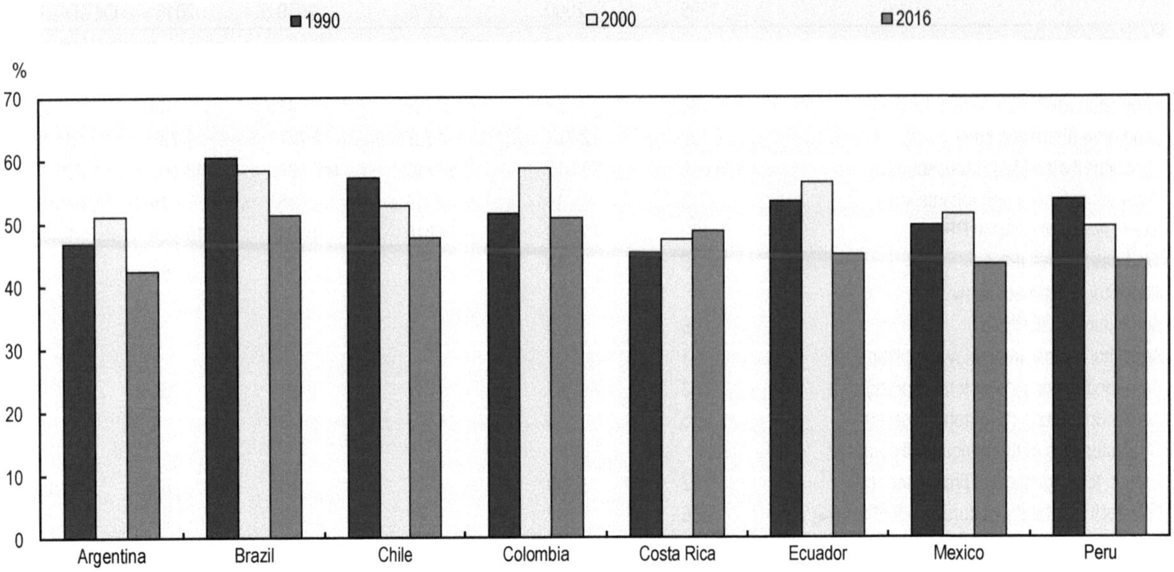

Note: 1990 or closest available year.
Source: World Development Indicators of the World Bank (WDI, 2018[6]).
StatLink https://doi.org/10.1787/888933907602

The incidence of extreme poverty measured as the percentage of the population (headcount ratio in urban areas) living under the USD 1.90 a day (2011 PPP) poverty line is very small, at 1.7% in 2014 (WDI, 2018[6]). However, according to the national poverty line[2], almost a third of the population is considered to live in poverty in urban areas: 32.2% in 2016 and 28.6% in 2017. Despite these relatively high rates, the country has witnessed progress in reducing poverty in recent years (INDEC, 2017[9]). The rate of the national poverty line reached its highest level (53% in 2002) in the years after the financial and economic crisis of 2001 (Figure 2.2). Contrary to Latin American countries, rural poverty is relatively low; most poverty is located in urban areas (INDEC, 2017[9]); (Ministerio de Agroindustria, 2018[10]).

Figure 2.2. National urban poverty rates, selected points in time

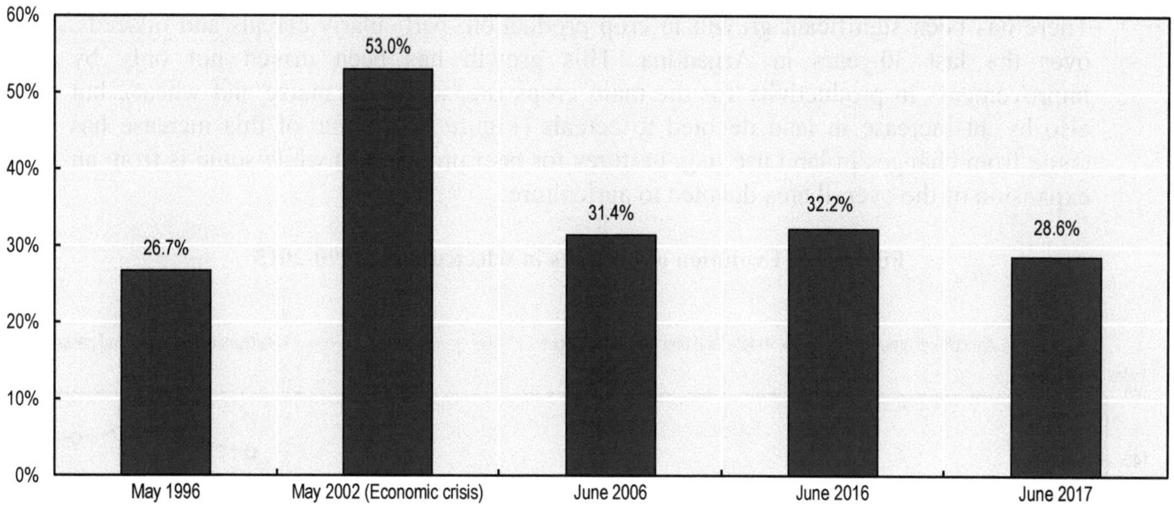

Source: (INDEC, 2017[12]).

StatLink http://dx.doi.org/10.1787/888933907621

Argentina has relatively high standards of human development in terms of human capital, education, health, housing and security compared to other countries in the Latin American region. In 2016, the country ranked 45th on the UNDP Human Development Index, the only country in the region apart from Chile (ranked 38th) in the category of "*very high human development*" (UNDP, 2017[11]). Over the years, the Argentine government has demonstrated sustained commitment to the provision of basic public services. For instance, public spending on health amounted to 2.7% of GDP in 2014 (WDI, 2018[6]); average life expectancy at birth was 76.5 years in 2015 (UNDP, 2017[11]); and access to electricity is approximately 99% (WDI, 2018[6]).

The country also has high literacy rates and full school enrolment for primary education, with literacy rates of 98% for ages of 15 and above (WDI, 2018[6]). Furthermore, around 58% of the rural population has at least seven years of schooling; at the national level (urban and rural) this figure rises to 86% of the population (INDEC, 2010[8]). Public expenditure on education was around 5.3% of GDP in 2014 (WDI, 2018[6]). Argentina's well-educated labour force in agriculture, with an average of 12 years of schooling, has been and remains an important factor for the development of the sector (Ministerio de Agroindustria, 2018[10]). A 2012 survey from Austral University estimates that in the Pampas region 70% of producers were younger than 55% and 37% had a university degree (Feeney et al., 2012[12]).

2.3. Dynamic grain and oilseed production but other sectors lagging

There has been significant growth in crop production, particularly cereals and oilseeds, over the last 30 years in Argentina. This growth has been driven not only by improvements in productivity for the main crops (i.e. soybeans, maize and wheat), but also by an increase in land devoted to cereals (Figure 2.3). Some of this increase has come from changes in land use (e.g. pastures for beef production) while some is from an expansion of the overall area devoted to agriculture.

Figure 2.3. Evolution of hectares in selected uses, 1990-2015

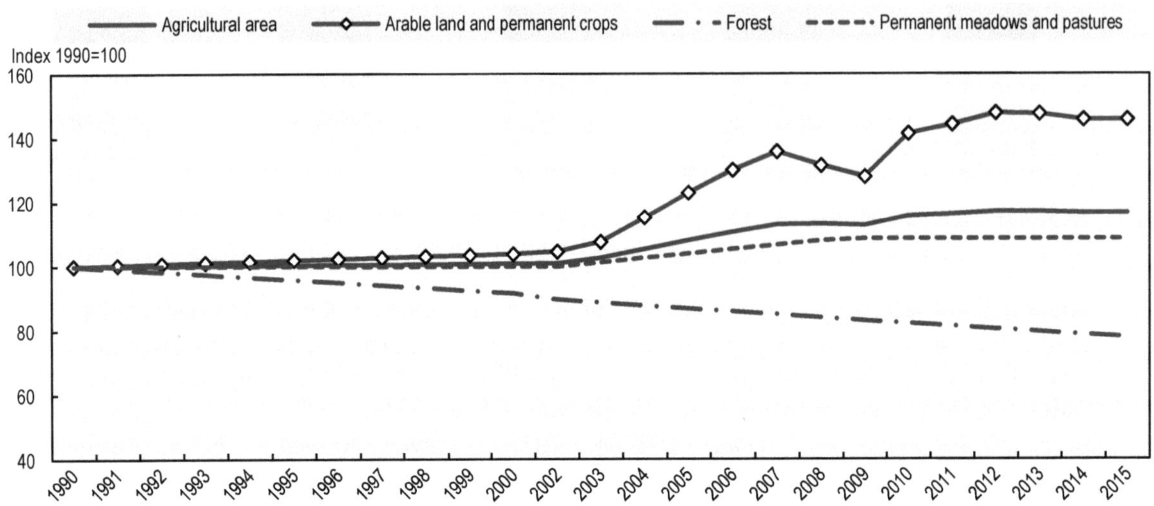

Source: Land Use Data (FAOSTAT, 2018[13]).

StatLink https://doi.org/10.1787/888933907640

Land used for the production of soybeans has seen the biggest change, from 2 million in 1980 to 20 million hectares in 2017, followed by maize, from 3.3 to 8.4 million hectares during the same period. The impressive growth of crops is also reflected in production: soybeans increased from 3.5 to 55 million of tonnes in the period 1980-2017, and maize also experienced a large increase, from 6.4 to 49.5 million tonnes (Figure 2.4.A).

Livestock production has also experienced growth. For example, poultry increased from 335 720 tonnes in 1990 to 2 055 000 tonnes in 2016 Figure 2.4.B). Pigmeat also saw a significant increase: from 140 548 tonnes to 522 429 tonnes over the same period. Bovine meat, on the other hand, experienced a significant decrease in recent years, from 3 007 000 tonnes to 2 643 000 tonnes between 1990 and 2016. This decrease was due to a reduction in the number of animals, resulting from policies such as an export ban, taxes and macroeconomic policy uncertainty. These policies discouraged domestic livestock production and favoured crop production, which has shorter cycles and requires less upfront investment.

Figure 2.4. Evolution of production of selected crops and livestock products, 1980-2016

A. Selected crops

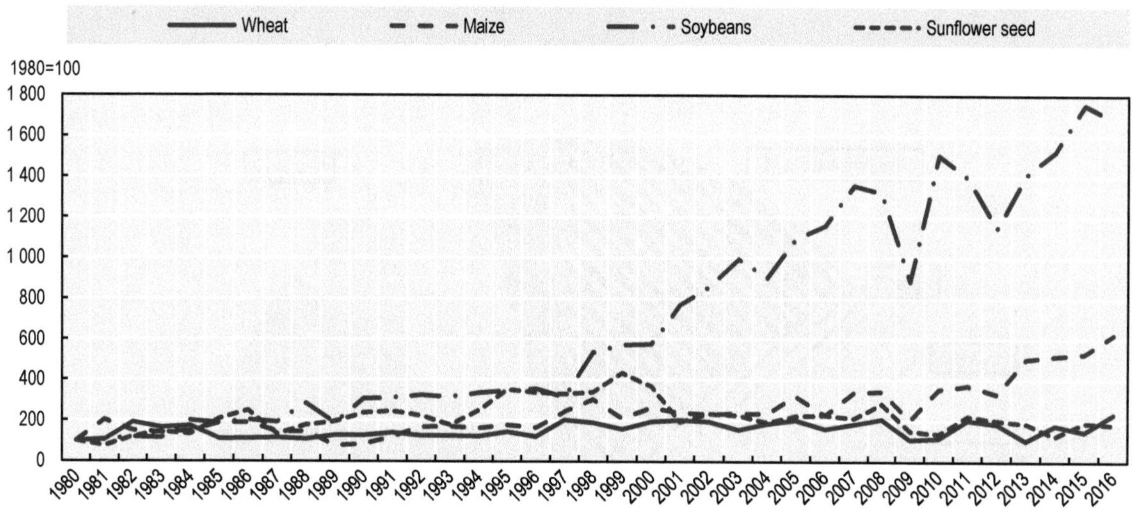

B. Selected livestock

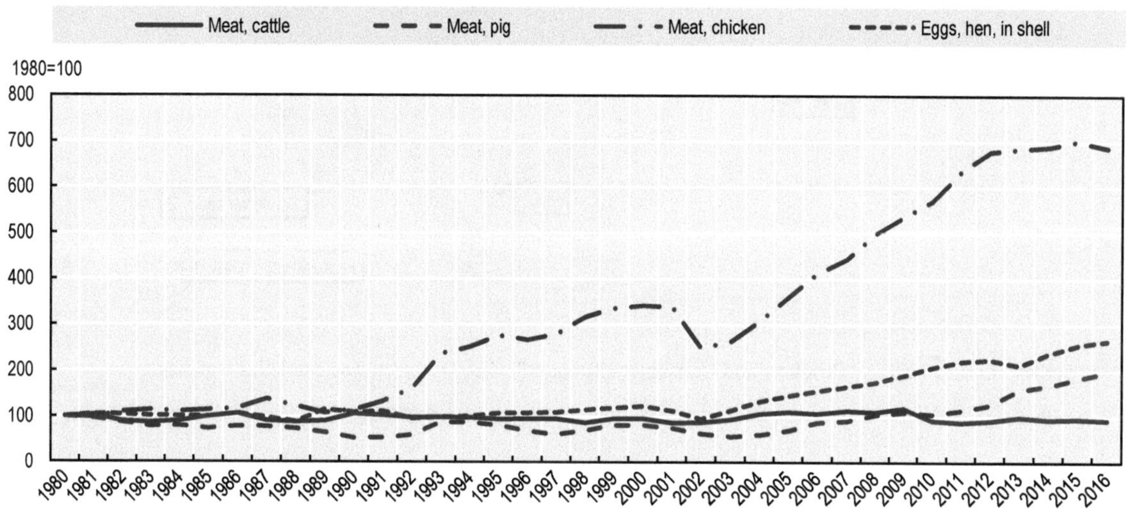

Source: (FAOSTAT, 2018[13]).

StatLink https://doi.org/10.1787/888933907659

Figure 2.5 shows the contribution of leading products to the value of agricultural production. Soybean is the first commodity and has experienced an increase in its contribution in the last two decades, but recent evidence suggests a partial reversal of this trend since 2016.

Figure 2.5. Contribution of selected commodities to agricultural value of production, 2015-17

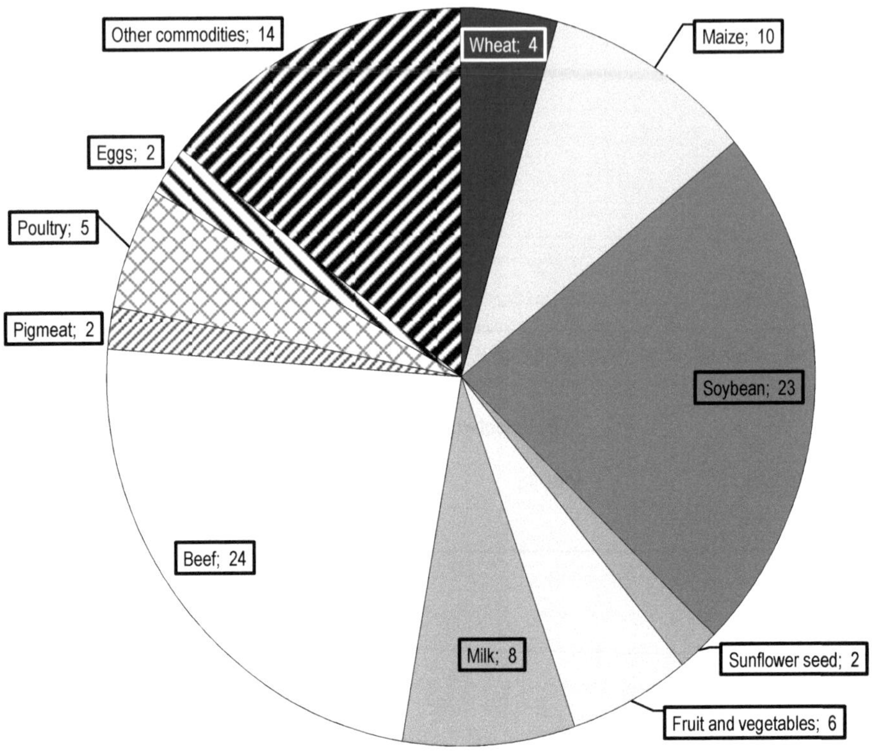

Source: OECD (2018), "Producer and Consumer Estimates", OECD Agriculture Statistics Database.

StatLink https://doi.org/10.1787/888933907678

The Total Factor Productivity (TFP) of agriculture has grown in Argentina at an average annual rate of 1.4% over the last twenty years. This rate is less than half that of Brazil and below the performance of Chile and the United States (Figure 2.6A). That said, it is in line with productivity growth across the Southern Cone countries and that of Australia. The use of inputs on agricultural production also increased at 1.4% on average, adding to a total growth of agricultural production of 2.8% in the last two decades. However, the rates of production growth and TFP growth have decelerated in the last ten years compared to the previous decade.

Figure 2.6. Total Factor Productivity of agriculture in Argentina

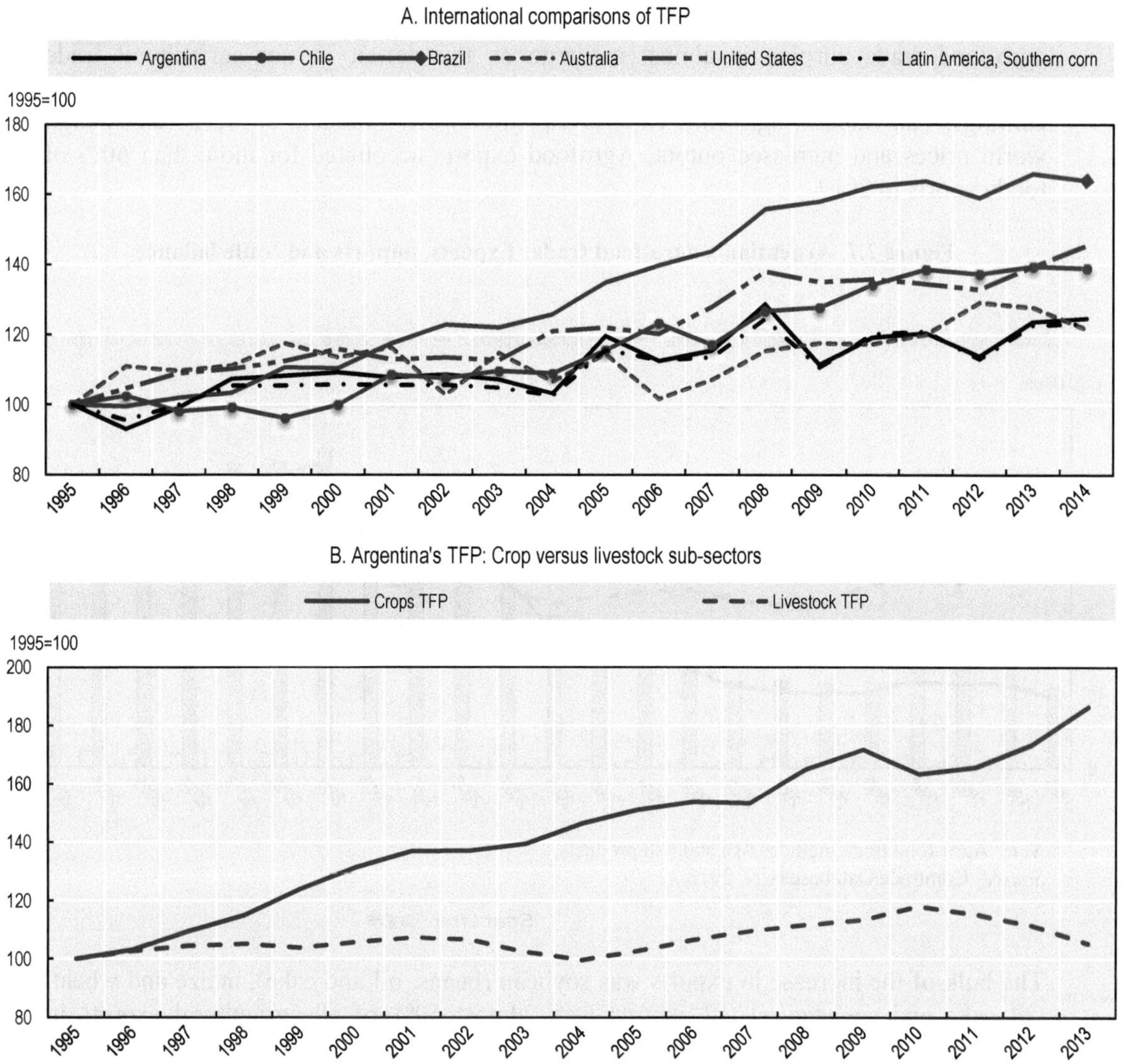

Source: International Comparisons from (Fuglie, 2012[17]); Argentina's crops and livestock (Lema, 2015[18]).

StatLink https://doi.org/10.1787/888933907697

According to estimations by the World Bank (Lema, 2015[14]) this total productivity growth hides significant differences between plant and animal products. Productivity growth in plant products has been higher than 2% over the last two decades, above that of other countries in the Southern Cone, while animal production and overall TFP were well below 1% on average (Figure 2.6.B).

This differentiated behaviour of TFP, with high increases in crops and stagnation in livestock, reflects the duality of innovation in Argentina's agriculture. New technological packages for production systems – including GMO seeds, no-till farming and increased use of pesticides – have rapidly been adopted in crop production in the Pampas, together with large-scale contract farming; meanwhile, livestock and other regional products have not encountered a similar situation.

2.4. A changing export profile and participation in value chains

In 2016, Argentina exports were valued at 10.6% of GDP and its imports at 10.2%. The agro-food trade surplus is almost as large as the deficit in non-agricultural trade (Figure 2.7). The role of the agro-food sector is crucial as a source of foreign exchange earnings. The value of agro-food exports tripled between 2002 and 2017, driven by high world prices and increased output. Agrofood exports accounted for more than 60% of total exports in 2017.

Figure 2.7. Argentina's agro-food trade: Exports, imports and trade balance

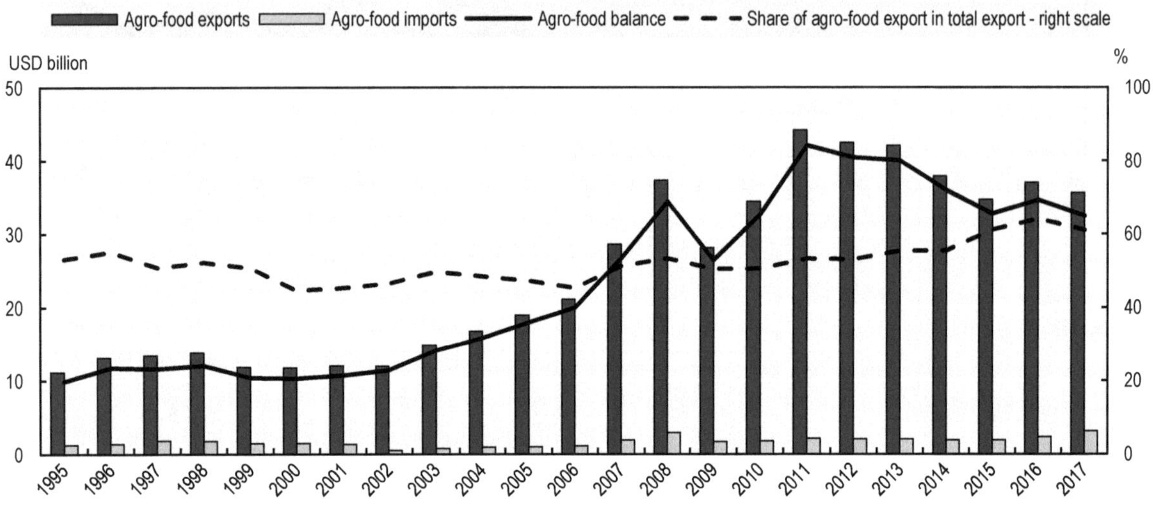

Note: Agro-food trade includes fish and fish products.
Source: Comtrade Database (UN, 2018[7]).

StatLink https://doi.org/10.1787/888933907716

The bulk of the increase in exports was soybean (beans, oil and cake), maize and wheat. Oil cake and soybean-related exports were almost 50% of all agricultural exports in 2015-17. Other significant export products are maize, wheat, fruits and vegetables (fresh and prepared), followed by bovine meat and wine (Figure 2.8). According to the OECD Agricultural Outlook, bovine exports are likely to grow in the upcoming decade (Box 2.1). However, there may be risks associated with the duration and uncertainties in biosafety regulatory in main importing countries such as the European Union and China. The adoption of genetically modified crops and the use of certain agrochemicals are becoming a major concern in some countries and, if brought to labelling or biosafety legislations, may condition the seeds and inputs to be used and the functioning of the whole value chain in Argentina.

Figure 2.8. Share of main commodities in Argentina's agro-food exports

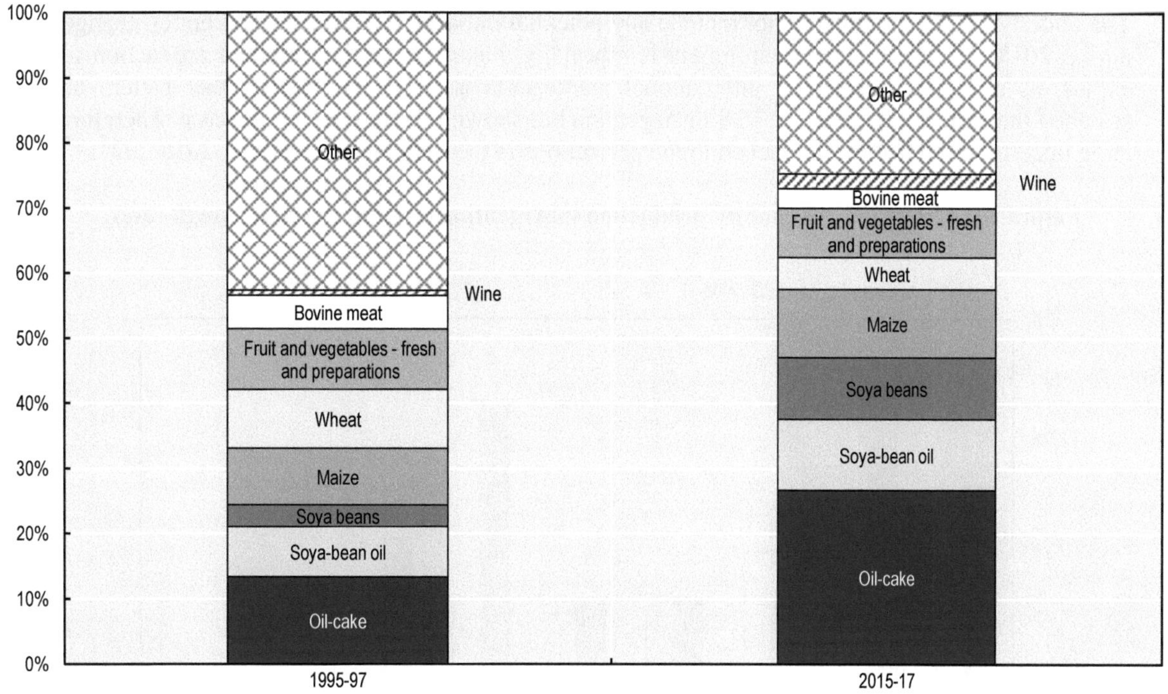

Source: Comtrade Database (UN, 2018[7]).

StatLink https://doi.org/10.1787/888933907735

Box 2.1. The agricultural outlook for Argentina: Beef is back to growth

The *Agricultural Outlook 2018-2027* is a collaborative effort of the Organisation for Economic Co-operation and Development (OECD) and the Food and Agriculture Organization (FAO) of the United Nations. The baseline projection is not a forecast about the future, but rather a plausible scenario based on specific assumptions regarding the macroeconomic conditions, the agriculture and trade policy settings, weather conditions, longer-term productivity trends and international market developments.

The *Agricultural Outlook* projects that production in Argentina will increase faster than consumption. Consequently, exports will continue to grow as for the Americas as a region. More and more of these exports are destined towards Asia and Africa.

In the case of Argentina, the annual growth rate of major crops, soybeans, maize, wheat and barley (other coarse grains) will be smaller than over the last ten years. Area planted of major crops will expand at slower pace. In case of sunflowers (other oilseeds), area planted will increase in contrast to a declining trend over the past decade. Crushing of soybeans and other oilseeds is projected to grow at a faster rate than production, enhancing the effect of domestic processing.

Poultry and pigmeat production will continue to grow fast but at lower rates than over the previous decade. In contrast, beef and milk production are projected to grow considerably fast in the coming decade, reversing years of decline. Milk production remained almost constant over the last ten years and will grow now considerably at 1.3% p.a. Thus, exports of especially whole milk powder (WMP) will expand rapidly. The turnaround in beef production is even stronger as it had been declining over the last ten years and a solid increase by 1.6% p.a. is projected forward. This will result in a considerable expansion of beef exports.

The underlying assumptions do not include any potential impact of the turmoil and policy changes during 2018. A stable policy environment is especially important for the ruminant production for export, as it requires access to international markets. In addition, normal weather pattern are assumed but as the crop year 2017/18 in Argentina has shown this may not be the case. Therefore, large uncertainties need to be attached to the projections in the Agricultural Outlook 2018-2027.

Figure 2.9. Growth in commodity production in Argentina (annual average growth rates)

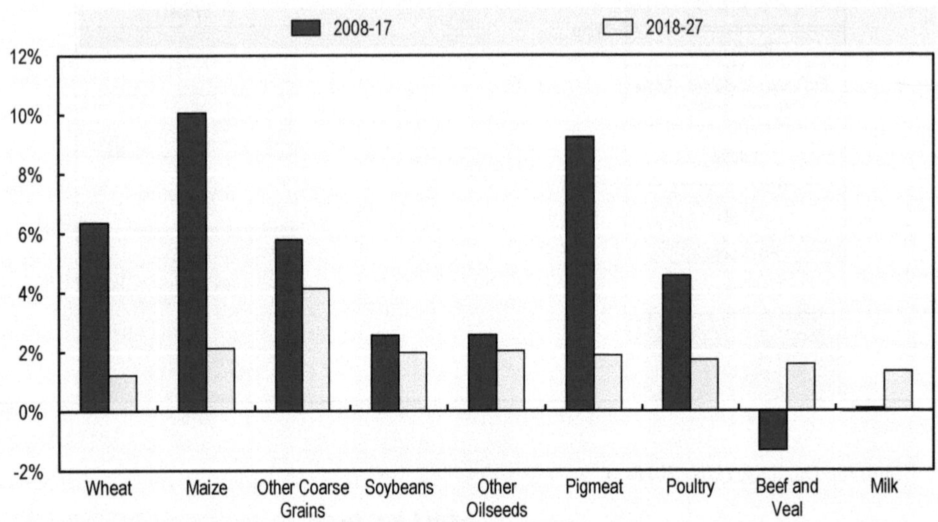

Source: OECD/FAO (2018), "OECD-FAO Agricultural Outlook", OECD Agriculture Statistics Database.

StatLink https://doi.org/10.1787/888933907754

The last two decades have also seen a marked change in the main destinations for agro-food exports. In line with a broader trend in Latin America towards a more intense trade and investment relationship with China (OECD/CAF/ECLAC, 2015[15]), the share of most OECD countries and of Brazil in Argentine exports has been reduced, while the share of Asian countries, in particular China but also Viet Nam and India, has significantly increased. China is now the primary market for Argentine agricultural exports (11.3%), well above Brazil at 8% (Figure 2.10). The countries in the European Union as a whole continue to be the first trading partner of Argentina, but their shares are falling.

Figure 2.10. Share of Argentina's agro-food exports by country of destination

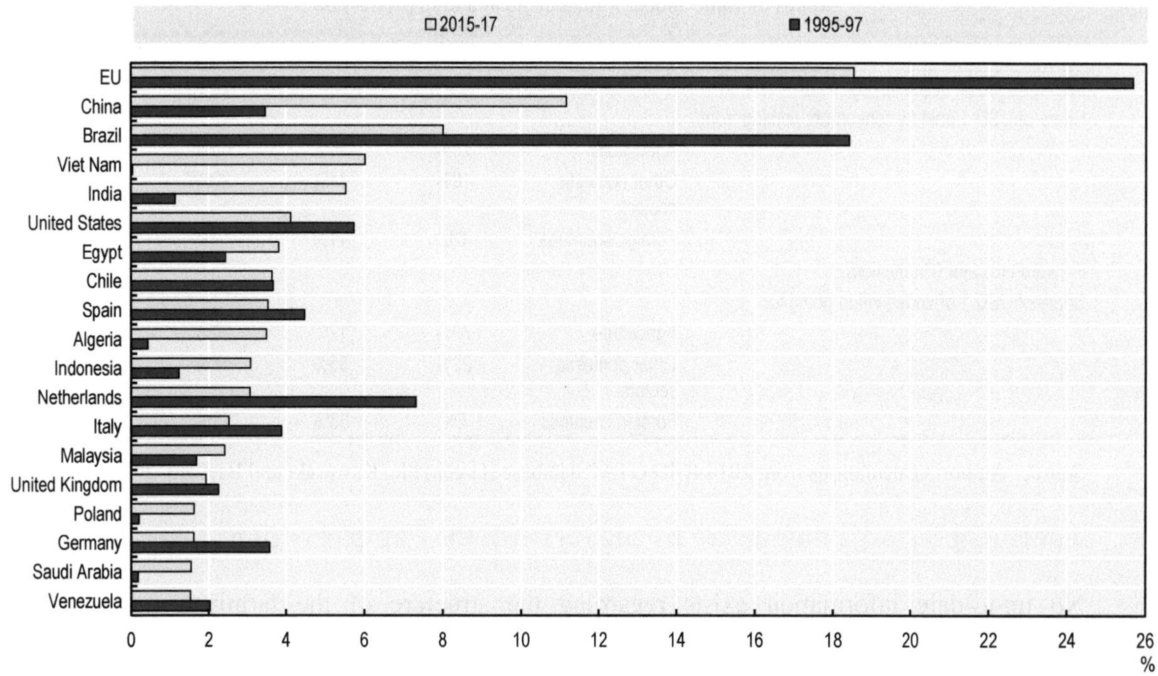

Notes: EU15 in 1995-97 and EU28 in 2015-17.
Source: Comtrade Database (UN, 2018[7]).

StatLink https://doi.org/10.1787/888933907773

Argentina's participation in general Global Value Chains across all sectors is low compared with other OECD and non-OECD countries. According to the OECD-WTO TiVA Database, in 2011 the total (forward plus backward) indicator of Argentina's participation in GVCs was 30%, compared with an average of 48% in both developing and developed economies (WTO, 2017[16]). The backward indicator (participation by buying foreign inputs) was relatively lower than the forward indicators (participation by selling inputs for other countries' exports). For the agricultural sector, backwards and forward GVC participation (10% and 14% respectively) is also low compared with other countries. For the food sector is even lower (Greenville, Kawasaki and Beaujeu, 2017[17]).

However, the value-added flows between Argentina's agriculture sector and other domestic and foreign sectors is larger than what these indicators may seem to reveal. For instance, 44% of agricultural value added is coming from other domestic sectors, which represents a significant backwards linkage to domestic value chains; and 33% of agricultural value added is exported compared to 23% in Brazil and 32% in Chile (Table 2.2), which represents a significant forward linkage with foreign value chains. The degree of forward integration of Argentine agriculture on value chains is particularly high when considering both domestic and foreign markets. An additional 55% of agricultural value added ends in the production of other sectors in the country, which makes a total 88% share of value added entering longer domestic or global value chains – one of the highest shares in the world.

Table 2.2. Agriculture backward and forward linkage with value chains

Shares of value added in final demand and in production

		World	Argentina	Brazil	Chile
Backward indicator (Demand)					
Share of USD 1 paid by consumers coming from:					
	Agriculture	74%	45%	65%	61%
	Other domestic sectors	18%	44%	29%	27%
	Foreign countries	8%	11%	7%	13%
Forward indicator (Production)					
Share of USD 1 of added value going to:					
	Agriculture	70%	12%	20%	34%
	Other domestic sectors	22%	55%	57%	34%
	Foreign countries	8%	33%	23%	32%

Source: Author's calculations from 2014 ICIO GTAP database (Greenville, Kawasaki and Beaujeu, 2017[17]).

2.5. The farming sector is dominated by big farms in the Pampas region

No up-to-date information exists regarding the structure of the farming sector in Argentina; the last agricultural census dates from 2002 (Box 2.2). According to this, the total number of agricultural holdings in the country was 297 425, with an average size of around 588 hectares (Table 2.3).The average size of farms devoted to grains tends to be higher, at 2 000 hectares, while farm size for land used for fruits and vegetables is relatively smaller, at 30 hectares.

Table 2.3. Farm structure and farm area in 2002

Hectares range	Holdings	Hectares	Contribution
0-5	40 957	105 895.1	0.1%
5.1-10	22 664	177 973.5	0.1%
10.1-25	39 833	714 584.2	0.4%
25.1-50	33 787	1 290 129.1	0.7%
50.1-100	34 881	2 660 005.5	1.5%
100.1-200	34 614	5 150 390.1	2.9%
200.1-500	40 211	13 113 229.4	7.5%
500.1-1 000	21 441	15 261 566.5	8.7%
1 001-2 500	16 621	26 489 560.0	15.2%
2 501-5 000	6 256	22 525 345.1	12.9%
5 001-7 500	2 088	12 962 493.8	7.4%
7 501-10 000	1 285	11 546 633.6	6.6%
10 001-20 000	1 851	27 296 370.2	15.6%
>20 000	936	35 514 388.0	20.3%
Total	297 425	174 808 564.1	100.0%

Source: INDEC, 2002.

Land ownership is generally high: almost 99% of all farm area is under the private system of land tenure, and property rights are secure. In 2002, around 74% of land in production was worked by the owner, and 11.5% was considered to be rented. The remainder was accounted for by other arrangements, including sharecropping.

Box 2.2. Official statistics in Argentina

The quality of Argentine statistics deteriorated over 2007-15. The frequency and quality of underlying censuses, surveys and procedures declined and some data on inflation, GDP and poverty levels became unreliable. In July 2011, the IMF found Argentina to be in breach of its minimum reporting requirements because of its inadequate provision of Consumer Price Index (CPI) and GDP data (IMF, 2013[18]). Since 2016, the national statistics institute INDEC has been completely reformed and its leadership changed. Argentina is now working with the OECD to improve the quality of its statistics.

In the case of agricultural statistics relevant for this study, several areas have been affected by the absence or unreliability of statistical data. This is particularly the case for household data and farming surveys, but also for the Agricultural Census, which has not been updated since 2002. Information on the value of agricultural production is incomplete, food inflation data is not reliable, and no information is available on rural poverty and farm structures. Production and trade information is more reliable. But the only available structural information on the farming sector dates from 2002 and, given the dynamic transformation of the sector in the last two decades, it is likely to provide an inaccurate picture of the current situation.

References

Bolt, J. and J. van Zanden (2014), "The Maddison Project: Collaborative research on historical national accounts", *The Economic History Review*, Vol. 67/3, http://dx.doi.org/10.1111/1468-0289.12032. [1]

FAOSTAT (2018), *Food and Agriculture Data*, Food and Agriculture Organization of the United Nations. [13]

Feeney, R. et al. (2012), *Encuesta Sobre las Necesidades del Productor Agropecuario Argentino 2012*, Centro de Estudios en Agronegocios y Alimentos, Universidad Ausral. [12]

Gerchunoff, P. (2016), *¿Por Que Argentina No Fue Australia?*, Siglo Veintiuno, http://www.sigloxxieditores.com.ar/fichaLibro.php?libro=978-987-629-699-1 (accessed on 06 April 2018). [2]

Greenville, J., K. Kawasaki and R. Beaujeu (2017), "A method for estimating global trade in value added within agriculture and food value chains", *OECD Food, Agriculture and Fisheries Papers*, No. 99, OECD Publishing, Paris, http://dx.doi.org/10.1787/f3a84910-en. [17]

IMF (2013), *Press Release: Statement by the IMF Executive Board on Argentina*, http://www.imf.org/en/News/Articles/2015/09/14/01/49/pr1333 (accessed on 05 June 2018). [18]

INDEC (2017), *Encuesta Permanente de Hogares*, Instituto Nacional de Estadística y Censos, República Argentina. [9]

INDEC (2010), *Censo Nacional de Poblacion, Hogares y Viviendas 2010*, Instituto Nacional de Estadistica y Censos, Republica Argentina. [8]

Lema, D. (2015), *Crecimiento y Productividad Total de Factores en la Agricultura: Argentina y Países del Cono Sur 1961-2013*, World Bank, Washington, DC. [14]

Lence, S. (2010), *The Agricultural Sector in Argentina: Major Trends and Recent Developments*, Iowa State University. [4]

Ministerio de Agroindustria (2018), *Sector background information provided by the Ministry of Agroindustry for the OECD Review of Agricultural Policies of Argentina*. [10]

OECD (2017), *OECD Economic Surveys: Argentina 2017: Multi-dimensional Economic Survey*, OECD Publishing, Paris, http://dx.doi.org/10.1787/eco_surveys-arg-2017-en. [3]

OECD/CAF/ECLAC (2015), *Latin American Economic Outlook 2016: Towards a New Partnership with China*, OECD Publishing, Paris, http://dx.doi.org/10.1787/9789264246218-en. [15]

Regúnaga, M. and A. Tejeda Rodriguez (2015), *Argentina's agricultural policies, trade and sustainable development objectives*, International Center for Trade and Sustainable Development (ICTSD). [5]

UN (2018), *UN Comtrade database*. [7]

UNDP (2017), *Human Development Report*, United Nations Development Programme. [11]

WDI (2018), *World Development Indicators*, World Bank, Washington, DC. [6]

WTO (2017), *Trade in value-added and global value chains: Statistical profile of Argentina*, https://www.wto.org/english/res_e/statis_e/miwi_e/countryprofiles_e.htm. [16]

Notes

[1] Urban refers to the population that resides in areas of 2 000 or more inhabitants; rural areas are, in turn, those with less than 2 000 inhabitants.

[2] The national official poverty line is based on the cost of the basic needs. It consists of establishing whether households have the capacity to satisfy – through the purchase of goods and services – a set of needs both food as non-food (including: clothing, transportation, health, housing, education, etc.) considered essential (INDEC, 2017[9]).

Chapter 3. Agricultural policy framework and objectives

Agricultural policies in Argentina have suffered the same volatility as other policies, especially macroeconomic and trade policies. The open economy approach of the 1990s was followed by a period of economic isolation with higher tariffs and export taxes over 2001-15. The current Government has renewed the open economy approach since 2015. The Ministry of Agriculture was only separated from the Ministry of Economy in 2009, while a broader focus on the whole value chain was introduced in 2015 and reflected in the new name of Ministry of Agroindustry, which is part of the Ministry of Production and Labour since September 2018. Several decentralised institutions with responsibility for implementing agricultural policies and services have a long tradition of professionalism; these include the research and extension institute, INTA, and the animal and plant health service, SENASA. There are very few input or output payments to producers in Argentina, with the exception of programmes under the Special Tobacco Fund (FET), preferential credit mainly to small producers through FINAGRO and some infrastructure programmes such as PROSAP.

3.1. A history of back and forths on trade openness

Since the beginning of the 20th century, Argentine agricultural policies have shifted back and forth between free trade and import substitution under different economic policy frameworks (Table 3.1). The country experienced a golden age between 1860 and 1915, when its agricultural exports boomed. But after the 1929 crash the country took a series of measures that ended free trade. The economy gradually opened again in the period leading up to World War II, but after 1945 the country decided to keep trade barriers (Lema, 2018[1]).

Temporary trade liberalisation took place in the late 1970s, and in the second half of the 1980s, Argentina explored ways to trade more with its neighbours and with the world. The first step was economic integration within MERCOSUR in 1991 and then signature of the WTO agreement in 1994. This was followed by substantial liberalisation of trade throughout the 1990s, the biggest opening of the economy in more than 60 years. A key measure was the substantial reduction of tariffs, with an average external tariff of 11% by the late 1990s and no export restrictions (Lema, 2018[1]).

Table 3.1. Main developments in agricultural policies

Years	Economic framework	Key agricultural policy measures	Long term agricultural initiatives and policies
1860-1932	Open economy	Low import tariffs and export taxes. High levels of investments in transport and agricultural infrastructure (railroads, ports).	Promotion of commodity production.
1933-40	Open economy with increasing regulations	Searching for low food prices for final consumers. Import tariffs. Price stabilisation measures: support prices, public stockholding policies, trade regulations, exchange rate market controls.	Creation of National Boards (Grains/Meat).
1941-70	Closed economy	Price interventions on main agricultural products, mandatory public stockholding, export taxes on agricultural trade, tariffs on imports of agricultural inputs such as fertiliser, low levels of investment in *private* agricultural R&D, and in general infrastructure.	Creation of several farmer organisations and regulation of the land tenure system. Creation of agricultural R&D and extension services INTA (1956) AACREA (1960).
1971-90	Attempts to open the economy	Export taxes on agricultural products and high anti-trade bias continues. Initial attempts to open up to trade. Low levels of investment in R&D and agricultural infrastructure, roads, and electrification.	Initial conversations towards regional trade agreements: MERCOSUR (1985). Private organisations created or grow to take over tasks provided by the government, AAPRESID (1989).
1991-2001	Open economy	Dismantling stockholding and price-setting public institutions, reduction of import and export tariffs, free trade agreements. Price stabilisation, reduction of barriers to trade, privatisation and deregulation of markets.	Starting of MERCOSUR (1994) and WTO (1995). SENASA merges with the Institute for Plant Health IASCAV and strengthens the control of Foot-and-Mouth Disease. Creation of INASE. Dissolution of National Boards (1991)
2002-15	Closed economy	Implementation of export taxes. Search for low food prices for final consumers, high import tariffs, and high export taxes, value chains subject to regulations as export quotas and price controls at the retail level. The National Office of Agricultural Trade Control (ONCCA) implements ROEs and other trade restrictions.	INTA increasing budget and personnel staff. SENASA extends its control to plant species (previously only animals). ONCCA is dissolved in 2011.
2016-	Open economy	Elimination of export taxes for all agricultural commodities, except soybean, which are reduced.	CFA (Federal Agricultural Council) reformed.

Source: Authors based on Lema (2018[1]).

However, after experiencing a financial crisis in 2001, the country once again changed its policy paradigm and moved back to closed markets. With a strong real depreciation of the peso, domestic price stability and the fiscal balance were at stake, and export taxes on agricultural products were reintroduced. Taxes on agricultural exports were the preferred instrument to maintain the fiscal balance because they were easy to implement and effective in raising revenue (Chapter 5). In the context of rising international agricultural prices, these taxes enabled an increase in government revenues.

In 2015, the new government reversed the previous agricultural policies by eliminating export taxes for most agricultural and livestock products (except those for soybeans and soybean oil, which were significantly reduced)[1]. All export quotas were eliminated, and the exchange rate was deregulated (i.e. allowed to float). This resulted in favourable changes in relative prices and increased revenues for grain and meat producers. Agricultural policy is now focused on integration in world markets. When the new government came into power in 2015, it carried out a process of consultation and consensus-building with different stakeholders in the agro-industrial subsectors, with provincial and local governments, and national Ministries that relate to the sector. On the basis of this consultation process, a strategic agricultural policy plan was developed for the 2015-20 period.

The main objective of this plan is to make Argentina a benchmark country in the agro-industrial development of food, based on productivity, competitiveness and development in technology and innovation, with actions that lead to the productive and commercial integration of the sector in international markets (Ministerio de Agroindustria, 2018[2]). To achieve this general objective, five strategic guidelines were developed:

- Achieving the maximum productive potential of the regions in a sustainable way, by preserving biodiversity and improving the quality of natural resources.
- Promoting product differentiation and value-adding, by fostering national development in the whole agroindustry sector.
- Improving the competitiveness and transparency of the agroindustrial chain and increasing value added and exports through market diversification.
- Promoting territorial development with a focus on family farmers, small- and medium-scale farmers, and rural workers.
- Contributing to global food security by improving diversity and access to food, and ensuring food safety and quality.

Furthermore, the general objective was supported by two high-level initiatives the "Agroindustry Strengthening Plan" (*Plan de Fortalecimiento de la Agroindustria*) and the "Irrigation Plan" (*Plan de Riego*). These initiatives are part of the long-term development framework of the national government under the objectives of "National Productive Agreement" (*Acuerdo Productivo Nacional*) and "Infrastructure Development" (*Desarrollo de la Infraestructura*), respectively.[2] Moreover, other public investments impacting the sector fall under the national public investments strategy of *Belgrano Plan*, which prioritises social, productive and infrastructure investments in the less developed regions in the north of Argentina (Box 3.1).

Box 3.1. The Belgrano Plan

The Belgrano Plan is a set of initiatives to promote the development of the Northern region of Argentina, which includes the provinces of Jujuy, Salta, Tucumán, Santiago del Estero, Catamarca, La Rioja, Formosa, Chaco, Corrientes and Misiones. These provinces have lower levels of economic and social development than the rest of the country. The Plan focuses on social, infrastructure and production areas. The Plan, run by the Chief of the Cabinet of Ministers and set out in Decree 435/2016, has no specific budget; rather, it co-ordinates all infrastructure and social actions in the Northern provinces. The Plan works in an articulated way with the different national ministries, through established working groups, following up on projects, programmes and works carried out throughout the Northern region.

There are four working boards: Social Development, Productive Development, Infrastructure and Regional Integration. Each board has a different composition of Ministries. The Secretariat of Agroindustry is represented only on the Productive Development Board.

The Belgrano Plan co-ordinates actions of all the national agencies in the provinces to enhance policies for the region, as well as initiatives not focused on the region but which have an impact on it.

The Plan seeks to improve: 1) The Human Development Index (10 provinces that comprise the Belgrano Plan are lower on the Index than the rest of the country); 2) Housing, especially sewerage, for 61% of the population in the region; 3) Exports (the region represents only 10% of the country's total exports).

The national government has developed actions in the following areas: improve social and housing conditions, housing infrastructure and urban planning; investments to consolidate the connectivity and social and economic integration of the region; rehabilitation and renewal of roads and corridors, including the General Belgrano Cargas Railroad; investments in transportation services; construction of roads beyond the national road network; infrastructure for a rational, integral, and equitable multiple use of water resources, including for productive purposes in the agro-industrial sector, where 34% of the investments fall under "Policies for increasing production and productivity in agro-industrial chains in a sustainable manner"; and tourism development. 35% of the Federal Solidarity Fund for infrastructure works is transferred to the Belgrano provinces.

3.2. Institutional arrangements[3]

In Argentina the Secretariat of Agroindustry (Ministry of Agroindustry up to September 2018) is responsible for the management, formulation and implementation of agricultural policies. Up to 2009, responsibility for agricultural policies lay with the Ministry of the Economy. The Ministry of Agroindustry was created in 2016 after an institutional reform of the previous Ministry of Agriculture (Decrees 13/15, 32/2016 and 302/2017), with the aim of broadening the scope of the Ministry from just focusing on primary production to the agroindustry sector as a whole. This change reflects the view that the primary productive sector and related industries are key strategic participants in the economic development of the country (Ministerio de Agroindustria, 2018[2]). The reform also responded to efficiency needs to cut red tape, improve co-ordination and avoid overlapping functions among national and provincial public agencies. Argentina is a federal country and some policy competencies and their implementation correspond to the provinces. Provincial governments have a leading role on regional cross-sector development strategies (OECD, 2016[3]).

The competences of the Ministry of Agroindustry did not completely change in 2016 nor in 2018 when it became a Secretariat of the Ministry of Production, only the emphasis in the areas of action and the implementation and co-ordination mechanisms. The Secretariat of Agroindustry had four secretariats and seven sub-secretariats. Each secretariat has its own remit and assists the Secretary of Government of Agroindustry in the design, implementation and co-ordination of different policies and actions. The four secretariats are the Secretariat of Agriculture, Livestock and Fisheries, the Secretariat of Food and Bio-economy, the Secretariat of Family Agriculture, Coordination and Territorial Development, and the Secretariat of Agro-Industrial Markets.

Figure 3.1. Organigram of the Secretariat of Agroindustry of Argentina

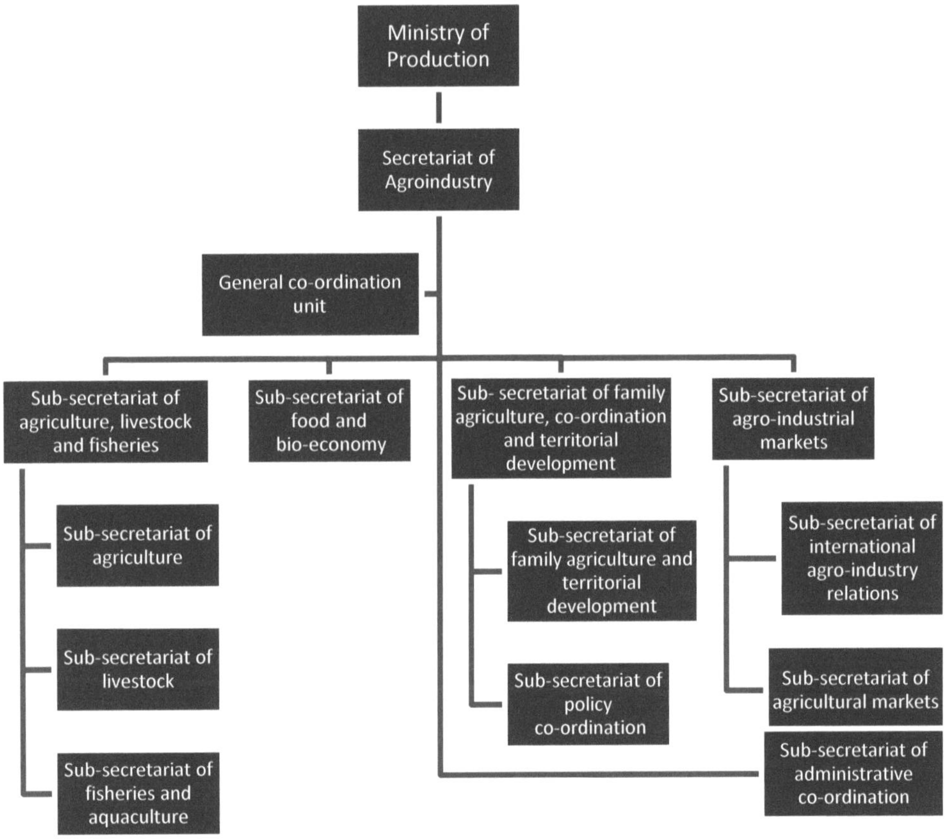

Note: In early September 2018, several institutional arrangements in the government changed, including the integration of the former Ministry of Agroindustry into the Ministry of Production. Several changes are still underway and therefore the current organisation does not include institutional adjustments that will eventually take place.
Source: (Ministerio de Agroindustria, 2018[2]).

As part of the institutional reforms undertaken by the new Government in 2016, the Federal Agricultural Council (CFA) was strengthened and broadened to improve the dialogue with the agro-industrial sector in the provinces. The CFA aims to foster dialogue between national and provincial authorities by identifying, prioritising and addressing problems at local, regional and national levels and by providing support and technical co-operation. The CFA is a consultative advisory and sectoral co-ordination body to the National Executive Branch (created by the Law No. 23843/1990). It approves the sectoral plan and budget and meets every six months. The CFA is chaired by the Minister of Agroindustry and includes the heads of Ministries of each province. The CFA has five regional commissions: the Northwest, the Northeast, New Cuyo, the Pampas, and Patagonia. The CFA's main responsibilities include: 1) preparation of legislative initiatives with federal application and of administrative regulations; 2) identification of instruments for the promotion of regional economies (agricultural production outside of the Pampas region); 3) strategic design of public policies aimed at provincial, regional and national development; 4) definition of productive strategies by value chain.

Other institutional reforms implemented in 2016 focused on reducing red tape in the sector. The creation of the Platform of Procedures at Distance (*Trámites a distancia*, TAD) allows all procedures related to a ministry to be carried out remotely. Similarly, National Executive Order 1079/2016 created the Foreign Trade Exclusive Desk (*Ventanilla Única de Comercio Exterior, VUCE*) aimed at optimising and digitally unifying the information and documentation for import, export and customs transit (Ministerio de Agroindustria, 2018[2]).

Decentralised agencies

The public institutional framework in Argentina is relatively straightforward and comprises five main institutions under the Secretariat of Agroindustry (Figure 3.2): the National Agricultural Technology Institute (Instituto Nacional de Tecnología Agropecuaria, INTA), the National Service for Agro-Food Health and Quality (Servicio Nacional de Sanidad y Calidad Agroalimentaria, SENASA), the National Institute of Seeds (Instituto Nacional de Semillas, INASE), the National Institute of Viticulture (Instituto Nacional de Vitivinicultura, INV) and the National Institute of Research and Development of Fisheries (Instituto Nacional de Investigación y Desarrollo Pesquero, INIDEP). These institutions are financially and politically independent but have to follow the main guidelines of agricultural policy and to report to the Secretary of Agroindustry for guidance.

INTA is by far the most important institution within the public system, in terms of both budgetary allocation and number of employees. INTA was created in 1956 by Decree-Law No. 21680/56 and has two main functions: agricultural research and development and extension services. INTA is a decentralised institution with operational and financial autonomy and is mainly funded by a budgetary allocation of 0.45% of the Cost Insurance and Freight (CIF) value of imports (Law No. 25641). INTA serves a wide spectrum of farmers, ranging from those who produce for own-consumption to those producing for international markets. INTA has played a key role in the generation and transfer of knowledge and is present throughout the country. However, in recent years its main activities have shifted towards the implementation of social rural policies funded by different ministries, at both national and provincial levels. This can impact its effectiveness in providing innovation services (Chapter 6).

SENASA's functions date back at the end of the 19th century and are basically to provide sanitary guarantees for exports. However, SENASA was formally created in 1996 (Decree No. 660 and Law No. 24629) to merge the separate animal and plant health institutes. SENASA is financially autonomous and is funded by budgetary allocation and by fees charged to farmers for services provided. SENASA's mission is to plan, regulate, execute, supervise and certify processes and products, as well as to implement controls on animal and plant health, food safety, hygiene and quality, safety of products and associated inputs, across the different stages of primary production, processing, transformation, transport and trade. SENASA's main challenge is ensuring the capacity and reach of its technical personnel to cover the entire country, and to enforce the laws related to its objectives (Chapter 8).

Figure 3.2. The institutional agricultural framework of Argentina

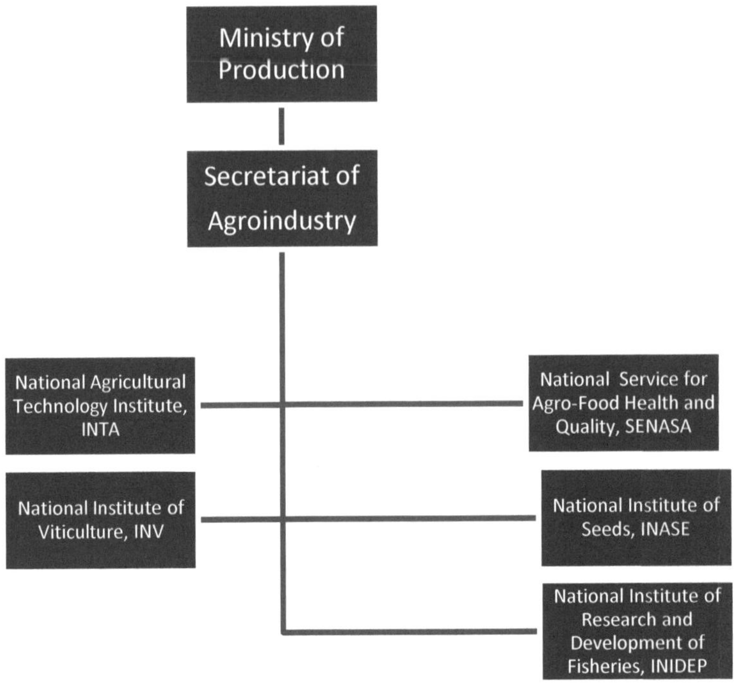

Source: Authors based on information from the (Ministerio de Agroindustria, 2018[2]).

The seeds institute INASE was originally created in 1973 (Law. No. 20247/73) but later renamed and its functions redirected in 1991 (Decree 2817/91). Dismantled (Decree 1104) in 2000 and recreated in 2003 under the original Decree (2817/73), its main function is to promote the efficient production and commercialisation of seeds, while guaranteeing the identity and quality of seeds acquired and protecting the property rights of phyto-genetic creations. INASE reports directly to the Minister of Agroindustry and is publicly funded.

INASE's main objectives are: i) to interpret and apply the Seed Law and Phyto-genetic Creations Law (N°20247); ii) to exercise the law enforcement derived from its implementation; iii) to issue national and international certifications for any plant organ destined for sowing, planting or propagation, while complying with any relevant agreement signed by Argentina; iv) to protect and register the intellectual property of seeds and phyto-genetic and biotechnological creations; v) to propose and apply regulations regarding the identity and quality of seeds. INASE's main challenge is to improve the enforcement of intellectual property rights (IPR) laws (Chapter 6).

The viticulture institute INV oversees the technical control of production, industrialisation and commercialisation of grape and wine making, and the control of production, circulation, and trading of ethyl alcohol and methanol. INV regulates and implements several laws: Law No. 14878 on wine; Law No. 24566 on alcoholic beverages; Law No. 25163 on general rules for the designation and presentation of wines and spirit drinks, their indication of geographical origin and their controlled designation of origin; Law No. 26093 on regulation and promotion for the sustainable production and use of biofuels. INV is funded through fees for the services it provides and from the fines it applies (Chapters 6 and 9).

The fisheries institute, INIDEP, is a decentralised institution created by Law No. 21673 that carries out fisheries research and development. INIDEP is fully resourced with public funds. Law No. 24922 provides that the Federal Fisheries Council sets the objectives, policies and requirements of scientific and technical research related to marine-living resources, while INIDEP carries out planning and execution of scientific and technical activities with the provinces and other bodies or entities. The INIDEP research programme generates and adapts knowledge, information, methods and technology for the development, use and conservation of Argentine marine fisheries (Ministerio de Agroindustria, 2018[2]).

Private institutions

Argentina has a long history of private institutions that organise stakeholders and farmers. These include co-operatives, confederations, federations, supply chain farmer organisations, chambers and societies, among others. Some of these private institutions are: Confederación Inter-cooperativa Agropecuaria Limitada (CONINAGRO); Confederaciones Rurales Argentinas (CRA); Federación Agraria Argentina (FAA); Sociedad Rural Argentina (SRA); Asociación Argentina De Consorcios Regionales De Experimentación Agrícola (AACREA); Asociación Argentina de Productores en Siembra Directa (AAPRESID); Coordinadora De Las Industrias De Productos Alimenticios (COPAL); Confederación Argentina De La Mediana Empresa (CAME); Asociación De La Cadena De La Soja Argentina (ACSOJA); Asociación Maíz Argentino (MAIZAR); Asociación Argentina De Trigo (ARGENTRIGO); Asociación Argentina De Girasol (ASAGIR); Cámara de la Sanidad Agropecuaria y Fertilizantes (CASAFE); Cámara de la Industria Argentina de Fertilizantes y Agroquímicos (CIAFA); Fertilizar Asociación Civil (FERTILIZAR); Asociación de Cooperativas Argentinas (ACA); Instituto de Promoción de la Carne Vacuna Argentina (IPCVA); Corporación Vitivinícola Argentina (COVIAR) among others (Chapters 4 and 9, and Annex A).

These private institutions have played an important role in the development of the agricultural sector; for example, in the establishment of land tenure, the generation and adoption of new technologies, and in the design of long-term agricultural policies. On several occasions they have served as a counterbalance to unstable policies.

3.3. Overview of the main agricultural policy areas

The policy measures that provide support to agriculture in Argentina are decided and implemented not only by the Secretariat of Agroindustry, but also by other ministries and government agencies. Following the OECD methodology to estimate the support to the sector based on implementation criteria, policy measures can be classified under different categories (OECD, 2016[4]). The first main distinction is between: policies that provide direct positive or negative support to farmers for example, via minimum reference prices, taxes, subsidies or payments; and policies that provide support to the agricultural sector as a whole, such as public expenditures on R&D and extension services or animal and plant health. Argentina concentrates most of the budgetary programmes on the provisions of general services such as agricultural innovation system or inspection services. Compared with producer support, these programmes are less distorting and better targeted to enhance the productivity and sustainability of the sector. The country provides few payments to farmers or highly distorting measures, except for the export taxes.

Support to producers

In Argentina, the majority of agricultural products do not receive price support; on the contrary, export taxes and restrictions were imposed on several agricultural products over the past decades, until 2015. An exception is the positive support provided to tobacco producers in the form of a supplement to market prices (payment based on output) as part of a broader policy arrangement called the Special Tobacco Fund (*Fondo Especial del Tabaco* FET, Box 3.2).

Box 3.2. The Special Tobacco Fund (FET)

The Special Tobacco Fund (*Fondo Especial del Tabaco* FET) was created in 1972 (Decree Law 19.800) to provide additional revenue to producers. The fund is financed by a tax of 7% on all tobacco sold in Argentina, which goes directly to the Secretariat of Agroindustry. These funds are not mixed with the regular budget: 20% of the funds are spent by the Secretariat of Agroindustry and 80% are transferred to the tobacco producing provinces proportionally to their share in national production. The beneficiary provinces are, in decreasing order, Jujuy, Salta, Misiones, Tucuman, Corrientes, Chaco and Catamarca. The sector is dominated by small producers with critical economic and social difficulties, and the benefiting regions are all also included under the Belgrano Plan.

Historically, the share of the fund managed by the provinces was mainly spent to supplement prices to producers. However, after the signature of the WTO agreement in 1994, Argentina committed to reduce this support by 1.3% yearly over three years. Argentina's Total Aggregate Measurement of Support (Total AMS) commitment level in WTO constrains expenditure to support the tobacco producer price. Currently only 20% of the FET funds spent by the provinces are dedicated to support tobacco prices, with the rest being spent on programmes to support producers' fixed and working capital, to provide technical assistance, to invest in local infrastructure and even to provide social and health assistance. These programmes are declared under the Green Box in WTO; according to the PSE methodology, they cover payments based on inputs, general services, and some are not specific to agriculture even if they are implemented in tobacco producing areas.

Each province approves its set of Annual Operative Projects (POAs) that are then approved by the Secretariat of Agroindustry before the funds are transferred. Each province distributes the funds with different criteria on the basis of their POA.

In 2017, the total FET was ARS 5 762 million (Argentina pesos) in 2017, the same order of magnitude as expenditures on INTA. The fund was initially focused on supporting tobacco producers in poor provinces, but its implementation is now constrained by the WTO and its objectives are blurred. The programme would need to redefine its objectives and implementation towards facilitating the adjustment and economic development of tobacco producers and their families.

Argentina provides very limited input subsidies, mostly in the form of implicit interest rate subsidies through preferential credit provided by FINAGRO. These credits are targeted to a range of products and finance investment and working capital. A new fund, FONDAGRO, was created in 2017 to finance investment in the sector at preferential interest rates, but its scope is presently limited.

There are almost no direct payments to producers in Argentina. Limited amounts are provided as disaster assistance in response to extreme weather events, mainly droughts (Chapter 8). There are no national direct payments for agri-environmental services, and few at provincial level. Among these, since 2017, voluntary payments on area have been provided in the province of Cordoba subject to the application of good agricultural practices.

General services to the sector

A significant share of public expenditure in the agricultural sector is directed to general services, mainly agricultural knowledge and innovation, and food inspection and control. Research and development and extension services are mainly provided by INTA, while animal and plant health and input control services are provided mainly by SENASA.

Agricultural and rural infrastructure has received very little investment over the past decades, and limited large-scale irrigation works have been undertaken. The Agricultural Provincial Services Programme (PROSAP), financed by the Inter-American Development Bank (IADB) and managed by the Secretariat of Agroindustry has been the exception, investing mainly in large agricultural irrigation infrastructure.

Consumer measures

During the period 2007-10, the National Office of Agricultural Trade Control (ONCCA) subsidised the price of some food commodities bought by first processors, including wheat, beef and milk. Argentina has no social protection programmes to support food consumption or distribute food among households in need. However, the country has a long history of providing free services to its population, such as public health care and basic education, and subsidies for utilities like electrification, fuel and water. These latter are currently being phased out.

Biofuel policy

Argentina is a large exporter of biodiesel produced from soya and has an active biofuel policy. The Biofuel Law 26.093 approved in 2006 establishes compulsory blend mandates since 2010, starting at 5% but then progressive increased to 10% for diesel and 12% for gasoline. The Law also assures that, up to the end-term of the Law in 2021, the biofuel production supplied in the domestic market will be purchased at a price calculated according to a formula. Biofuel production can also benefit from some fiscal measures. First, exports of biofuels have historically had a lower tax rate than the export of grains and oilseeds, creating incentives for processing rather than exporting raw inputs (Chapter 5). Secondly, the Law establishes that domestic consumption of biofuels benefits from a VAT rebates under certain conditions, which, however, have not been met by exporting companies.

References

Lema, D. (2018), *Agricultural policies in Argentina*, Insituto de Economía- INTA, Buenos Aires. [1]

Ministerio de Agroindustria (2018), *Sector background information provided by the Ministry of Agroindustry for the OECD Review of Agricultural Policies of Argentina*. [2]

OECD (2016), *OECD Territorial Reviews: Córdoba, Argentina*, https://doi.org/10.1787/19900759. [3]

OECD (2016), *OECD's Producer Support Estimate and Related Indicators of Agriculture Suport: Concepts, Calculations, Interpretation and Use (The PSE Manual)*, Trade and Agriculture Directorate, http://www.oecd.org/tad/agricultural-policies/full%20text.pdf (accessed on 07 June 2018). [4]

Notes

[1] In early September 2018, while this review was being written, the government decided several policy measures in response to an economic turmoil triggered by a large depreciation of the peso. Among these measures, the introduction of taxes on all exports will directly affect the agricultural sector and the estimate of support.

[2] Similarly, the national development framework of the "State Modernisation Plan" (*Plan de Modernización del Estado*) includes the objective of strengthening the National Agricultural Sanitary Service (*Servicio Nacional de Sanidad y Calidad Agroalimentaria*, SENASA) to improve food safety and simplify the process for agro-industrial exports (Ministerio de Agroindustria, 2018[2]).

[3] Among the policy measures taken in early September 2018, the reduction in the number of Ministries changes the institutional arrangements of the agricultural public sector. The Ministry of Agroindustry is now under the auspices of the Ministry of Production and Labour as a Secretariat which has a lower institutional level. As these measures are still underway, this section could be subject of further changes to reflect the institutional changes.

Chapter 4. Benchmarking agricultural policies: PSE results

Argentina's policies have burdened the agro-food exporting sector for most of the last two decades. Producer support was estimated to have a negative value of -14% in 2015-17, showing the impact of these policies on farmers' receipts. The %PSE was as low as -39% in 2008-10. This negative value is an outlier compared with most other countries covered by OECD monitoring and evaluation. The current administration eliminated all export taxes with the exception of those on soybean in 2016, and this has been reflected in the reduction in the absolute value of the negative PSE. Given that soybeans represent a big share of the value of production in Argentina, the PSE is likely to remain negative if the export taxes on soybean remain. The new temporary tax on all exports introduced in September 2018 is not yet reflected in the estimates of support. Direct payments to farmers are marginal. General services on Knowledge and Innovation and Inspection are significant. However, the Total Support Estimate (TSE) remains negative.

4.1. Introduction

This section provides a quantitative evaluation of support allocated to Argentinian agriculture between 1997 and 2017. This evaluation is based on OECD indicators of agricultural support, including the Producer Support Estimate (PSE), Consumer Support Estimate (CSE), Total Support Estimate (TSE), General Services Support Estimate (GSSE), and others indicators (Box 4.1). The definitions of these indicators are presented in Annex C. The "PSE Manual" (OECD, 2016[1]), a detailed description of the methodology applied by the OECD to estimate agricultural support, as well as the comprehensive databases for OECD countries and a number of non-OECD countries are available at www.oecd.org/tad/support/psecse. The methodology applied in this study is consistent with that used in OECD reports that monitor and evaluate agricultural policies in other countries (OECD, 2017[2]). Technical details of the calculations for all support indicators in Argentina are set out in Box 4.1.

4.2. Unlike most other countries Argentina has negative producer support

The percentage Producer Support Estimate (%PSE) is the OECD's key indicator to measure support to agricultural producers. It expresses the monetary value of support transfers to agricultural producers as a percentage of producer gross receipts. As it is neither affected by inflation nor the size of the sector, it allows comparisons in the level of support to be made both over time and among countries. This indicator provides insights into the support or burden that agricultural policies place on producers, consumers and on taxpayers, through negative or positive market price support or through budgetary transfers.

In most of the countries studied by the OECD, market price support (MPS) is positive or zero. A positive MPS reflects that the support measures make domestic prices higher than international reference prices. MPS close to zero indicates that domestic prices are aligned with world prices. Negative MPS reflects interventions on prices that lead to domestic prices below international reference prices. Argentina's estimations show that the agricultural sector has been heavily burdened over the last two decades, with domestic prices below world market levels, resulting in negative MPS. This implies transfers from producers to first consumers or buyers of the primary agricultural product, i.e. millers and processors in the industry, who can buy cheaper inputs. Taxpayers also benefit via the government revenues from export taxes.

The average level of producer support in Argentina, expressed as a share of gross farm receipts (%PSE) was -14% for the 2015-17 period. This negative number indicates how much public policies have reduced producers' gross farm receipts. Negative MPS has been the main component of the PSE in Argentina, while budgetary support (different types of subsidies) has been relatively low and offset only marginally the negative MPS. This negative level of support is an outlier in comparison with OECD countries, as well as other emerging economies, where the agricultural sectors receive significant support (Figure 4.1). Only Ukraine, India and Viet Nam have also a negative level of support as measured by the %PSE (OECD, 2018[3]).

Figure 4.1. Producer Support Estimate (PSE) in Argentina and selected countries, 2015-17

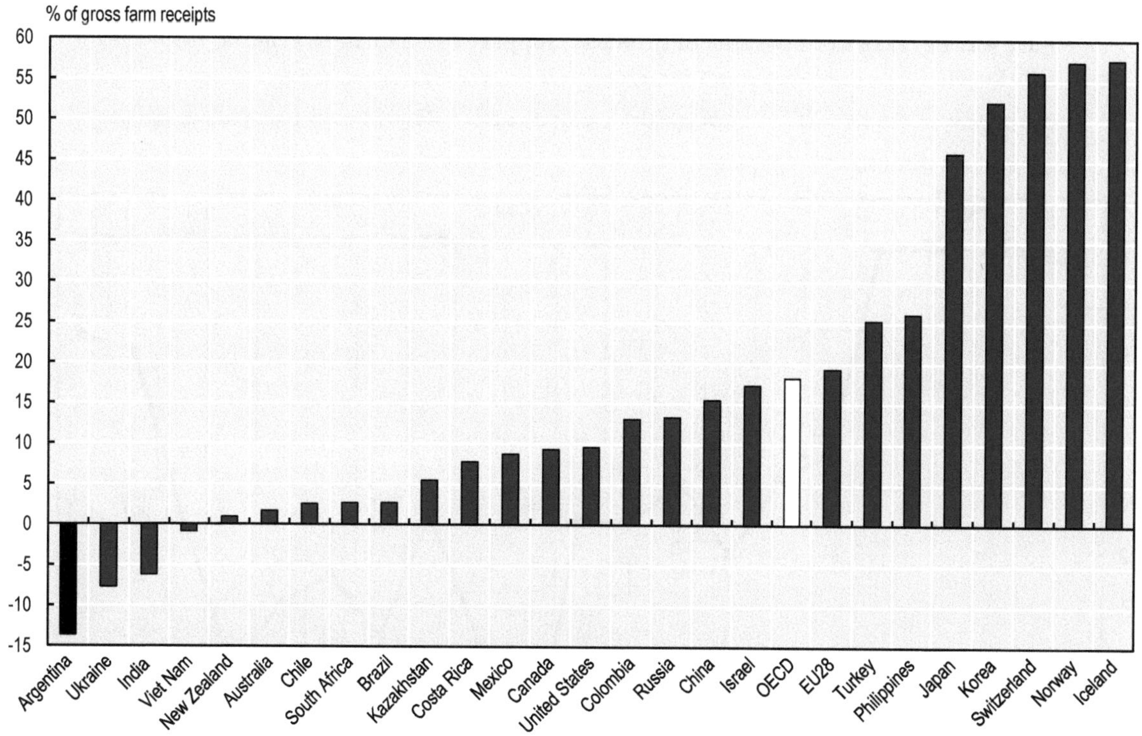

1. The statistical data for Israel are supplied by and under the responsibility of the relevant Israeli authorities. The use of such data by the OECD is without prejudice to the status of the Golan Heights, East Jerusalem and Israeli settlements in the West Bank under the terms of international law.
2. The OECD total does not include the non-OECD EU member states.
3. 2014-16 instead of 2015-17 for India.
Source: (OECD, 2018) "Producer and Consumer Estimates", OECD Agriculture Statistics Database.

StatLink https://doi.org/10.1787/888933907792

Argentina's negative %PSE represents the sum of a large negative price support (derived from export taxes) and a small positive support (certain types of subsidies or budgetary payments provided to farmers and a relatively small positive MPS for certain products). Both components to some extent offset each other and therefore need to be interpreted carefully (Figure 4.2). The negative MPS is a consequence of different measures, but is mainly due to export taxes on key agricultural products such as soybean, wheat, maize, sunflower and beef. The positive part of the support represents mainly subsidies for tobacco and other subsidies for variable and fixed inputs, including those provided through preferential interest rates. When these two components (negative and positive support) are added up, they only partially cancel each other out, and negative results largely dominate the policy effects in Argentina.

Argentina systematically has negative %PSE values since 2002 when export taxes on its main commodities were introduced, with high negative support of around -30% over 2002-15. The largest negative value coincides with the world price spike of 2008 that resulted in a record high level of export taxes in Argentina (Figure 4.2). This type of policies and their continuous adjustments create uncertainty and may exacerbate the volatility of world prices (FAO, IFAD, IMF,OECD, UNCTAD, WFP, the World Bank, the WTO, 2011[4]). Under the reforms introduced by the new government, negative price support has been gradually reduced since 2016.

Figure 4.2. Level and composition of Producer Support Estimate in Argentina, 1997-2017

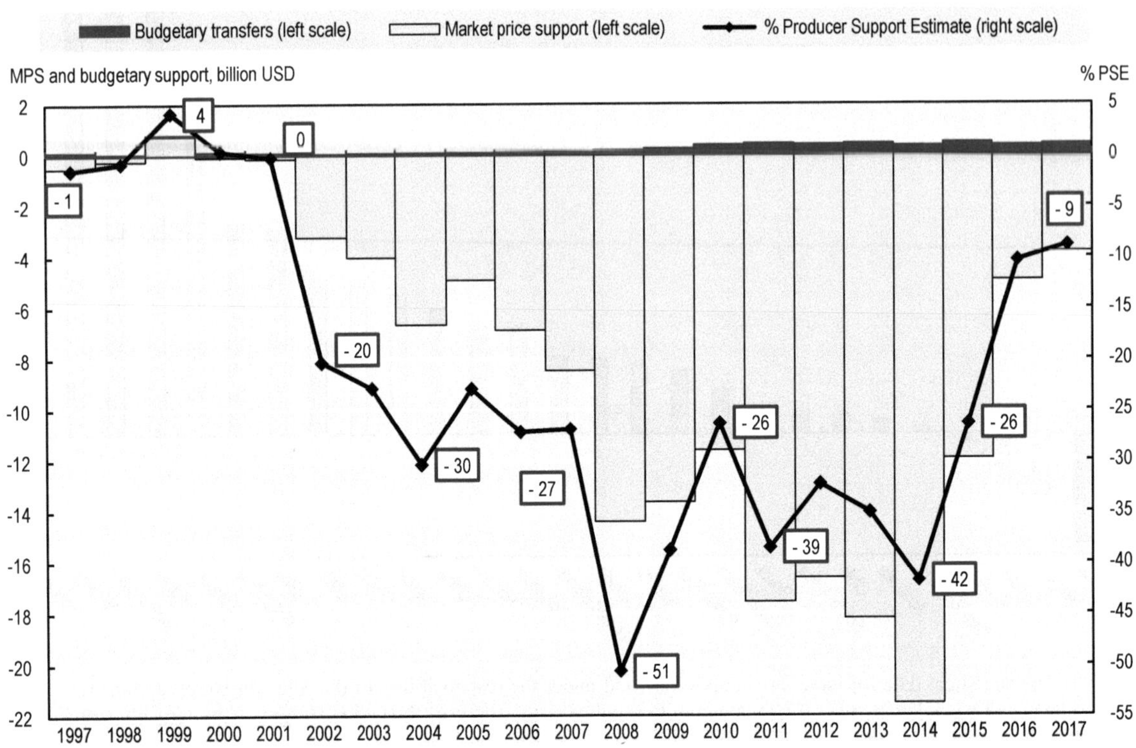

Source: (OECD, 2018), "Producer and Consumer Estimates", OECD Agriculture Statistics Database.

4.3. Most negative producer support is a reflection of highly distorting export taxes

The way in which support is delivered to farmers merits as much attention as the level of support itself (whether positive or negative). The composition of support shows how positive producer support is provided and negative producer support is imposed, with different impacts on the agricultural sector and on the distribution of benefits across society. Support may be given through MPS or input subsidies, it may take the form of a payment per hectare or per animal, of compensation to producer income or through export refunds. On the other hand, instruments such as export bans and export taxes are taxing the sector (negative support). These distinctions are important: depending on how it is delivered, support has varying impacts on agricultural production, trade and incomes.

Market price support is directly linked to commodity output and can have a significant effect on production and trade. This type of support – be it positive or negative – qualifies as the most trade-distorting form of support. Moreover, MPS is less effective in increasing (or decreasing) producer income than other types of support, such as direct payments to farmers or taxes on assets that are less attached to commodity output. Negative market price support "taxes" producers with low prices, creating at once a disincentive to produce and a transfer from producers to government through public tax revenues (if there is a tax) and to first consumers through lower prices. Both positive and negative market price support, either of which by definition applies on a commodity-by-commodity basis, distort relative production incentives across individual commodities.

Negative market price support imposes additional consequences on domestic consumers by providing a positive transfer to first buyers, i.e. processors, who buy their inputs at lower prices than those in the world markets. However, this transfer is less efficient in improving poor consumers' welfare than targeted measures like social policies focused on the poor. Negative MPS mainly benefits the processing industry and other elements of the value chain which only partially passes through the price reduction to final consumers. While positive MPS typically has negative impacts on the environment, there is no evidence that negative support improves environmental outcomes, which often depend on more targeted regulations and environmental measures.

For Argentina, the major components of the MPS are the price differential (the negative gap between domestic producer price and reference price) for soybeans, maize, wheat, sunflowers, beef, and poultry. The aggregate value of MPS is the outcome of implicit taxation through negative price gaps for some commodities (a negative MPS) and small price support of others (a positive MPS). Annual variations depend on movements in world prices, domestic prices and exchange rates, changes in production levels and, in the case of Argentina, the rates of the export taxes (Chapter 5).

Figure 4.3. Level and composition of budgetary transfers to producers in Argentina, 1997-2017

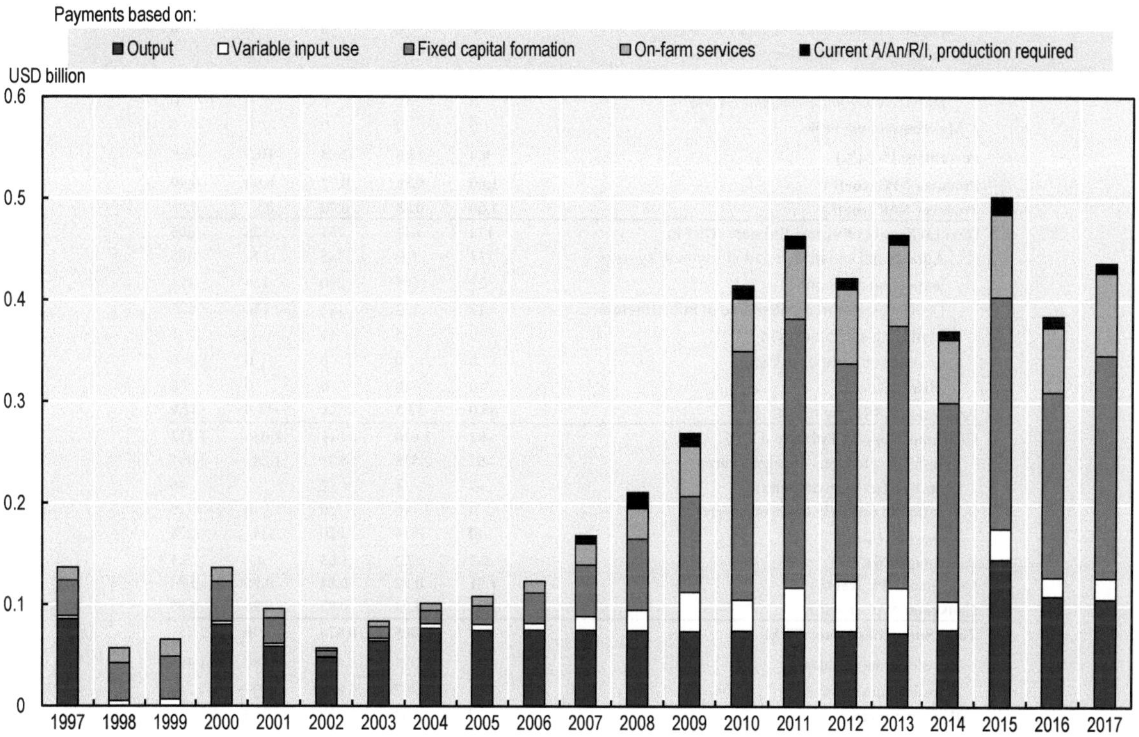

Note: A (area planted), An (animal numbers), R (receipts), I (income).
Source: OECD (2018), "Producer and Consumer Estimates", OECD Agriculture Statistics Database.

StatLink https://doi.org/10.1787/888933907811

Table 4.1. Argentina: Estimates of support to agriculture (provisional), USD million

	1997-99	2015-17	2015	2016	2017
Total value of production (at farm gate)	**22 043**	**41 220**	**42 867**	**43 408**	**37 385**
of which: share of MPS commodities (%)	*76.5*	*85.6*	*82.7*	*86.2*	*87.9*
Total value of consumption (at farm gate)	**11 407**	**24 542**	**26 223**	**23 737**	**23 666**
Producer Support Estimate (PSE)	**94**	**-6 436**	**-11 424**	**-4 526**	**-3 357**
Support based on commodity output	36	-6 757	-11 782	-4 801	-3 688
Market Price Support [1]	*7*	*-6 877*	*-11 927*	*-4 910*	*-3 794*
Payments based on output	*29*	*120*	*145*	*109*	*106*
Payments based on input use	58	309	340	265	321
Based on variable input use	*5*	*23*	*30*	*19*	*21*
with input constraints	*0*	*0*	*0*	*0*	*0*
Based on fixed capital formation	*38*	*210*	*228*	*182*	*219*
with input constraints	*0*	*0*	*0*	*0*	*0*
Based on on-farm services	*15*	*76*	*82*	*64*	*81*
with input constraints	*0*	*0*	*0*	*0*	*0*
Payments based on current A/An/R/I, production required	0	12	17	11	10
Based on Receipts / Income	0	0	0	0	0
Based on Area planted / Animal numbers	0	12	17	11	10
with input constraints	0	12	17	11	10
Payments based on non-current A/An/R/I, production required	0	0	0	0	0
Payments based on non-current A/An/R/I, production not required	0	0	0	0	0
With variable payment rates	0	0	0	0	0
with commodity exceptions	0	0	0	0	0
With fixed payment rates	0	0	0	0	0
with commodity exceptions	0	0	0	0	0
Payments based on non-commodity criteria	0	0	0	0	0
Based on long-term resource retirement	0	0	0	0	0
Based on a specific non-commodity output	0	0	0	0	0
Based on other non-commodity criteria	0	0	0	0	0
Miscellaneous payments	0	0	0	0	0
Percentage PSE (%)	**0.4**	**-13.6**	**-26.3**	**-10.3**	**-8.9**
Producer NPC (coeff.)	**1.00**	**0.86**	**0.77**	**0.90**	**0.90**
Producer NAC (coeff.)	**1.00**	**0.88**	**0.79**	**0.91**	**0.92**
General Services Support Estimate (GSSE)	**174**	**631**	**751**	**535**	**606**
Agricultural knowledge and innovation system	133	309	345	276	305
Inspection and control	23	165	200	124	171
Development and maintenance of infrastructure	17	152	195	134	125
Marketing and promotion	0	5	11	1	5
Cost of public stockholding	0	0	0	0	0
Miscellaneous	0	0	0	0	0
Percentage GSSE (% of TSE)	**65.0**	**-12.3**	**-7.0**	**-13.4**	**-22.0**
Consumer Support Estimate (CSE)	**-82**	**2 020**	**3 811**	**1 036**	**1 213**
Transfers to producers from consumers	-65	2 538	4 833	1 283	1 497
Other transfers from consumers	-7	-4	-2	-3	-6
Transfers to consumers from taxpayers	0	0	0	0	0
Excess feed cost	-10	-514	-1 020	-244	-278
Percentage CSE (%)	**-0.7**	**7.2**	**14.5**	**4.4**	**5.1**
Consumer NPC (coeff.)	**1.01**	**0.92**	**0.84**	**0.95**	**0.94**
Consumer NAC (coeff.)	**1.01**	**0.93**	**0.87**	**0.96**	**0.95**
Total Support Estimate (TSE)	**267**	**-5 805**	**-10 674**	**-3 990**	**-2 751**
Transfers from consumers	72	-2 534	-4 831	-1 280	-1 491
Transfers from taxpayers	203	-3 267	-5 841	-2 707	-1 253
Budget revenues	-7	-4	-2	-3	-6
Percentage TSE (% of GDP)	**0.1**	**-0.8**	**-1.7**	**-0.7**	**-0.4**
GDP deflator 1997-99 = 100	**100**	**1 916**	**1 383**	**1 937**	**2 428**

Note: NPC: Nominal Protection Coefficient. NAC: Nominal Assistance Coefficient.
A=area planted), An=animal numbers, R=receipts, I=income.

1. MPS commodities for Argentina are: wheat, maize, soybean, sunflower, fruit and vegetables, milk, beef, pigmeat, poultry and eggs. MPS is net of producer levies and Excess Feed Cost.

Source: OECD (2018), "Producer and Consumer Estimates", OECD Agriculture Statistics Database.

Budgetary transfers account for almost all the positive producer support to the sector in Argentina and comprises different types of payments (Figure 4.3, Table 4.1 and Annex D). Payments based on output are made to tobacco farmers through the Special Tobacco Fund (FET), and some milk payments also exist. Most of the payments based on input are in the form of preferential interest rates for agricultural credit from FINAGRO, FONDAGRO, PROSAP and FET. These credits serve to finance fixed capital formation such as the acquisition of machinery and equipment, but also working capital and variable inputs, particularly for seeds and fertilisers, as well as other payments to farmers based on the provision of services. The majority of all these subsidies is provided to small-scale farmers that produce other agricultural products than grains and beef, and who are embedded in "regional economies" (*Economias Regionales*) surrounding the Pampas region. Furthermore, these transfers are relatively modest in the overall scale of support. Argentina provides almost no payments per hectare, or any direct income support of the kind that is common in some OECD countries.

4.4. Support is provided to first buyers of primary agricultural products

The Consumer Support Estimate (CSE) measures the cost (or benefit) to consumers arising from market price support policies and food subsidies, and is measured at the farm gate level. A negative CSE indicates an implicit tax on consumers (i.e. consumers pay domestic prices that are higher than international prices), while a positive CSE suggests an implicit support (i.e. consumers pay domestic prices lower than the international prices). In the OECD methodology, the consumer is understood to be the first buyer of these products, which can be a processor or wholesaler, or a retailer and in some cases a final consumer. In the absence of consumer support policies, CSE generally mirrors MPS in broad terms. The CSE also includes budgetary food subsidies for consumers where they exist, which is not the case in Argentina in recent years.

When the CSE is positive, first buyers are able to purchase the product at a cheaper price in the domestic market (an implicit subsidy). This is the case in Argentina. First buyers of agricultural products (e.g. processors) benefit from lower prices of grains, meat and oilseeds. Similar to the PSE, the CSE can be expressed in relative terms as a percentage of consumption expenditures (%CSE). A negative CSE indicates that consumers are paying more than they would in comparison to border prices (an implicit tax). In the majority of countries monitored by the OECD, consumers (i.e. first buyers) are taxed in this way. In some countries this burden is partly or fully compensated through direct budgetary subsidies to poor consumers or various forms of food assistance, such as the food stamps policy in the United States or Liconsa in Mexico. A positive CSE (as in the case of Argentina) does not translate into an effective social policy of low final consumer prices: this is due to weak price transmission in the value chain and lack of targeting to the poor (Chapter 5).

The average percentage CSE for Argentina is estimated at 7% for 2015-17. This indicates that first-stage consumers pay farm gate prices that, on average, are reduced by 7% due to public policies (Figure 4.4). In other words, policies that depressed farm prices – in Argentina mostly export taxes – reduced consumption expenditure by 7% on average across all commodities, compared to what consumption expenditure would have been in the absence of these policies and subsidies. This contrasts sharply with the average of -7% observed in OECD countries on in 2015-17, which acted as a tax on consumers.

Figure 4.4. Consumer Support Estimate (CSE) in Argentina and selected countries, 2015-17

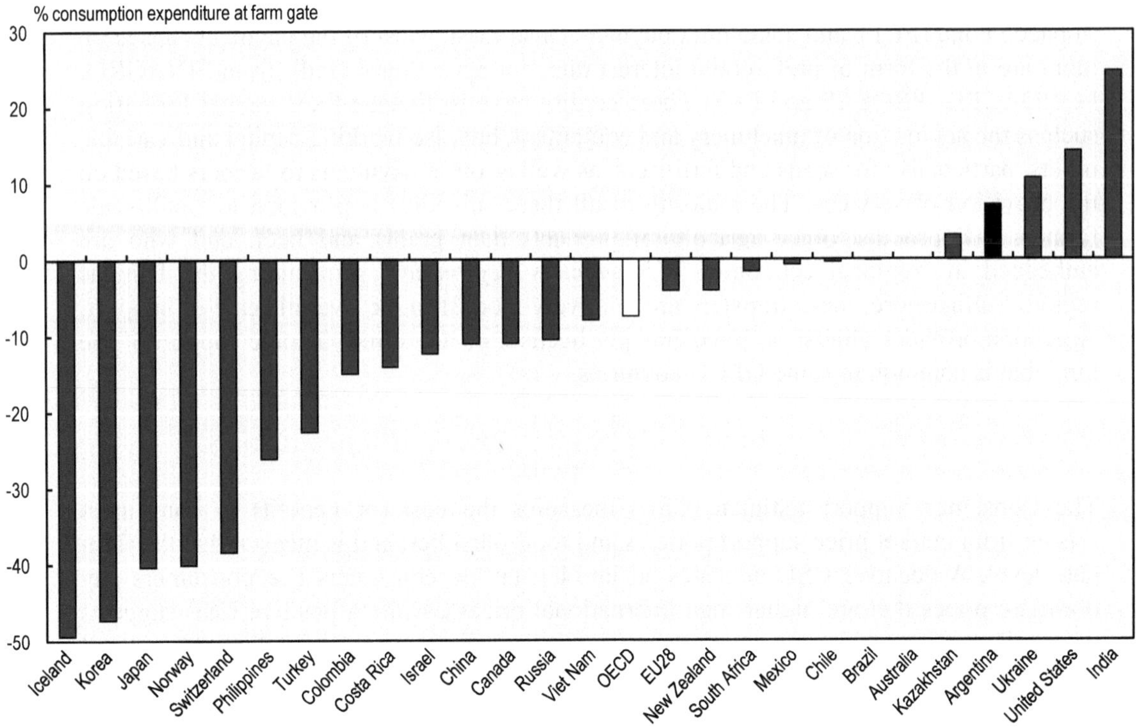

1. The statistical data for Israel are supplied by and under the responsibility of the relevant Israeli authorities. The use of such data by the OECD is without prejudice to the status of the Golan Heights, East Jerusalem and Israeli settlements in the West Bank under the terms of international law.
2. The OECD total does not include the non-OECD EU member states.
3. 2014-16 instead of 2015-17 for India.
Source: OECD (2018), "Producer and Consumer Estimates", OECD Agriculture Statistics Database.

StatLink https://doi.org/10.1787/888933907830

4.5. Argentina provides significant support for general services for agriculture

In addition to support provided to producers individually, the agricultural sector is assisted through the investments in activities that provide general benefits, such as agricultural research and development, training, inspection, marketing and promotion, and public stockholding. This support is considered not to be trade- or production-distorting, and it is, in general terms, well oriented to the provision of public goods, investments and services for the sector. It is measured by the General Services Support Estimate (GSSE) (as distinct from the PSE, which measures support for individual farmers).

Unlike many OECD countries, most of the budgetary expenditure on agriculture in Argentina goes to general services (GSSE) to improve the competitiveness of the sector rather than to producers (PSE). Public expenditure on such general services for agriculture in Argentina constituted around 59% of total budgetary expenditure for the sector in 2015-17, breaking down into three main categories (Figure 4.5). About 50% of total GSSE outlays were allocated to agricultural knowledge and innovation systems, in particular to the agricultural R&D and extension services institution, INTA (Chapter 6). Approximately 26% of total GSSE was provided to inspection and control services or to the animal and plant health public institution SENASA (Chapter 8). The majority of the remainder was provided for the development and maintenance of infrastructure, in particular, irrigation and rural roads. Argentina is one of the few countries evaluated by the OECD where most of the budgetary transfers are allocated to GSSE, joining Australia, Costa Rica, New Zealand and Chile.

Figure 4.5. Level and composition of General Services Support Estimate (GSSE) in Argentina, 1997-2017

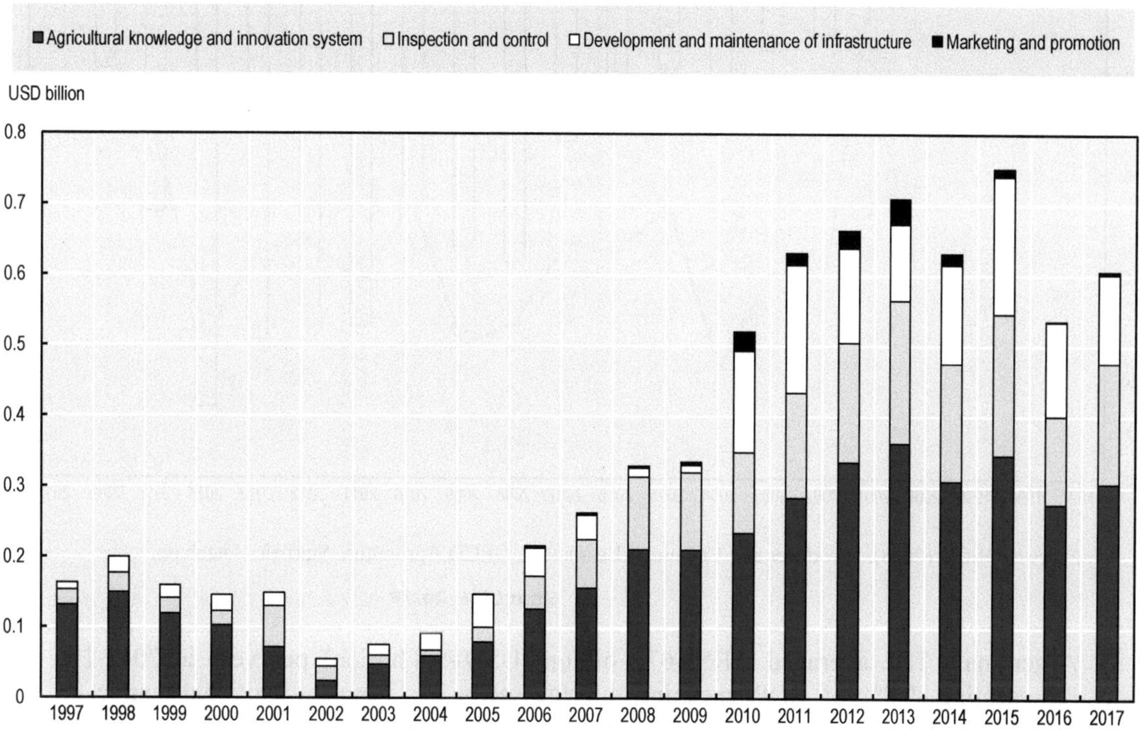

Source: OECD (2018), "Producer and Consumer Estimates", OECD Agriculture Statistics Database.

StatLink https://doi.org/10.1787/888933907849

4.6. Support to the agricultural sector as a whole is still negative

The Total Support Estimate (TSE) is the broadest indicator of support, representing the sum of transfers to agricultural producers both individually (PSE) and collectively (GSSE), it also includes transfers from taxpayers to consumers. Expressed as a percentage of GDP, the percentage TSE (%TSE) provides an indication of the support to (or taxation of) the agricultural sector in the whole economy. Its value depends on the degree to which the agricultural sector is supported or taxed in a country, the size of this sector and its importance relative to the overall economy.

Figure 4.6 shows the composition of the TSE for the period 1997-2017, where negative levels of MPS are the largest component. Positive budgetary transfers were relatively small, representing only 7% of the negative MPS in 2015-17.

Figure 4.6. Level and composition of Total Support Estimate in Argentina, 1997-2017

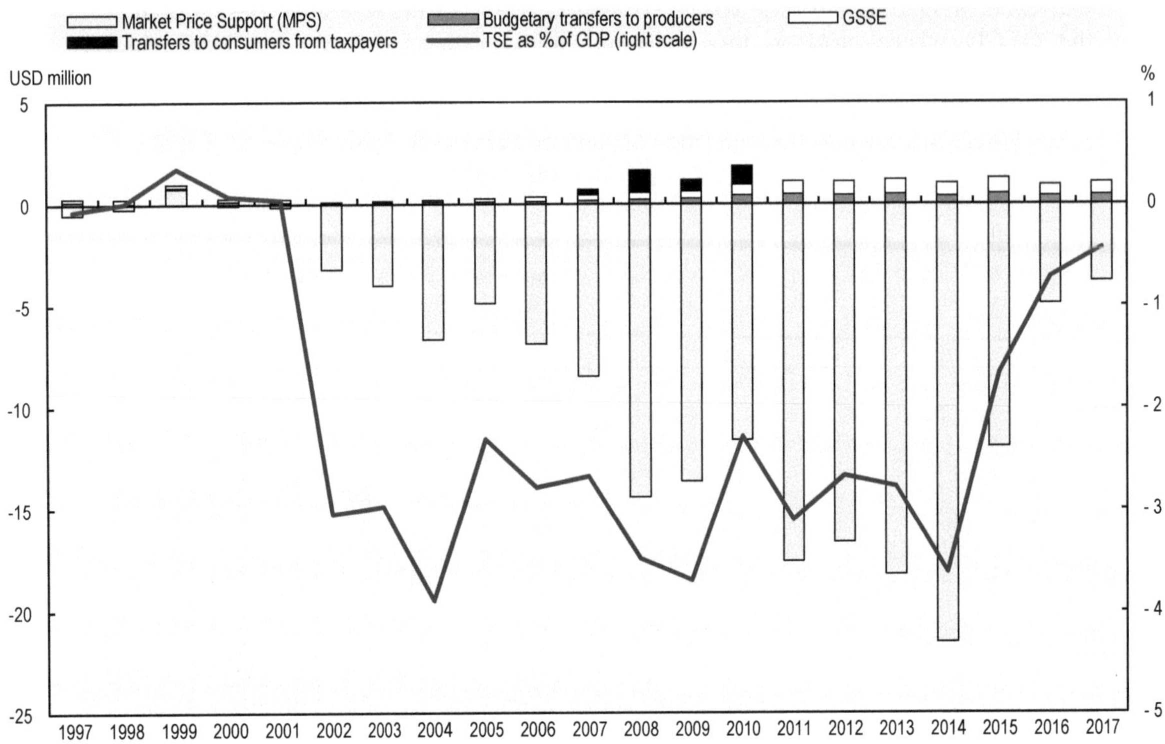

Source: OECD (2018), "Producer and Consumer Estimates", OECD Agriculture Statistics Database.

StatLink https://doi.org/10.1787/888933907868

Argentina's TSE averaged ARS -67.7 billion (USD -5.8 billion) per year in 2015-17, representing -0.8% of GDP, meaning that the sector has been a significant source of public tax revenue. Large negative MPS values in most of the period 1997-2017 made the %TSE also large and negative, becoming less negative only in 2016 when several export taxes were removed or reduced. However, there have been transfers to the sector both through some payments to farmers and, in particular, through investments in public goods or general services (Figure 4.6). In contrast with the case of Argentina, all OECD countries and emerging economies have a positive TSE, with the exception of Ukraine (Figure 4.7). Taxing the sector could lead to negative consequences, such as low long-term investments and lower productivity and competitiveness in world markets.

In total, positive transfers (i.e. the sum of budgetary transfers to producers, GSSE and transfers to consumers from taxpayers, and not counting the negative market price support) amounted to 0.2% of Argentina's GDP in 2015-17, or about 2.4% of the value of agricultural production.

Figure 4.7. Total Support Estimate in Argentina and selected countries, 2015-17

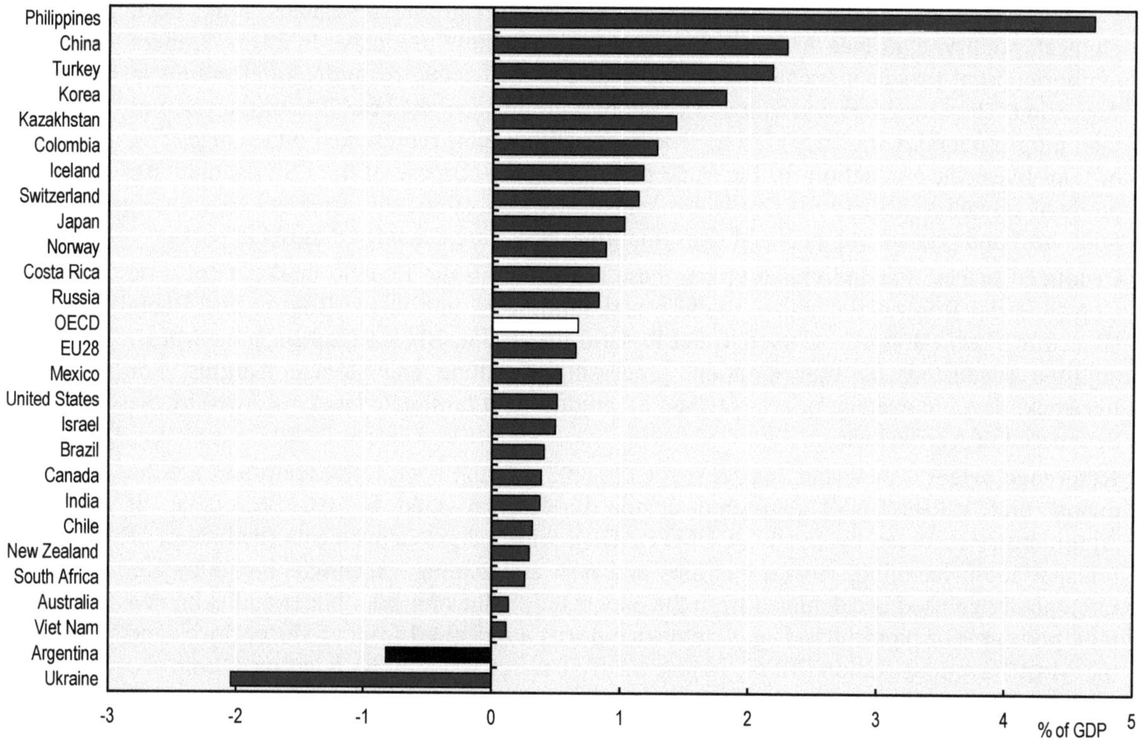

1. The statistical data for Israel are supplied by and under the responsibility of the relevant Israeli authorities. The use of such data by the OECD is without prejudice to the status of the Golan Heights, East Jerusalem and Israeli settlements in the West Bank under the terms of international law.
2. 2014-16 instead of 2015-17 for India.
Source: OECD (2018), "Producer and Consumer Estimates", OECD Agriculture Statistics Database.

StatLink https://doi.org/10.1787/888933907887

Box 4.1. Calculation of PSE for Argentina

The PSE is composed of two elements: market price support and budgetary transfers to individual farmers.

1) Market Price Support

Market price support (MPS) is based on the measurement of the gap between a country's domestic prices and international reference prices. This price gap results from a variety of policy measures that prevent domestic prices from aligning with international levels. These policies include trade measures such as export taxes, export licences, import tariffs, import quotas, tariff quotas, Sanitary and Phytosanitary (SPS) measures, export subsidies, as well as quantitative restrictions on exports. Policies creating a price gap also include domestic measures, such as administered prices, market interventions, or public stockholding. In emerging and developing economies, the gaps between domestic and international prices may also reflect factors that are not strictly policy related, e.g. deficiencies in physical infrastructure, inadequate information and weak market institutions. Market price support creates a financial transfer from consumers through higher prices, or to consumers if domestic prices are lower than in the world market. In the case of Argentina, the MPS is calculated on the basis of the following information:

Period covered: 1997-2017

Products covered: Wheat, maize, soybean, sunflower, fruit and vegetables, milk, beef, pigmeat, poultry, eggs (see Annex B for more details on these products). In 2015-17, these ten agricultural products accounted for 85% of the total value of agricultural output in Argentina. The four crops and fruit and vegetables group accounted for 79% of the value of total crop production in 2015-17. The five livestock products represented on average 93% of total livestock production for the same period. For the purpose of the PSE estimations, products treated as net exports are: wheat, maize, soybean, sunflower, fruit and vegetables, milk, beef and poultry. Pigmeat and eggs (marginal trade) are considered as net imports.

Producer prices: For individual crops, these are prices in the Rosario market (Bolsa de Comercio del Rosario for maize, soybean and sunflower), and in the Rosario and Bahia Blanca markets (Bolsa de Comercio del Rosario and Bahía Blanca Exchange for wheat) adjusted (deducted) by transportation, processing, handling and storage margins. For livestock, they are average prices received by producers at farm gate level, recorded by the Secretariat of Agroindustry.

Reference prices: For wheat, maize, soybean (2002-17) and beef, reference prices are the export unit values (EUV) registered at the border, provided by the Secretariat of Agroindustry (sourced by INDEC/COMTRADE), with margin adjustments (deduction of transportation, handling, storage margins and port and trading expenses). For milk, the reference price used is calculated from the export unit values for both butter and skimmed milk powder. For pigmeat and eggs, reference prices are derived from producer prices and the Most Favoured Nation (MFN) import tariff. The reference price is derived from the export tax for sunflowers and for soybean before 2002. The US producer price is used for poultry.

Marketing margins: Marketing margins are estimations of processing, handling and transportation costs for a given commodity and estimated from data provided by the Secretariat of Agroindustry, sourced by Bolsa de Comercio del Rosario and the *Márgenes Agropecuarios* magazine. For milk, the processing margin of butter and skim milk powder is an average margin of four major milk exporters: Australia, New Zealand, the European Union and the United States (average margin of AUS, NZ, EU and US). For beef margins, processing costs were estimated as a percentage of the border price. Handling and transportation costs from the border to the wholesale markets and from the farm gate to the wholesale markets were also estimated as a percentage of the border price. For sunflower, pigmeat, poultry and eggs, margins were not used, as import tariffs, export tax or producer price from another country were used to calculate the market price differential. Different margins were used to estimate producer prices and reference prices of different commodities (Table 4.2).

Price gap estimates. For all the individual products, price gaps are calculated as the difference between the producer price and the reference price, except for sunflower, for which the export tax rate is used, and for pigmeat and eggs, for which import tariffs are used. In line with the OECD methodology, the negative market price differential was set to zero for milk as from 2016, for beef in 2016 and 2017, for maize in 2017 and for wheat in 2016-17 as no export tax nor other market price policies taxing producers were applied to milk or beef producers during these periods.

A "zero price gap" was used for beef when positive gaps were obtained (1997 to 2001) and for maize (2016), as the estimated positive price gap was not reflecting the actual policy to beef and maize over these years. The price gap for the group of fruits and vegetables has been set at zero for the whole period 1997-2017. The large majority of the fruits and vegetables in this group are exportable and no tax or support policies have been identified for the exported fruits and vegetables.

Table 4.2. Market Price Support calculations in Argentina's PSEs

Commodity	Trade Position	Policies	Producer Price (PP)	Margin	Reference Price (RP)	Margin	Market Price Differential (MPD)
Soybean	Exporter	Export Taxes & Permits / quotas	Rosario/ Bahía Blanca – M1	M1=transport, handling, storage, processing	EUV-M1-M2	M2='port' and trading expenses	PP-RP (negative) Export tax used before 2002
Maize	Exporter	Export Taxes & Permits / quotas	Rosario – M1	M1=transport, handling, storage, processing	EUV-M1-M2	M2='port' and trading expenses	PP-RP (negative-- MPD set to zero in 2016-17)
Wheat	Exporter	Export Taxes & Permits / quotas	Rosario – M1	M1=transport, handling, storage processing	EUV-M1-M2	M2='port' and trading expense	PP-RP (negative-- MPD set to zero in 2016-17))
Sunflower	Exporter	Export Taxes & Permits / quotas	Rosario – M1	M1=transport, handling, storage, processing	PP - MPD		(PP * Tax rate) (negative)
Fruit and Vegetables	Exporter	No policies for exported fruit and vegetables	n.a.	n.a.	n.a.	n.a.	Set to zero
Milk	Exporter	Export Taxes & Permits / quotas	Farm gate by Secretariat of Agroindustry		EUV-M3	M3= average margin of AUS, NZ, EU and US	PP-RP (negative, MPD set to zero in 2016-17)
Beef	Exporter	Export Taxes & Permits / quotas	Farm gate by Secretariat of Agroindustry		EUV-M4	M4=processing costs, Handling transport	PP-RP (negative-- MPD set to 0 before 2002 and in 2016-17)
Poultry	Exporter	Export Taxes & permits / quotas	Farm gate by Secretariat of Agroindustry		US pp		PP-RP (negative)
Pigmeat	Importer	Import tariffs 10%	Farm gate by Secretariat of Agroindustry		PP - MDP		PP*(t/(1+t)) (positive)
Eggs	Marginal net Exporter	Import tariffs 5%	Farm gate by Secretariat of Agroindustry		PP - MDP		PP*(t/(1+t)) (positive)

n.a.: not applicable.
Source: Authors based on the PSE calculations of Argentina.

2) Budgetary support

Budgetary support comes from government revenues. Budgetary information for 1997-2017 was provided by the former Secretariat of Agroindustry, now Secretariat of Agroindustry.

References

FAO, IFAD, IMF,OECD, UNCTAD, WFP, the World Bank, the WTO, I. (2011), *Price Volatility in Food and Agricultural Markets: Policy Responses*, Interagency report for the G20. [4]

OECD (2018), *Producer and Consumer Suport Estimates*, OECD Statistics Database. [3]

OECD (2017), *Agricultural Policy Monitoring and Evaluation 2017*, OECD Publishing, Paris, http://dx.doi.org/10.1787/agr_pol-297-en. [2]

OECD (2016), *OECD's Producer Support Estimate and Related Indicators of Agriculture Suport: Concepts, Calculations, Interpretation and Use (The PSE Manual)*, Trade and Agriculture Directorate, http://www.oecd.org/tad/agricultural-policies/full%20text.pdf (accessed on 07 June 2018). [1]

Chapter 5. Export taxes generate distortions and negative support to the sector

Export restrictions and taxes on soybean, sunflower, wheat, corn, beef, milk and poultry have depressed producer prices for most of the last two decades in Argentina. Export taxes were typically lower for processed products, while quantitative restrictions and export licences have particularly affected wheat and beef. Export restrictions have proved not to be an effective and sustainable instrument for reducing food inflation, although they did generate fiscal revenue, notably in years of high food prices on world markets. This type of measures may contribute to world market price volatility. Federal revenue from export taxes is not shared with the provincial governments and represented as much as 13% of all tax revenues and 3% of GDP in 2008, a year of particularly high world food prices. Since the end of 2015, policy changes to reduce or eliminate taxes on agricultural products moved in the right direction of reducing distortions. The more recent decision to tax all exports in response to the economic turmoil of August-September 2018 should help macroeconomic stability and set the stage for more sustainable fiscal revenue over the longer term. The new export tax does not discriminate a specific sector like agriculture and has a sunset clause by the end of 2020. It should be part of an on-going process to improve the tax system.

5.1. Introduction

The largest agricultural policy transfers in Argentina are derived from trade policies, in particular export taxes, as shown by the PSE analysis in Chapter 4. Export restrictions have been used almost continuously for the last two decades in Argentina, and included not only taxes, but also a system of licences and quantitative export restrictions. The motivations behind these measures were threefold. First, generating fiscal revenue for the Federal Government, which has limited alternatives for collecting progressive taxes due to a small fiscal base, potential tax avoidance, and the particularities of sharing tax revenues with provinces. Second, promoting domestic processing industries with cheaper agricultural inputs and lower export taxes for processed products. Finally, depressing domestic food prices by restricting their export, as a social measure to benefit the urban poor. Notwithstanding this threefold motivation for the imposition of export taxes, this distorting policy has ultimately hampered primary producers and created significant policy uncertainties.

5.2. Export tax rates have been high and unpredictable

Policies which disadvantaged Argentina's agro-food sector began in 1933, when a differentiated exchange rate was applied to agro-food exports (Colomé, Freitag and Fusta, 2010[1]). The application of export taxes on agro-food products began in 1955, when the exchange rates for exports and imports were realigned. Subsequently, export taxes were maintained at different rates until they were almost eliminated in the 1990s for one decade, before being re-introduced in 2002 (Figure 5.1).

Figure 5.1. Export tax rates in Argentina

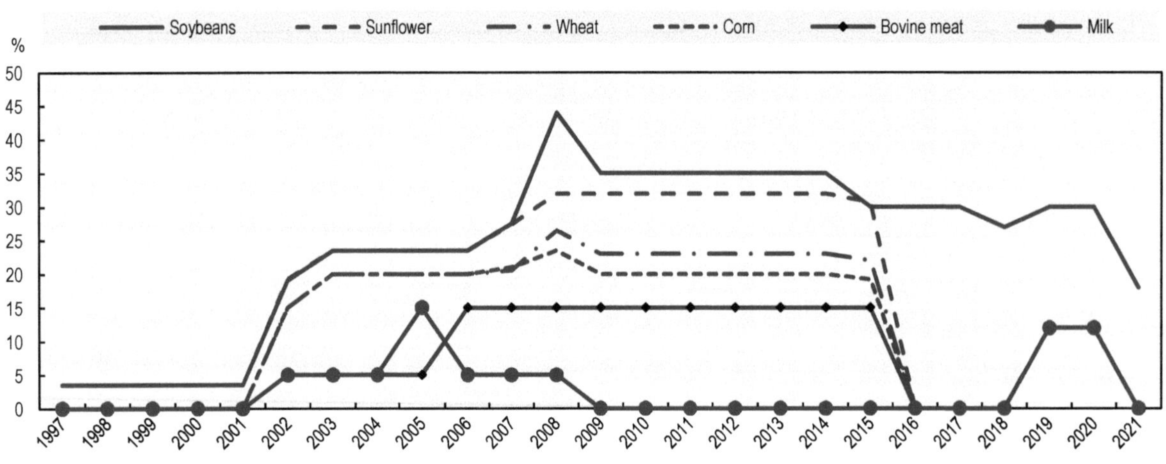

Note: The export tax rates on soybean, oil and flour were being reduced by 0.5% every month from January 2018 to September 2018. Since then a 12% tax on all exports is applied with a maximum of ARS per USD of export value.

Source: (Ministerio de Agroindustria, 2018[2]); (Regúnaga and Tejeda Rodriguez, 2015[3]).

StatLink https://doi.org/10.1787/888933907906

In the last two decades, the export tax rates of agricultural commodities have been variable over time, decided in a discretionary manner through government decrees. The increase in export tax rates from 2002 to 2012 coincided with increases in the international prices of the main Argentinian export commodities. Some of these commodities – such as wheat, corn and bovine meat – are part of the basic diet of most Argentinians, and the government of the time introduced these and other export restricting measures with the explicit aim of reducing the price for domestic consumers. For a few months in 2008 a variable export tax system was established, with tax rates increasing with international prices, reaching record rates of up to 44% for soybeans. The simple average export tax rates for the period 2002-15 were: 30% on soybeans, 28% on sunflower, 22% on wheat, 20% on maize, 12% on bovine meat and 3% on milk. In 2016 export taxes were eliminated except for soybean, for which there were reduced. To increase fiscal revenues the government established in September 2018 a temporary tax on all exports until December 31, 2020. The tax rate will be 12% and applied to all the goods and services exported including products from agriculture (Decree 793/2018). The tax rate will not exceed a maximum of ARS 4 per each dollar of exports of primary agricultural goods, and ARS 3 per dollar for the rest of products.

The export tax on soybean has had the highest rates and the highest tax revenue. Two decades ago, soybean was not a traditional component of Argentinian agricultural production, animal feed or diet. Export taxes on this oilseed had the explicit aim of raising fiscal revenue from increasingly profitable exports, whose international price had more than doubled during the 2000s. The tax rate on soybean exports climbed from 3.5% in 2001 to reach a peak value of 44% in March 2008; the rate was being gradually reduced in monthly steps of 0.5% to 30% in January 2018. In September 2018 the export rate specific for soybeans was reduced to 18% but the new tax rate on all exports is added on top. (Figure 5.1).

There is extensive literature on the damaging impact of Argentine export taxes on its agro-food sector (Baracat et al., 2013[4]; Lema and Gallacher, 2017[5]; Sturzenegger and Salazni, 2007[6]; Regúnaga and Tejeda Rodriguez, 2015[3]). Export taxes create disincentives to export and produce, reducing domestic prices for producers and first buyers[1] (Chapter 4). This is reflected in the Producer Support Estimates, with negative market price support (MPS) arising from the domestic prices for producers of main commodities being below the international prices at which exports compete (Figure 5.2). Only few commodities like pigmeat have positive market price support.

Market price support was relatively low (USD -142 million) in 2001, and its negative value peaked in 2014 at USD 22 billion, mostly from soybean and maize, followed by wheat and bovine meat. Export taxes began to be dismantled in 2015 and since then the negative MPS has been reduced significantly until 2017.

In almost all the value chains, export taxes varied with the degree of transformation. Exports of primary products were taxed at higher rates than processed ones. This was done to promote domestic processing industries and exports of products with higher domestic value added. For instance, the export tax on pasta used to be half of that on wheat flour, which latter was half of that on wheat grain. The "escalation" of export tax rates persists for soybean (Figure 5.3): the rate for beans was 30% as 1 January 2018, but only 27% for flour and oil, and 15% for biofuels. This practice mirrors import tariff escalation as defined by WTO, and it could be labelled as "tariff escalation on exports" (Regúnaga and Tejeda Rodriguez, 2015[3]).

Figure 5.2. Level and composition of Market Price Support (MPS) in Argentina

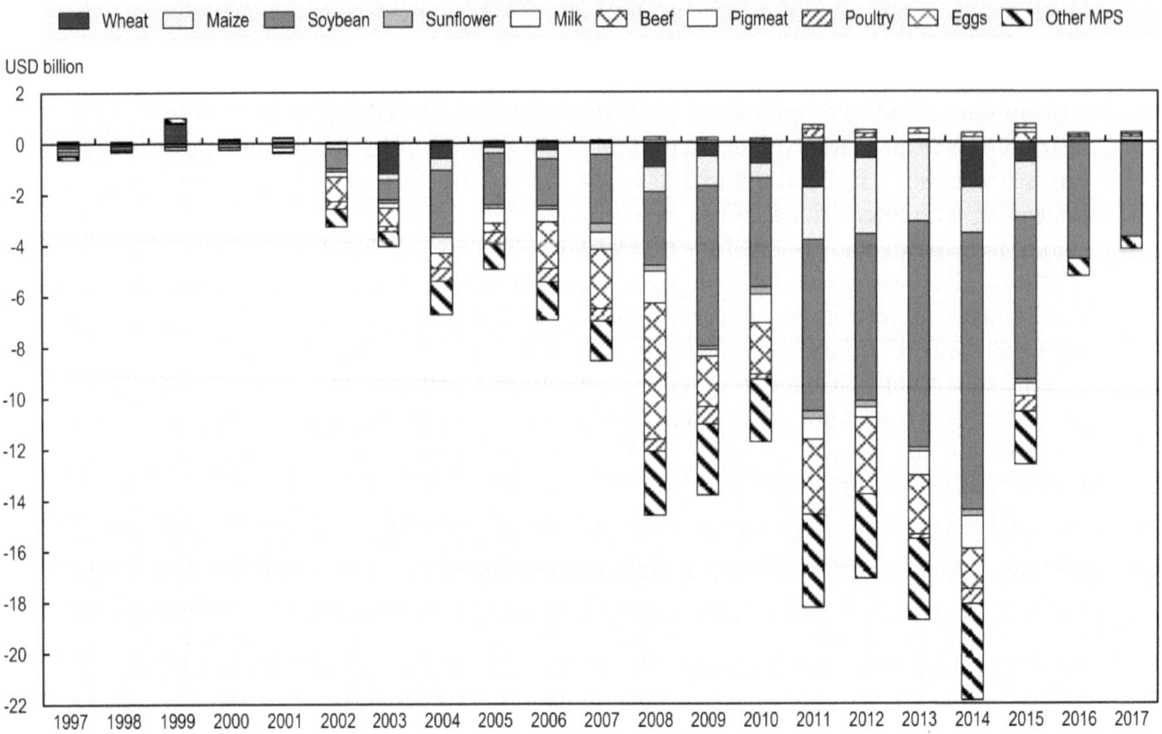

Note: MPS for fruit and vegetables was equal to zero over the period 1997-2017. See Annex C for the description of indicators.
Source: OECD (2018), "Producer and Consumer Estimates", OECD Agriculture Statistics Database.

StatLink https://doi.org/10.1787/888933907925

Figure 5.3. Export tax escalation

Soybean export tax rates as of 1 July 2018

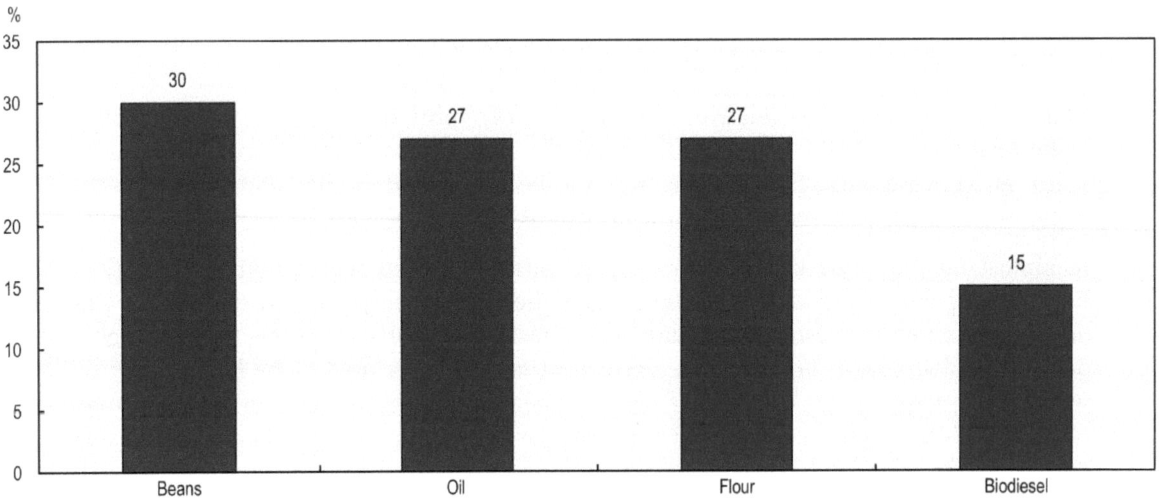

Source: Decrees of Ministry of Agri-Industry 133/2015, 1343/2016.

StatLink https://doi.org/10.1787/888933907944

5.3. Export taxes have been a significant source of revenue for the federal government

Even if tax rates have varied over the years, export tax revenues have generally represented high shares of GDP and of total fiscal revenue in most of the years in the decades of the 1960s, 70s and 80s (Nogués, 2010[7]). Only during the 1990s were they hardly used. As export tax rates were increased in the 2000s, they became a significant source of revenue for the government, representing more than 10% of total fiscal revenue and an average of 2% of GDP in the period 2002-15, peaking at 3.1% of GDP in 2008 (Figure 5.4). After the government decree of 2015, only export taxes on soybean remained, representing 0.6% of GDP. The persistence of export tax revenues reflect structural factors that make export taxes a readily available source of fiscal revenue for the government, and therefore difficult to reform.

Export taxes are part of a tax system that is characterised by weak enforcement with "low tax bases and highly distorting tax design", "few people paying income taxes" and contributing "comparably little to reducing inequalities and creating strong incentives for informality" (OECD, 2017[8]). The system is complex with many taxes, the revenue of which is shared between the federal and the provincial governments. In this context, export taxes can be seen as an imperfect and distortionary alternative to tax rents from agricultural exports.

Figure 5.4. Revenue from export taxes

As a percentage of GDP and of total fiscal revenue

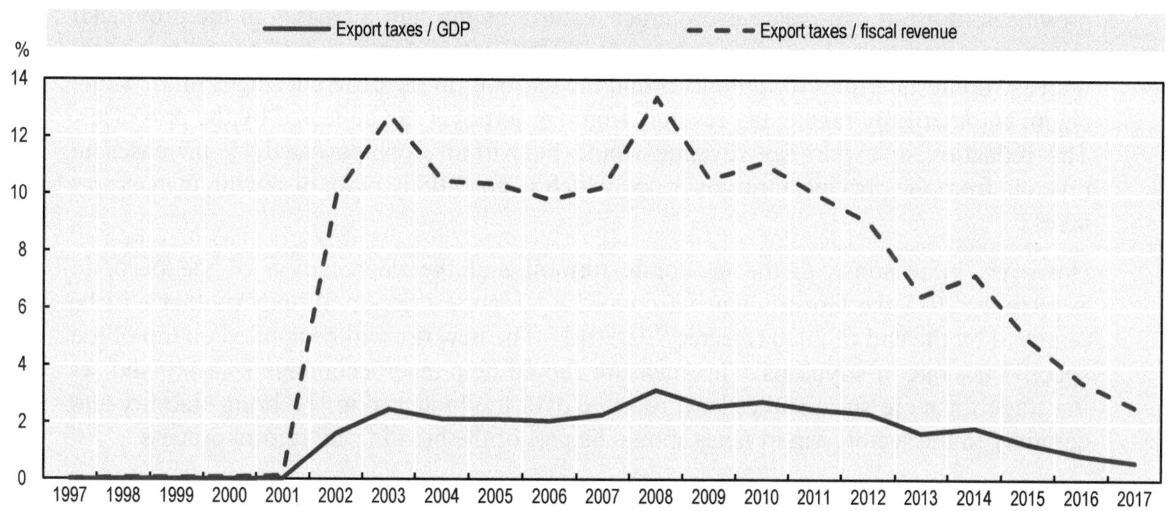

Source: Calculations by the authors based on official data (Ministerio de Hacienda, 2018[9]).

StatLink https://doi.org/10.1787/888933907963

OECD (2017[8]) recommended to "undertake a revenue neutral tax reform". In December 2017 a tax reform was approved as part of a process of improving the tax system (Law 27.430). The tax reform included: a gradual reduction over time in the maximum turnover tax rates to be applied by the provinces; a graduate reduction of the corporate income tax; phase-out of the financial transactions tax; and a reduction on employer social security charges for low income earners. The reform of export taxes was decided separately by successive decrees implying the elimination of agricultural export taxes except soybeans, which were subject to a gradual reduction planned for 2018 and 2019 (Decrees 133/2015, 1343/2016 and 486/2018). These measures were part of the effort to diminish distortions while at the same time meeting tight fiscal deficit objectives.

As part of Argentina's federal structure, the revenue from most taxes is shared between the two main levels of government – federal and provincial – according to predefined parameters. This is the case of the corporate income tax or the value added tax. However, two taxes belong to only one of the two levels of government, and they are highly distortive measures: the export tax, imposed by the federal government, and the turnover tax, imposed by the provincial one.

Export taxes are decided by decree in a discretionary manner by the treasury and the executive of the federal government, and their revenue does not need to be shared between the central government and the provinces (Ministerio de Hacienda, 2018[9]). This circumstance has encouraged the recurrent use of export taxes as a rapid way to raise federal tax revenue. On the other hand, the provincial turnover tax (*Impuesto sobre los ingresos brutos*) is under the full responsibility of the provinces. This turnover tax is particularly distorting because it is levied on sales at every stage in the supply chain, without any deduction for the tax paid in earlier stages. This creates incentives for vertical integration and for avoiding the inter-provincial addition of value, and it acts like an interprovincial tariff barrier. The agro-food sector, as well as other sectors, is significantly burdened with these distortions.

The elimination of export taxes has far-reaching impacts in terms of total tax revenue and how it is distributed between levels of government. First, it reduces total tax revenue; second, it disproportionally affects the revenue of the federal government compared to the provinces; third, it can create even larger distortions through increases in the provincial turnover tax revenue. According to Nogués (2015[10]), the elimination of export taxes will increase domestic prices for producers and the turnover in the different stages of the value chain, automatically raising tax revenue from the turnover tax collected by the provinces. The reduction in export tax revenue would be partially compensated by increases in revenue from the provincial turnover tax, which is potentially more distorting than export taxes.

However, in response to the economic turmoil and the depreciation of the peso, in September 2018 the Government introduced a temporary tax on all exports that will be removed by the end of 2020 (Decree 793/2018). The new tax will be applied on top of the specific tax rate of soybeans. This measure should help macroeconomic stability and set the stage for more sustainable fiscal revenue over the longer term. To bring stability and certainty to the sector, export taxes should be part of the broad fiscal reform process.

An additional tax uncertainty for agricultural exporters arises from the tax refund system. Exporters are entitled to a total or partial refund of some of the domestic taxes paid, in particular of the VAT and the provincial turnover tax. However, these reimbursements have also created distortions and uncertainties on their own as they have tended to be discretionary, subject to political negotiations and often received after long delays (OECD, 2017[8]). The recent decree 1341/2016 has defined in a more transparent manner the maximum refund percentages for each group of commodities.

For Argentina, the decisions about how to eliminate distorting taxes have to be taken as part of the ongoing tax reform process, including federal and provincial taxes. Furthermore, fiscal reforms in a federal state such as Argentina are politically challenging due to their implications for the distribution of revenue collected by different levels of government. However, in the short term, export taxes – particularly if applied to all exports in the context of a large depreciation– may create lower distortions and be more effective to raise revenue than any other available alternative.

5.4. Quantitative restrictions on exports created additional disincentives

Export taxes are only one form of export restriction. Other restrictions include export licencing, export bans and quotas, and other non-tax measures. Quantitative restrictions on exports of some products comprising the basic food basket of Argentinians were imposed from 2006, including on wheat, maize, bovine meat and milk. These quotas were subject to discretionary management by the Ministry of the Economy and the National Office of Agricultural Trade Control (ONCCA), an agency within the Ministry of Agriculture, through a system of Export Operation Registers (ROEs). In 2011 ONCCA was dismantled and the management of the scheme was allocated to the Ministry of the Economy. Quantitative restrictions ceased to be applied in 2015 with the elimination of the ROEs for grains and the creation of a more agile system of Declaration of Sales Abroad (DJVE).

During the period 2002-15, export quotas were subjected to significant uncertainty and lack of transparency due to the absence of a domestic law governing both the restrictions and the allocation of export licences (Baracat et al., 2013[4]). On several occasions in this period, the government decided to ban exports of some products (bovine meat in 2006, and wheat in 2007 and 2013), or to close the export registers (ROEs). This distorted competition by creating economic rents for exporting companies that were awarded the licence, estimated at between 20% (Nogués, 2014[11]) and 26% (Baracat et al., 2013[4]) of the price, while leaving other companies with lower domestic prices.

These quantitative restrictions on exports are an additional barrier to trade that is reflected in the market price differentials between the domestic Argentinian and world markets. The calculation of the market price differential for the Producer Support Estimate (PSE) reveals that the observed export unit value (adjusted EUV or reference price) of wheat was for many years significantly higher than the producer price augmented by the export tax (Figure 5.5).

Most products have negative commodity-specific support that, as percentage of farm revenues, is larger than the corresponding export taxes (Figure 5.6). In the case of maize, soybeans and wheat the %SCT (Single Commodity Transfers) represented a burden for producers of more than 50% of gross receipts in the peak years, well above the export tax rates. Furthermore, Argentina has not provided any payments to producers that could compensate for this negative support. The only payments based on output are for tobacco producers.

Some animal products like bovine meat and milk were also subject to export restrictions. However, their SCT is only marginally negative or even positive. This is due to the positive support that these producers receive in the form of cheaper feed crops. This partially compensates the negative support caused by export restrictions and the subsequent lower output prices. In some years the lower cost of feed fully compensates for the lower output prices and brings MPS and SCT for milk and bovine meat to virtually zero or even into positive territory. In spite of this positive support, bovine meat was substantially affected by the policy uncertainty and drought in livestock producing areas, and the number of animals decreased by almost ten million or 17% between 2008 and 2011. Pigmeat is the main commodity with a systematically positive SCT in Argentina.

Figure 5.5. Wheat price differentials: Export taxes vs quantitative restrictions

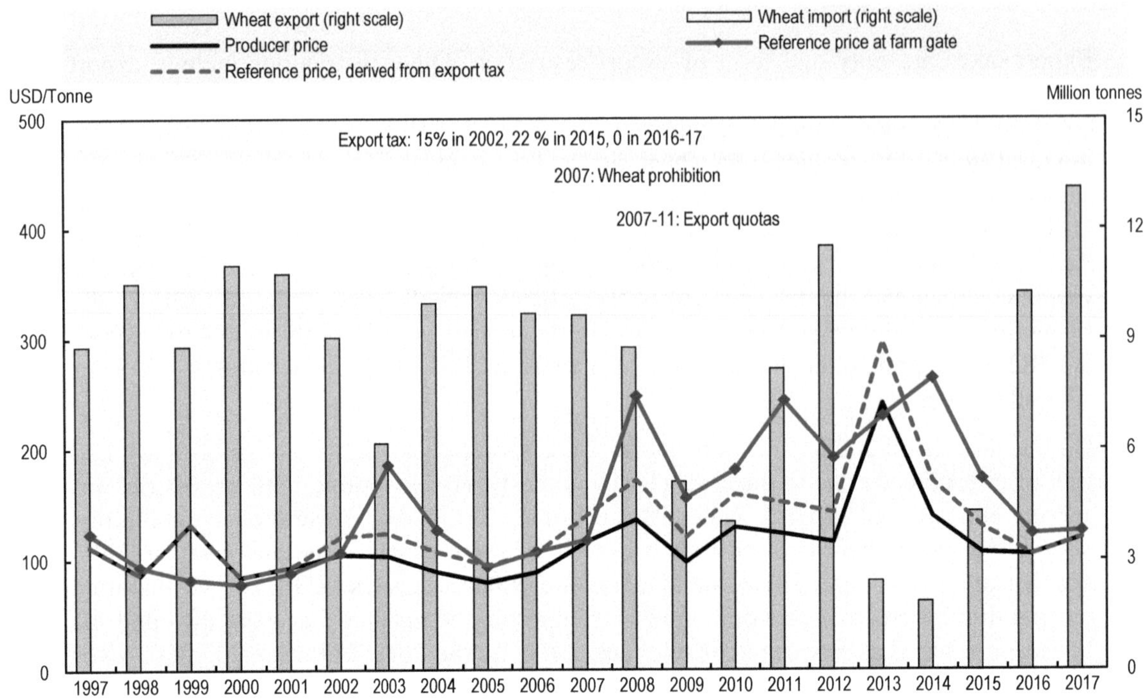

Source: OECD (2018), "Producer and Consumer Estimates", OECD Agriculture Statistics Database.
StatLink https://doi.org/10.1787/888933907982

Figure 5.6. Single Commodity Transfers, Argentina and all countries, 2000-02 and 2015-17

Percentage of gross receipts for each commodity

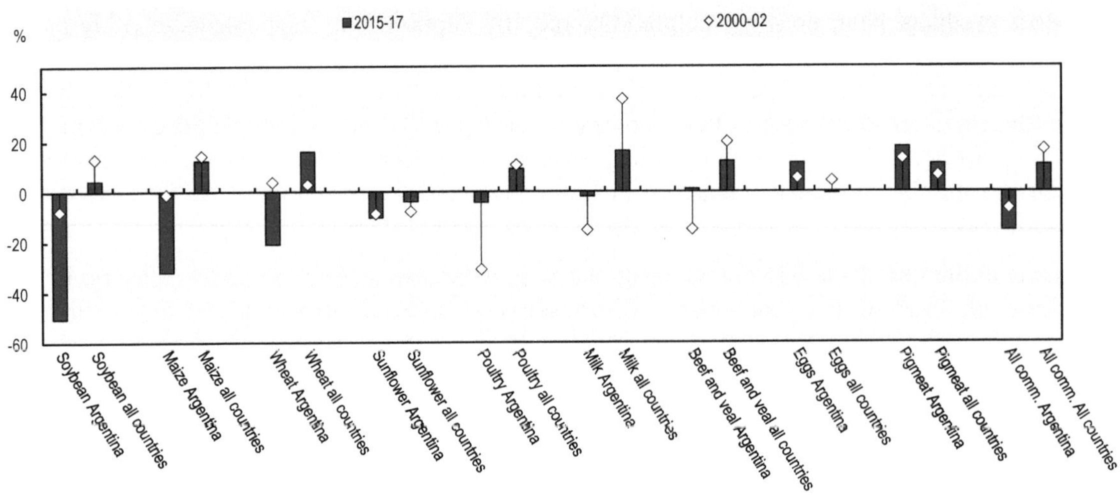

Note: Commodities are ranked according to the value of % SCT in 2015-17 in Argentina.
Source: OECD (2018), "Producer and Consumer Support Estimates", OECD Agriculture Statistics Database.
StatLink https://doi.org/10.1787/888933908001

The negative values of the SCT for most commodities reflects the fact that farmers in Argentina were not supported with policies, unlike farmers in most other emerging economies and in OECD ones. Furthermore, there have been significant transfers from producers to the government and the processing industries. For example, wheat and maize producers were supported by OECD and emerging economies with policy transfers, mostly highly distorting, that represented 16% and 12% of the value of production in 2015-17, respectively, while Argentine producers were burdened with negative transfers of more than 20% (Figure 5.6). Agricultural policies have harmed Argentine's position in its main exporting markets: its exporters, who are subject to negative policy transfers, need to compete with those from other countries, some of whom benefit from distorting positive support from their governments.

5.5. Export restrictions distorted production without controlling food inflation

Some of the above export taxes and trade restrictions were implemented with the aim of reducing Argentinian consumer prices for the basic food basket. From 2007, the National Office of Agricultural Trade Control (ONCCA) provided subsidies to food processors as first buyers of mainly wheat, beef and milk, but also poultry, pork, maize and soybean (Figure 5.7). These subsidies were small compared to the size of market transfer, except for wheat and milk. After a congressional inquiry into its activities, ONCCA was closed in 2011. During the period 2007-10, the subsidies – together with export taxes and restrictions – had a direct impact on reducing the price at which the primary commodity was purchased by the first processor (Grundke and Foders, 2010[12]).

Figure 5.7. Consumer transfers

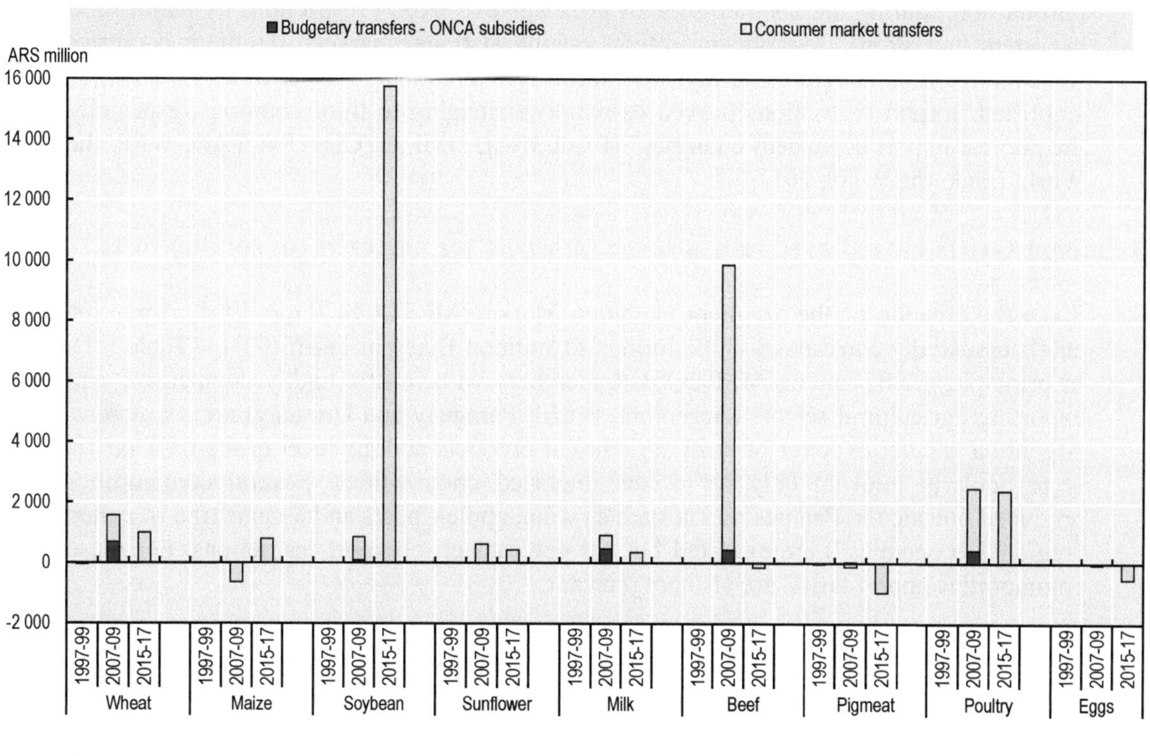

Source: OECD (2018), "Producer and Consumer Estimates", OECD Agriculture Statistics Database.

StatLink https://doi.org/10.1787/888933908020

However, the impact of these polices on the food prices for final consumers is much smaller, even if this is difficult to assess in Argentina due to the absence of reliable Consumer Price Indexes for the period 2002-15, in particular for food prices. Inflation started to rise to double digits in 2007 and reached 40% in 2014, while the Central Bank increasingly printed money to finance the fiscal deficit (OECD, 2017[8]). Inflation was starting to be contained up to 2017 and the national statistics institute, INDEC, began the publication of a new series in 2016.

Despite this lack of statistical information, there is evidence that the use of trade policies to control inflationary pressures has not been effective. The share of the primary product in the price of the final product is too insignificant for these measures to have a relevant impact on consumer prices. For instance, wheat flour represents only 10% of the price of bread, and export restrictions were reported to reduce the domestic price of wheat and flour, but not of bread and other derived products (Regúnaga and Tejeda Rodriguez, 2015[3]). These results are confirmed by econometric analysis that estimate an impact of only 1% on the consumer prices for wheat-derived products (Calvo, 2014[13])

The large size of export taxes is likely to have had significant impacts on production decisions. It has been argued that, despite the higher tax rates on soybean, the market for this product was more predictable than that for wheat or maize, which were subject to uncertain quantitative restrictions. This predictability, together with higher international prices and lower requirements on investment and working capital, could have created additional incentives for the expansion of soybean production compared to other crops (Baracat et al., 2013[4]). There is also evidence that export taxes created a bias against yield-enhancing technologies and in favour of cost-reducing ones, favouring soybean production (Cristini, Chisari and Bermúdez, 2009[14]).

Furthermore, during the 2008 episode of price spikes, "export restrictions by major food exporters had strong destabilising effects on international markets. As more countries followed the first movers, volatility was exacerbated and the upward price movement was amplified. Export restrictions proved extremely damaging to third countries, especially the poorest import dependent countries" (FAO, IFAD, IMF,OECD, UNCTAD, WFP, the World Bank, the WTO, 2011[15]).

5.6. Import tariffs have played only a secondary role for agricultural commodities

Since the creation of the Southern Common Market (MERCOSUR) in 1991, Argentine tariffs essentially correspond to the former's Common External Tariff (CET) (Table 5.1). In principle, tariffs among MERCOSUR members with mostly highly competitive and exporting agricultural sectors (Argentina, Brazil, Paraguay and Uruguay) are set at zero. Argentina is a net exporter of most agricultural products and the level of the CET tariffs is particularly relevant only for a few imported commodities. Several commodities produced outside the Pampas region such as wine, apples, pears and lemons (the so called "regional economies") are exported but are not subject to export restrictions. For these commodities import tariffs are also not relevant.

Average and maximum applied import tariffs are lower for agriculture than for other products (Table 5.1). Only certain imported agricultural commodities are subject to import tariffs. For instance, pigmeat is the most significant imported commodity and the applied MFN tariff is 10%. In the past ONCCA also managed the Import Operation Register ROI that included pigmeat products. This is the only commodity that contributes with a positive market price support to the PSE. However, the magnitude of this positive support is small compared with the size of the negative support to most exporting commodities.

Import restrictions and tariffs affect agriculture's access to inputs. Argentina has systematically used non-automatic import licenses since 1999 for a large set of manufactured products, including agriculture machinery and agrochemicals. There is evidence that during the period 2002-15 the licence mechanism created significant delays and administrative uncertainty (Baracat et al., 2013[4]). The Argentinian import licensing system has been the subject of several disputes in the WTO. The protection (through import tariffs) of the domestic production of agro-chemicals, fertilisers and machinery have created additional input costs that have been growing in recent years due to the increasing use of all these inputs in the new technological packages adopted by agriculture in the Pampas region (Sturzenegger and Salazni, 2007[6]).

Table 5.1. Tariffs on imports by product groups

	Final bound duties			MFN applied duties		
Product groups	Average	Duty-free in %	Max	Average	Duty-free in %	Max
Animal products	26.5	0	35	8.3	6.5	16
Dairy products	35	0	35	18.3	0	28
Fruit, vegetables, plants	33.8	0	35	10.0	5.6	35
Coffee, tea	34.2	0	35	14.3	0	35
Cereals & preparations	33	0	35	10.9	14.7	31
Oilseeds, fats & oils	34.6	0	35	8.5	10.8	35
Sugars and confectionery	33.3	0	35	17.6	0	20
Beverages & tobacco	35	0	35	17.8	0	35
Cotton	35	0	35	6.4	0	8
Other agricultural products	31	0.7	35	7.7	10.4	20
Fish & fish products	34.5	0	35	10.4	3.9	16
Minerals & metals	33.8	0	35	10.1	7.2	35
Petroleum	33.6	0	35	0.1	97.2	6
Chemicals	21.4	0	35	8.2	1.4	35
Wood, paper, etc.	30.2	0	35	11.2	3.3	35
Textiles	34.9	0	35	23.3	0	35
Clothing	35	0	35	35.0	0	35
Leather, footwear, etc.	35	0	35	16.0	2.8	35
Non-electrical machinery	34.9	0	35	13.4	11.8	35
Electrical machinery	34.9	0	35	14.8	10.1	35
Transport equipment	34.5	0	35	18.5	12.0	35
Manufactures, n.e.s.	33.5	0	35	15.7	8.8	35

Source: WTO (2018).

5.7. Overall policy assessment and recommendations

Market Price Support (MPS) policies – either negative or positive – are among the most distorting forms of support to agriculture. Previously in Argentina, export restrictions and taxes were used heavily in pursuit of policy objectives related to fiscal revenue and control of food inflation to favour consumers and food processors. During agricultural price spikes, export taxes accounted for 13% of all fiscal revenue, but they were not effective in controlling food inflation. In this sense, the reduction of export taxes for agricultural products undertaken in 2015 and 2016 were movements in the right direction.

They significantly reduced the size of market distortions created by negative market price support. Only soybean export remained taxed, which may affect relative incentives across the sector. The large size of the agro-food sector in Argentina makes the elimination of export taxes more challenging: it is likely to have positive impacts on GDP while increasing the government deficit and decreasing the world price of some of its exporting commodities (Piñeiro et al., 2018[16])[2]. The new temporary tax on all exports was introduced in September 2018 to raise government revenue and reduce its deficit.

Export restrictions are not only market distorting, they also generate uncertainty because they are decided and implemented in an ad hoc discretionary manner through government decrees with low transparency and predictability. This uncertainty creates additional distortions and disincentives for long-term investment. Furthermore, export restrictions and policy uncertainty have direct spillover effects in exacerbating volatility in agricultural world markets.

The first priority for agricultural export taxes in Argentina would be to accompany the gradual reduction in the tax rates with more certainty in the way they are determined, modified and implemented, in order to improve the investment decision environment in the agricultural sector and in the whole economy. The soybean exporting subsector and the rest of the agriculture sector could be more appropriately taxed through non-sectoral, less distorting taxes for the whole economy, such as corporate and income taxes.

A first-best policy option is a fiscal system that replaces export taxes with less distorting measures. The tax system in Argentina should in the long term phase out distorting taxes like the provincial turnover tax and the federal export tax. The discussion about the potential substitution of these distorting taxes by other measures is not new in Argentina. Piffano and Sturzenegger (2010[17]) proposed the substitution of export taxes by less distorting taxes on rural property. OECD (2017[8]) proposes a phase-out and integration of the turnover tax into the existing VAT. The 2017 tax reform (Law 27.430) gradually reduces maximum turnover tax rates, while export taxes were reduced and modified by a succession of decrees: 133/2015, 1343/2016 and 486/2018. The decree 793/2018 introduced in September 2018 a temporary tax on all exports in response to economic turmoil when the economy began to stall and the currency depreciated.

Tax reforms need to combine the long-term objective of phasing out distorting taxes with short-term measures that facilitate the path to the long term and permit financing the government deficit. The decisions about the reduction of distorting taxes have to be taken considering the limited capacity of the whole system to collect fiscal revenues in a progressive and non-distorting manner. Additionally, the tax reform faces political and institutional complexities and needs to ensure that the new distribution of revenues is acceptable for both federal and provincial governments.

The long term reduction of export taxes should be part of the ongoing more ambitious tax reform process beyond agricultural policies, providing more stability and certainty as part of structural reforms, and preventing their future use as discretionary arrangements to close public revenue gaps. As part of such a package, provisions could be made to facilitate the consistent achievement of long- and short-term objectives such as the sunset clause in the Decree 793/2018 that expires in 2021, or temporary compensation arrangements.

Finally, the reduction in the taxes to the sector has to be undertaken in a manner consistent with other objectives. The expansion of the production of the main commodities and the use of existing or new technological packages could potentially increase environmental sustainability pressures (negative externalities). Those who increase these pressures should be subject to the "polluter pays principle" PPP rights (OECD, 2001[18]), It is therefore essential that any export tax reform should be accompanied by measures to offset potential negative environmental consequences and ensure any eventual costs to society as a whole are borne by those who generate them, strengthening the responsibility of producers in reducing negative agri-environmental impacts, as discussed in Chapter 7.

References

Baracat, E. et al. (2013), *Sustaining Trade Reform Institutional Lessons from Argentina and Peru*, World Bank, Washington, DC. [4]

Calvo, P. (2014), *Welfare Impact of Wheat Export Restrictions in Argentina: Non-parametric Analysis on Urban Households*, UNCTAD. [13]

Cicowiez, M., C. Diaz-Bonilla and E. Diaz-Bonilla (2010), "Impacts of trade liberalization on poverty and inequality in Argentina: Policy insights from a non-parametric CGE microsimulation analysis", *International Journal of Microsimulations*, Vol. 3/(1), pp. 118-122. [19]

Colomé, R., J. Freitag and G. Fusta (2010), "Tipos de cambio real y tasas de " protección " a la agricultura argentina en el período 1930-1959", *Anales de la Asociación Argentina de Economía Política. XLV Reunión Anual: Tipos de Cambio Real y Tasas de Protección a la Agricultural Argentina.* [1]

Cristini, M., O. Chisari and G. Bermúdez (2009), "Agricultural and macroeconomic policies, technology adoption and agro-industrial development in Argentina: Old and new facts", *Argentine Agricultural Economics Review*, Vol. XI/2, pp. 95-114. [14]

FAO, IFAD, IMF,OECD, UNCTAD, WFP, the World Bank, the WTO, I. (2011), *Price Volatility in Food and Agricultural Markets: Policy Responses*, Interagency report for the G20. [15]

Grundke, R. and F. Foders (2010), "The economic and social consequences of agricultural export taxes: A CGE – analysis for Argentina", GTAP Conference paper. [12]

Lema, D. and M. Gallacher (2017), *Producer Support Estimates: Argentine Agriculture 2007-16*, The Inter American Development Bank. [5]

Ministerio de Agroindustria (2018), *Sector background information provided by the Ministry of Agroindustry for the OECD Review of Agricultural Policies of Argentina.* [2]

Ministerio de Hacienda (2018), *Destino de la Recaudacion de los Impuestos al 30/03/2018*, Dirección Nacional de Investigaciones y Analisis Fiscal, Subsecretaría de Política Tributaria, Ministerio de Hacienda de la Republica Argentina. [9]

Nogués, J. (2015), "Bareras sobre las exportaciones agropecuarias: Impactos económicos y sociales de su eliminación", *Serie de Informes Técnicos del Banco Mundial en Argentina, Paraguay y Uruguay* No. 3. [10]

Nogués, J. (2014), "Rentas proteccionistas generadas por las políticas restrictivas sobre las exportaciones: Argentina". [11]

Nogués, J. (2010), "Agro e Industria una interpretacion de la decadencia Argentina ente dos centenarios". [7]

OECD (2017), *OECD Economic Surveys: Argentina 2017: Multi-dimensional Economic Survey*, OECD Publishing, Paris, http://dx.doi.org/10.1787/eco_surveys-arg-2017-en. [8]

OECD (2001), *Improving the Environmental Performance of Agriculture: Policy options and market approaches*, OECD Publishing, Paris, http://dx.doi.org/10.1787/9789264033801-en. [18]

Piffano, H. and A. Sturzenegger (2010), *Una Propuesta de Cambio Tributario: Sustitución de las Retenciones a las Exportaciones Agropecuarias y Agroindustriales por un Impuesto al Valor de la Propiedad Rural Libe de Mejoras Productivas*. [17]

Piñeiro, V. et al. (2018), *Looking at export tariffs and export restrictions: The case of Argentina*, IFPRI Discussion paper. [16]

Regúnaga, M. and A. Tejeda Rodriguez (2015), *Argentina's agricultural policies, trade and sustainable development objectives*, International Center for Trade and Sustainable Development (ICTSD). [3]

Sturzenegger, A. and M. Salazni (2007), *Distortions to Agricutural Incentives in Argentina*, World Bank, Washington, DC. [6]

Notes

[1] The total amount of the export tax may not be fully transmitted into lower prices, particularly in the case of a large exporting country or a situation of market power.

[2] Other quantitative studies also estimate small potential impacts in increasing poverty and inequality (Cicowiez, Diaz-Bonilla and Diaz-Bonilla, 2010[19]).

Chapter 6. Innovation success and the need for modernisation

During the last three decades, Argentina's agriculture went through a process of notable production and structural change and innovation. Outside the Pampas region, agriculture showed little dynamism during the last decades, but within it a remarkable increase in arable land area and productivity was associated with the widespread adoption of new technologies such as no-tillage and biological improvements, and the expansion of soybean production. With new roles and new actors such as large service contractors, sowing pools and farmers' innovation associations, the private sector has led the innovation process responding to economic incentives. The role of policy has been important in creating basic and applied knowledge and facilitating its diffusion and adoption, in particular through the National Institute of Agricultural Technology (INTA). Argentina benefited from access to genetic innovations in advantageous conditions that are unlikely to recur. However, the Agricultural Innovation System needs to improve its capacity to respond to new environments and growing sustainability challenges, focusing also on "regional economies" (agricultural production chains outside of the Pampas region), improving the enforcement of seed intellectual property rights, and enhancing INTA capacities to respond to new demands to create and transfer knowledge.

6.1. Introduction

Far-reaching innovation in Argentinian agriculture occurred during the 1990s and 2000s – a difficult period in terms of macroeconomic instability[1]. The national innovation system has changed its focus away from scientific objectives towards the whole innovation process, with a significant investment in institutional capacity. The performance of the Agricultural Innovation System (AIS) reflects the heterogeneous nature of Argentinian agriculture in terms of activities, actors and performance across the country. The production system developed in the Pampas region differs significantly from subsystems in other areas of the country, which are referred to as "regional economies".

6.2. Impressive productivity performance, but innovation duality

Total factor productivity (TFP) of agriculture in Argentina has grown at an average annual rate of 1.4% since 1995, less than half of that of Brazil and below the performance of Chile and the United States (Fuglie, 2012[1]). TFP increased strongly in crops but stagnated in livestock, reflecting the duality of innovation in Argentina's agriculture. While crop production was boosted by the adoption of new technologies, livestock as well as other regional production have been losing dynamism. Aggregate performance of TFP hides the difference between livestock and crops, but also and more importantly, between the Pampas and other regions.

Argentina has heterogeneous regions in terms of resource endowments, farming systems, and overall quality of life. While the Pampas region is very fertile and productive, the productive systems in other regions (*Economias Regionales*, henceforth "regional economies") lag behind. Although these regions have a high potential to grow a variety of products, they suffer from less favourable natural conditions, coupled with deficits in infrastructure and public-private investment, low access to services, low innovation-adoption rates, and poor social and economic conditions. In contrast with the impressive growth of the agricultural sector in the Pampas since the 1990s, most of the regional economies lacked innovation dynamics and followed erratic growth patterns with low productivity and an overall unsuccessful performance, with the exception of specific products such as the lemons in Tucumán and olives and wines in the Cuyo region.

Higher yields and a significant increase in planted area translated into an impressive growth in total production of oilseeds and cereals since the early 1990s (Figure 6.1). Area under crop cultivation in Argentina continuously increased until around 1930, when a complete expansion of the agricultural frontier was reached (around 20 million hectares that belong to the Pampas region), with fluctuations guided by differences in prices of crops and livestock because the Pampas is suitable for both in a mixed production system (Barsky and Gelman, 2001[2]). Between 1930 and 1960, the area under cultivation fell in favor of cattle and, conversely, it increased in the period 1960-90 in a process of abandoning the traditional crop-livestock rotation. Intensification of crop production flourished in the Pampas region while livestock activities moved outside it. By the end of the 1980s, this system had created severe soil degradation problems, affecting about 36% of the total area of the Pampas region to a greater or lesser extent by 1995 (Consejo General Agropecuario, 1995[3]). A response to this problem was provided by an innovative partnership scheme involving farmers, researchers, extension workers, and private companies, who came together in the 1990s to promote no-tillage as a resource-conserving cultivation practice (Trigo, Cap and Malach, 2009[4]).

Figure 6.1. Evolution of total production (in tonnes) and cultivated land (in hectares) of total oilseeds and cereals, 1900-2016

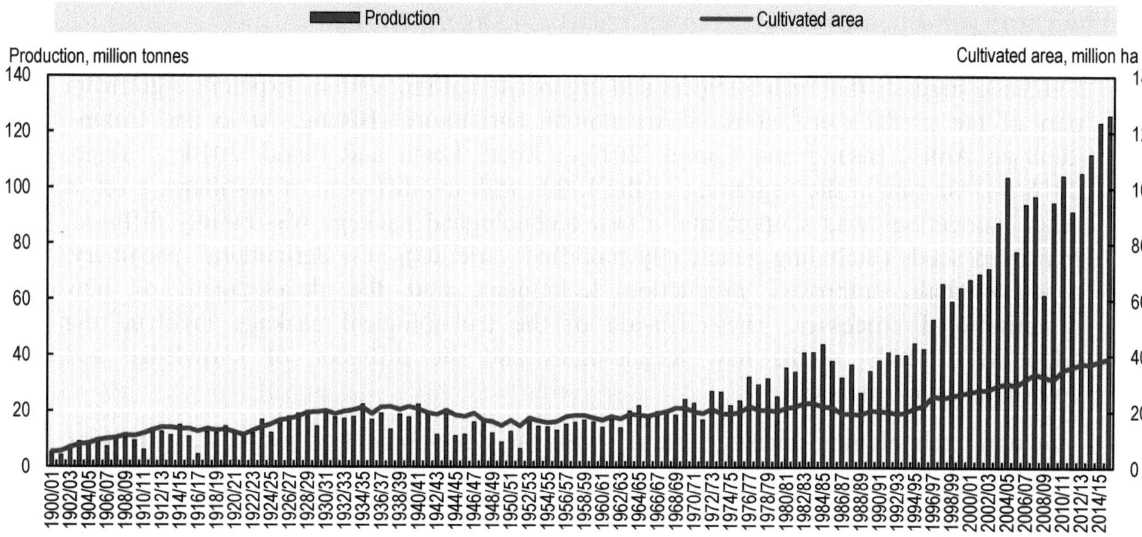

Source: (Anlló, Bisang and Campi, 2013[5]) and (Ministerio de Agroindustria, 2018[6]).

StatLink https://doi.org/10.1787/888933908039

The trade liberalisation of the 1990s improved the relative input-output prices, boosting investment and innovation in crop production, processing, and distribution. Total cereal and oilseed production almost tripled from 38.2 million tonnes in 1990/91 to 112.2 million tonnes in 2015/16, while cultivated area almost doubled from 19.9 to 39 million hectares. This expansion was possible with the development and adoption of innovations that allowed crop production in land that was previously not suitable for it and the expansion of double-cropping: in the Pampas region, for example, wheat followed by soybean (Regúnaga, 2010[7]; Bisang, Anlló and Campi, 2015[8]; Rocha and Villalobos, 2013[9]).

Argentinian productivity growth is associated with the expansion of the production of soybean, which was practically an unknown crop in Argentina in the 1960s with little relevance in the population's diet, animal feed, or Argentina's agriculture. Its massive diffusion started in the 1970s, when new varieties of seeds were mainly developed locally by the long-standing plant breeding industry and several public institutions, particularly the National Institute of Agricultural Technology (INTA). A significant growth of soybean production during the 1980s was boosted from the mid-1990s by the diffusion of genetically modified soybean varieties.

The lack of a substantive local demand for soybean made its expansion dependent on export markets. Consequently, Argentina's presence in certain markets gained worldwide significance: the share of Argentinian exports in total world exports increased between 1995 and 2015 from 6.7% to 11.1% in maize, 7.4% to 23.6% in soybeans, 23.6% to 41.7% in soybean oil, and 18% to 36.3% in soybean oil-cakes.[2] Also, in 2015 the share of Argentinian exports in total world trade of biodiesel was over 50%. Currently, the soybean subsystem in Argentina is one of the most efficient in the world in terms of productivity and technological development, but its rapid and remarkable expansion has real and relevant vulnerabilities derived from the occupation of areas previously dedicated to other crops, the tendency to monoculture, and concentration of production. It has generated several controversies related to its environmental, social, and economic sustainability (Anlló, Bisang and Campi, 2013[5]).

6.3. The rapid adoption of a new technological package for crops

Evidence suggests that technological and organisational innovations explain a significant part of the productivity gains in Argentinian agriculture (Bisang, Anlló and Campi, 2008[10]; Anlló, Bisang and Campi, 2013[5]; Reca, Lema and Flood, 2010[11]; Trigo, 2016[12]). Starting at the beginning of the 1990s with the diffusion of no-tillage, a set of other innovations was adopted and a new technological package was rapidly diffused: improved seeds (including genetically modified varieties), new agricultural machinery, agro-chemicals, improved production techniques, and the development of new organisational processes. The diffusion of the technological package involved the adoption of each of the new technologies and the diffusion of knowledge and co-ordination mechanisms.

The new technological package started with the development, adjustment, and quick diffusion of no-tillage practices at the beginning of the 1990s (Figure 6.2). In response to the increasing degradation of soils, crop management practices changed with an increasing reliance on technical assistance to adapt imported technologies (Alapin, 2008[13]). Public-sector agricultural researchers, innovative farmers and extension workers in association with manufacturing industries became the core of an innovation network to establish a new agricultural production strategy focused on soil management and conservation: no-till farming (Ekboir, 2002[14]).

Figure 6.2. Adoption rate of no-tillage and soybean GMO

% of cultivated land

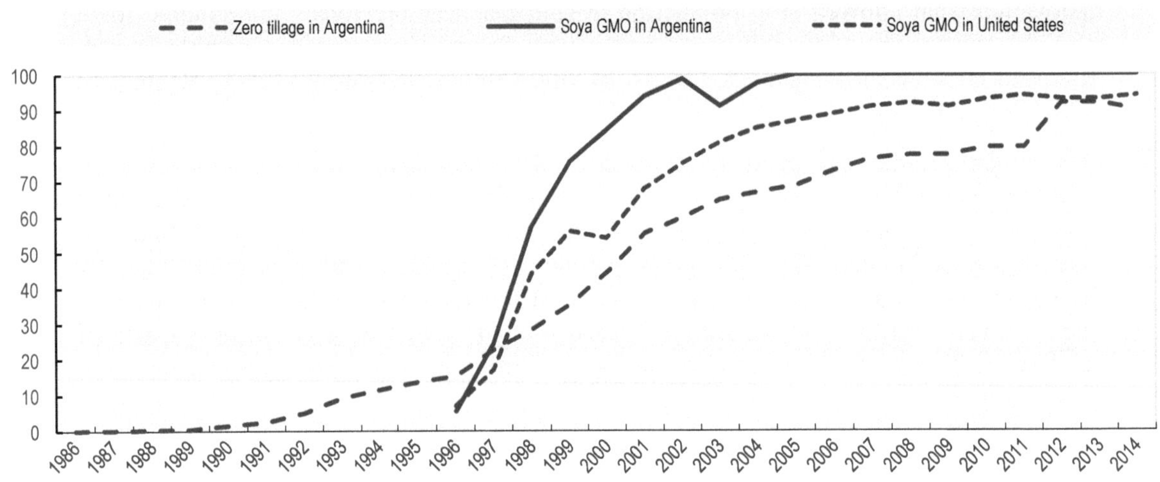

Source: (Trigo and Ciampi, 2018[56]) based on (Noceli Pac, 2016[57]). (Campi, 2016[58]) and (USDA ERS, 2018[59]).

StatLink https://doi.org/10.1787/888933908058

In 1986 a broad public policy effort, the Conservationist Agriculture Project (PAC), was initiated by INTA, to develop a response to the land degradation problems. New agricultural practices included a maize-wheat-soybeans rotation, reduced and vertical tilling, nutrient replacement through fertilisation and integrated pest and weed management. PAC also facilitated the integration and exchange of information among researchers, extension staff, private technical assistance providers, farmers, input suppliers, farm equipment manufacturers, and other related institutions (Senigagliesi and Massoni, 2002[15]).

Although most specialists recommended no-till only for soybeans as the second crop in a double-cropping scheme, a group of farmers and extension workers started trials with other crops, generating the information needed for an even higher adoption of the practice (Ekboir, 2002[14]). The adoption accelerated when glyphosate became commercially available in Argentina, greatly facilitating weed control and the launching a new no-till innovation cycle (Trigo, Cap and Malach, 2009[4]). The Argentinean Association of No-till Agriculture (AAPRESID) was created in 1989 by medium and small-scale farmers and technical assistance providers (see Annex A for further details). The Association, whose main focus was the diffusion and exchange of information regarding no-till practices among its members, grew very rapidly, becoming the pivot around which the development and expansion of no-till has continued to evolve (Trigo and Ciampi, 2018[16]).

The definitive increase in agricultural production in Argentina derived from the diffusion of genetically modified (GM) soybean, which deepened the adoption of technologies to reduce costs and maintain profitability (Bisang, 2003[17]). In the 1990s soybean was already a main crop in Argentina, but the introduction of the first GM soybean variety in 1996 dramatically increased its production. In 1991 Argentina's National Advisory Commission on Agricultural Biotechnology (CONABIA) was created as the regulatory body governing the testing and commercial release of GM events, which facilitated the process of diffusion of the new GM crops (Trigo, 2016[12]) (see Annex A for more details). The National Institute of Seeds (INASE) was also created in 1991 to protect the intellectual property (IP) in seeds, only to be dismantled in 2000 and recreated in 2003 (See Chapter 3 for more details). Between 1996 and 2017, forty-three GM events were approved for release in Argentina (Ministerio de Agroindustria, 2018[18]). As of October 2018, the Secretariat of Food and Bioeconomy had approved the commercialisation in Argentina of GM crop events for six commodities: afalfa, cotton, maize, potato, safflower and soybean (https://www.argentina.gob.ar/ogm-comerciales).

The first transgenic variety, named RR (Roundup Ready) soybean, was developed by Monsanto and contained a gene that provides resistance to glyphosate. This critical asset in the new technological package was patented in the United States and Europe in 1995, but it was introduced in Argentina without patent protection. The gene was licensed to Asgrow by Monsanto, and the Argentinean Company Nidera that acquired Asgrow Argentina had access to the gene. After obtaining approval in 1996, it released the RR soybean with Monsanto's agreement. Simultaneously, Monsanto applied for a patent for the gene, but patent authorities of the National Institute of Industrial Property (INPI) considered that the right had expired (Trigo et al., 2004[19]; Lopez, 2010[20]; Qaim and Traxler, 2005[21]).

The herbicide-tolerant soybean was authorised almost simultaneously in Argentina and the United States, and in both countries was rapidly adopted by farmers, but diffusion was faster in Argentina (Figure 6.2). Several factors considerably reduced the cost of GM seeds for Argentinian farmers. First, farmers did not have to pay royalties for their use; second, farmers had the legal possibility of saving seeds; and finally, there was a large illegal market of seeds (Trigo and Ciampi, 2018[16]). Nonetheless, even in the absence of a patent in Argentina, multinational companies and breeders started licensing agreements and, except for Nidera, companies releasing RR soybeans paid license fees to Monsanto (Traxler, 2006[22]). Additionally, some seed companies sell seeds through contracts in which farmers commit to pay royalties every time they plant. Monitoring these contracts is difficult and they are not as widespread as in the United States, where different legal provisions support their use. Despite this context increasing seed prices in Argentina, GM soybean seed prices were still below those in both the United States and Brazil. The case of RR soybean contrasts with that of Bt cotton which was introduced by Monsanto with a patent and a price too high for producers to adopt (Qaim and de Janvry, 2003[23]).

The success of the RR soybean in the main producing areas of Argentina is also associated with the development of improved varieties adapted to the different agro-ecological conditions of the country by the Argentine-based seed industry, which is not limited to multinational firms (Regúnaga, 2010[7]). The Argentinian seed industry has a long-standing tradition, and improved seeds have been historically the most important tool to increase productivity and competitiveness in the country (Barsky and Gelman, 2001[2]). Since the beginning of the twentieth century, private breeders achieved new hybrids by building on the freely available developments from public institutions (Anlló, Bisang and Campi, 2013[5]).

Currently the Argentine seed industry includes several domestic small- and medium-size firms, a few public research institutions, as well as the main international seed companies, which have increased their market shares during the last three decades. The global market for agricultural inputs has tended to concentrate in a few companies, and the actions of domestic companies depend on multinational companies that dominate in scientific knowledge and biotechnological techniques. While multinational companies control the most modern biotechnological techniques, domestic companies have most of the best locally adapted plant varieties. Domestic firms are still primarily responsible for the improvement of seeds, even of the most important crops such as soybean, maize and wheat (Marin and Stubrin, 2017[24]).

Despite changes in the seed industry, a large share of new cultivars was registered by Argentinian companies: an average of 64% in 1996-2005 and 91% in the most recent decade. The number of registered plant varieties grew, with an increasing share of genetically modified cultivars in total new cultivars (Figure 6.3). The seed industry has also an important role in technology transfer and in the financing of seeds. The private sector has been increasingly providing extension services, which were previously provided almost exclusively by the public sector, in particular by INTA.

Boosted by the adoption of improved seeds and no-tillage, other inputs for crop protection were also rapidly adopted – basically, fertilisers, herbicides and pesticides. According to CASAFE, herbicides represent 70% of total phytosanitary industry since 1994. Different herbicides were progressively replaced by glyphosate, produced locally and imported from different countries (mainly from China). The domestic agro-chemical market has been very dynamic since the early 1990s, with leading multinational companies like Monsanto, Syngenta, Basf, Dow Agrosciences, Advanta, Atanor, Bayer Cropscience, Nidera, Dupont, Nufarm, Merk, or Repsol-YPF, operating together with medium-size local and international firms that produce or import and distribute agro-chemicals (Regúnaga, 2010[7]).

Figure 6.3. Number of new conventional and genetically modified cultivars registered at the National Register of Cultivars (RNC), 1996-2017

Soybean and maize

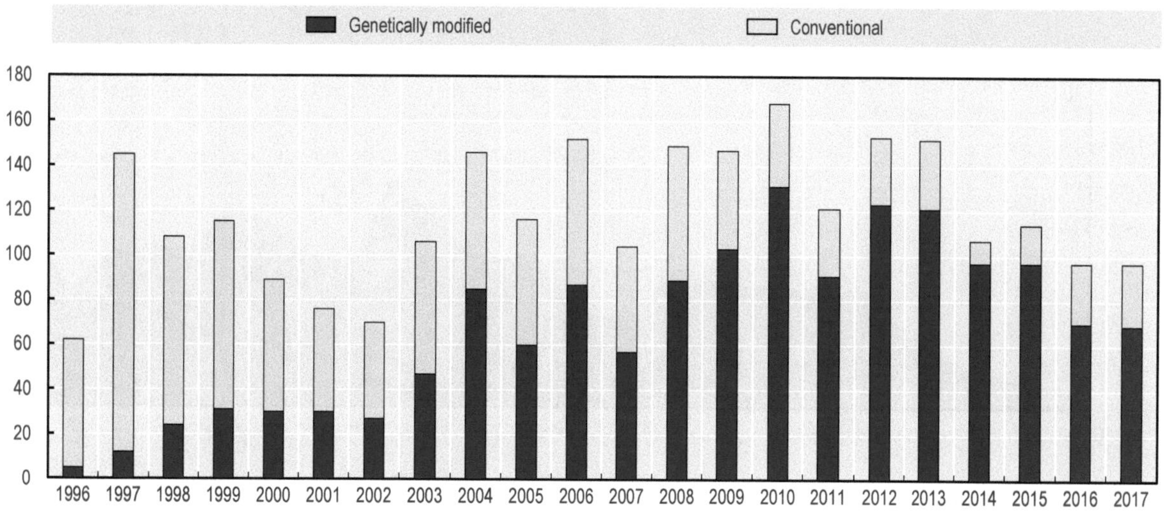

Source: (INASE, 2018[25]).

StatLink https://doi.org/10.1787/888933908077

In the 1970s and 1980s, the consumption of fertilisers was limited to a small part of wheat production. To some extent, the existence of the traditional crop-livestock rotation reduced the need for chemical fertilisation and the price of fertiliser was high due to restrictive import measures (Regúnaga, 2010[7]). This situation changed from the early 1990s and the use of fertilisers increased significantly between 1991 and 2006, reducing the gap with respect to other countries (Figure 6.4). Fertiliser use is concentrated, to a great extent, in the most dynamic crops: wheat, soybean, and corn. In addition, the increase in the consumption of fertilisers is related to the local development of massive fertiliser production based on the use of gas during the 1990s, giving rise to a competitive domestic market (Mercado, 1999[26]). However, a significant share of the growth of fertiliser consumption is explained by the increase in cultivated land. Empirical evidence suggests that the balance of nutrients in the soil for crops (particularly phosphorous) is negative, that is, agricultural soils lose more nutrients than they gain with fertilisation (Trigo, Cap and Malach, 2009[4]; Lavado and Taboada, 2009[27]; Cruzate and Casas, 2012[28]).

Another relevant innovation adopted in the agricultural sector is the silo-bag[3]. The increase in agricultural production since the 1990s accentuated the deficits in logistics and infrastructure for storage and transport of grains. The diffusion of silo-bags started at the beginning of the 1990s to gather fodder in the dairy activity and, some years later, to store cereals and oilseeds. Silo-bags became massively used after the devaluation registered in 2001 (Rocha and Villalobos, 2013[9]). The silo-bag increases the storage capacity in the place of the harvest, allowing farmers to decide when to sell depending on the market situation and financial needs. Macroeconomic instability and credit shortages after the devaluation made silo-bags more attractive, and their use increased from 1 to 41 million tonnes between 2001 and 2010 (Bragachini, 2011[29]).

Figure 6.4. Fertiliser consumption in Argentina

In thousands of tonnes. 1990-2016

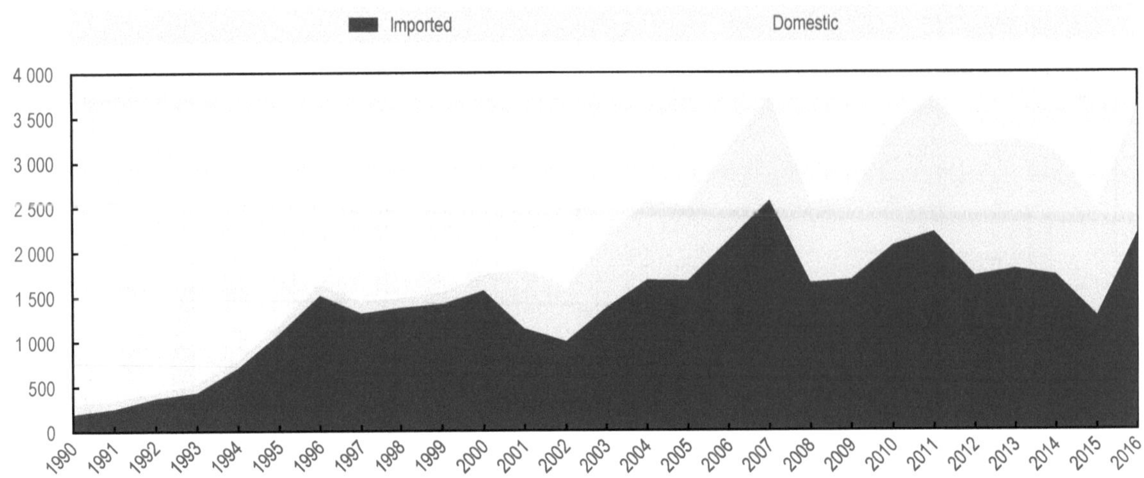

Source: CIAFA – Fertilizar AC, http://www.fertilizar.org.ar.

StatLink https://doi.org/10.1787/888933908096

Argentine agriculture has been mechanised since the beginning of the 20th century and there is a tradition of machinery and equipment industry. Since the 1990s, the use of specific machinery related to the diffusion of no-tillage – often domestically designed – steadily grew and, more recently, machinery changed, driven by the development of computerised controlling systems to implement precision agriculture. The open trade policies of the 1990s facilitated imports of innovative machinery. Despite external openness, some domestic manufacturers retain advantages over international competitors to adapt machinery to local conditions to provide technical support close to the users (Lódola, 2008[30]) (Bisang, 2003[17]). After the devaluation of 2001, sales of machinery increased again, expanding the installed capacity of the industry, and some companies became internationally competitive, offering local innovations as an integral part of the technological no-tillage package (Bragachini, 2011[29]).

The outsourcing of activities that involve the use of agricultural machinery increased significantly. The new technological package was adopted together with the development and diffusion of a new organisational model, which was driven by more interrelated actors – service contractors, sowing pools, new agricultural producers, input, service and knowledge suppliers – that together shaped and fueled the innovation process. In addition, this process took place in a new institutional and political context for the development of science, technology and innovation (SC&I) activities.

6.4. The changing role of different actors in the national innovation system

Argentina has a wide set of public and private institutions promoting science, technology and innovation (ST&I) activities throughout the economy. Agricultural innovation appears throughout this complex structure, reflecting the importance of the sector in the Argentinian economy. The ST&I system has a highly decentralised structure and many institutions have their own funding mechanism, contributing to weak linkages among the different components and, often, to the image of overlapping and disjointed efforts (Dahlman et al., 2003[31]).

The main system components are: the Ministry of Science, Technology and Productive Innovation (MINCYT), which is responsible for broader policy design and priority settings (reflected since the 1990s in the national science, technology and innovation plans); the National Agency for the Promotion of Science and Technology (ANPCYT), mainly responsible for the system's non-institutional funding instruments; the National Council for Scientific and Technological Research (CONICET), which together with the universities (public, private, national, and provincial) constitute the main R&D implementing capacities (human resources and infrastructure); and a whole host of specialised public research centres and institutions concentrating on specific sectors (such as agriculture, industry, defense, aerospace, and health) and private organisations of different types, in most cases focusing on the applied end of the R&D spectrum.

This structure is relatively recent and results from a system-wide review that took place in the early 1990s and the subsequent change in roles and actors refocusing existing science and technology activities to the development of technological solutions that have transformed production systems. This process started with the implementation of the Program for Technological Modernization (PTM) financed by the Inter-American Development Bank (IADB), which introduced project funding through the establishment of two specific funds under the ANPCYT, the National Fund for Scientific and Technological Research (FONCYT) to support scientific research, and the Argentinean Technological Fund (FONTAR) to facilitate public-private innovation in specific productive systems, following the model of FINEP in Brazil and FONDEF in Chile. This was complemented with the creation of policy co-ordination and stakeholders' participation mechanisms, which are responsible for the design of the national ST&I plans (Albornoz and Gordon, 2010[32]).

Two elements are at the core of this emerging system. One is the clear-cut separation of the funding and the implementation of R&D projects, with implementation staying within institutions such as the National Scientific and Technical Research Council (CONICET), the universities, INTA and the National Institute of Industrial Technology (INTI), which have high-quality human resources and infrastructure for successful implementation, and the funding deriving from ANPCYT. The second is the national strategic plans providing the priorities for public participation within the innovation system (Albornoz and Gordon, 2010[32]). Over time there have been three plans: 1998-2000 to consolidate the new institutions; the plan "Bicentenario" 2006-10 that made ST&I an active instrument of public policy to improve public-private partnerships; and the ongoing "Argentina Innovadora 2020" plan for 2012-20. These elements contributed to the deep transformation from a collection or organisations working independently with their own priorities and rules, to an interconnected system reflecting the recognition that science, technology and innovation are essential for economic and social development.

According to (Trigo and Ciampi, 2018[16]) the different guidance and co-ordination mechanisms and project funding instruments are widely known and perceived as effective and the new administration since 2015 has kept the same governance structure. However, there are a number of weaknesses: firstly, the system is still supply-driven, as the "demand" presence is weak and restricted to "advisory" functions and the private sector presence in FONTAR projects; and secondly, there is no formal monitoring and follow-up mechanisms except for the specific projects funded by the ANPCYT. The new administration has set up sectorial public-private platforms to discuss public policy and investment co-ordination, including ST&I issues.

Within the general system, the Agricultural Innovation System (AIS) is a relatively complex system in which technological and organisational innovation interact. Figure 6.5 presents a stylised version of the main actors of the system, highlighting how they come together for innovation to happen, with the agricultural producer at the centre of the process.

INTA is the cornerstone of the Argentinian agricultural innovation system. The INTA model is based on two key ideas: first, bringing under one roof all agricultural R&D activities; second, providing a "non-political" source of funding, initially with an *ad valorem* tax on agricultural exports, then changed to a percentage of the value of imports and exports; finally, incorporating the private and academic sectors into institutional decision-making through a board of trustees. INTA grew rapidly and, until the late 1990s, provided the bulk of agriculture R&D capacities. With the creation of the MINCYT, the strengthening of CONICET's centres, the consolidation of the project mechanisms administrated by ANPCYT, and the growth of the private sector, the relative weight of INTA has tended to diminish (Trigo and Ciampi, 2018[16]). However, it still represents the national structure dominating public sector contributions to the agricultural innovation processes.

Today's system (Figure 6.5) is quite different to that of 1990. At that time, the majority of farmers owned their land, and service suppliers had a minor role since farmers had capital and technical and tacit knowledge for the organisation of production. However, there were some public extension services, mainly INTA, and producer organisations, such as AACREA. Activities beyond the farm gate were looked after by marketing and other agroindustry complexes. Since then, the private sector role has grown significantly to become the main supplier of inputs, labour and extension services connected through different type of contracts and network.

Figure 6.5. The Argentinian agricultural innovation system

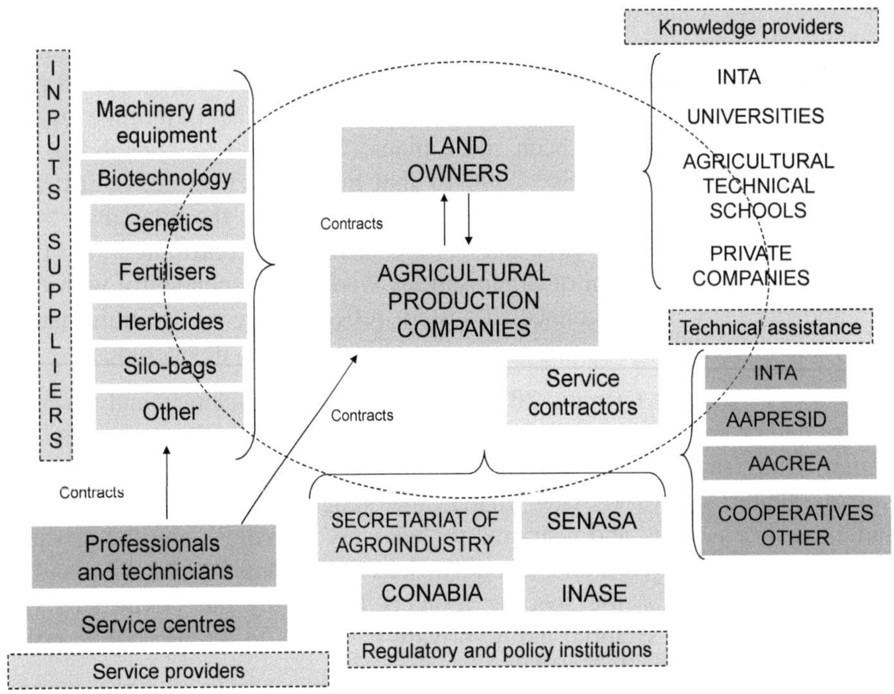

Source: (Trigo and Ciampi, 2018[16]) based on (Anlló, Bisang and Campi, 2013[5]).

The agricultural producer is at the centre of today's innovation system. The new farmer in the Pampas region manages a modern agricultural production company that accesses land in different ways; it can be a large vertically integrated company or a small producer, but it can also be a service contractor. The agricultural company does not necessarily own the land: around two thirds of the companies access this production factor through leasing (Chapter 8). Agricultural producers lease land in different locations to manage and reduce climatic risks. In addition, agricultural production companies outsource a relevant part of farming activities to service contractors.

Contractors own the latest machinery and provide skilled labour. Seeds are more commonly bought than reproduced at the farm. Part of the decisions related to the productive process – and innovations – are now taken by the inputs and services suppliers. Financial resources are obtained from extra-agrarian funders, as investors are attracted by the high profitability of the sector. The modern "farmer" is more connected and interdependent on different actors in the system that compete to provide high-quality inputs and services, and this competition is an essential component of the innovation process (Bisang and Gutman, 2005[33]).

Agricultural services contractors offer a wide range of services such as no-tillage, seed drills, planting, fumigation, monitoring, harvesting, storage, classification of grains, levelling or preparation of soil and pruning. They provide many innovations such as self-propelled spraying machines, displaced monitors and online yield information often linked to the application of ICTs to agricultural machinery and specialised operational management. The contractors move along the territory, offering their services and helping to homogenise the technological level in different farms; they implement innovations and are part of the learning process (Lódola, 2008[30]; Anlló, Bisang and Campi, 2013[5]). They harvest 90% of total grains cultivated in Argentina, and they are in charge of 70% of both sowing and the application of agro-chemicals (Ministerio de Agroindustria, 2018[34]). Agricultural services contractors also account for more than 60% of the purchases of agricultural machinery, regularly renewing their equipment.

During the 1990s, new forms of financing arose, such as mutual funds, direct investment funds, societies, temporary contracts for harvest, and financial trusts, most of them known today as sowing pools or *pools de siembra*. These pools responded to the weaknesses in the Argentine financial systems and funded producers with strong technical levels, allowing them to consolidate land area to an optimum scale for the use of the highest level of technology (Posada and Martínez de Ibarreta, 1998[35]). Land leasing allows producers to concentrate their investment in inputs of the highest technological level. These new forms of production are partly an expression of the process of concentration of the production that has been taking place since the 1990s. Many small or medium traditional producers became service providers or land leasers.

The emerging system has a high degree of decentralisation in decision-making and is, essentially, privately led in response to economic market incentives. The Argentinian AIS has no formal monitoring and performance evaluation mechanisms other than those implicit in the market mechanisms. However, the system has been able to respond to sustainability issues with the development of no-till agriculture and, more recently, the good practices network and other public or private initiatives promoting the adoption and certification of good agricultural practices.

6.5. The National Institute of Agricultural Technology (INTA)

The National Institute of Agricultural Technology (INTA) is the most relevant public-sector component of Argentina's agricultural innovation system (AIS). It was created "…to promote and co-ordinate agricultural research and extension and through the benefits of these activities, the technological improvement of the agricultural enterprise and rural life" through four main activities: (i) R&D on natural resources and production; (ii) R&D on the conservation and primary transformation of agricultural commodities; (iii) agricultural extension and training of farmers; and (iv) promotion needed for the implementation and diffusion of R&D results. INTA's main strengths are its presence in all the national territorial and the quality of its human resources.

INTA's territorial reach covers the whole of the country's geography and agricultural economy. It has over 50 Experimental Research Stations scattered around the country, a large Research Centre located in the outskirts of the city of Buenos Aires, focusing on basic and advanced applied research, and about 300 extension agencies. No region or natural resources/production sector escapes its attention and, in many cases, INTA represents the only territorial presence of the federal government. This is a clear source of institutional strength, but it is also a source of conflicts as it implies political pressures for the institution in the implementation of programmes and projects that are outside of its original R&D mandate.

Overall, total human resources at INTA have systematically increased during the last decade to reach a total of 7 562 agents in 2016, of which 2 966 were researchers (Figure 6.6). The rest of staff is technical and field support for research and extension, and "other staff" for rural development and other promotion activities. This latter residual group is the most significant in terms of increments during the period, having grown from about 1 200 in 2009 to over 2 175 in 2016. In terms of the education level of researchers, INTA has a relatively low number of PhDs – under 15% of total researchers – compared to 75% in EMBRAPA of Brazil and 50% in INIFAP of Mexico (Stads et al., 2016[36]) and an average of 30% in other Argentinian AIS R&D institutions (MINCYT, 2015[37]).

INTA's budgetary resources have significantly increased in nominal terms. It accounts for the highest expenditure among Argentinian budgetary programmes included in the PSE calculations as part of the General Service Support Estimate (GSSE). However, expenditure in real terms in 2017 was around 25% below than in 2012 (Trigo and Ciampi, 2018[16]). About 95% of INTA funding comes from the federal budget, currently set at 0.45% of the value of imports (exports before 2002). The rest of the budget comes from a variety of other public sources such as provincial and local governments, MINCYT and ANPCYT, and international organisations, with less than 1% coming from private entities. In the past the system redistributed in favour of the less developed regions outside the Pampas that hardly export. Currently the bulk of financial resources fully depend on central government decisions.

Up to the 1970s the role of INTA was clear: acquire and adapt agricultural technologies through R&D, and transfer know-how to farmers through extension services. During this time INTA played a central role as an "organiser" of innovation processes. This scenario changed in the following decades, as innovation processes shifted from the public to the private domains. INTA evolved, decentralising its activities into regional bodies and then leading the system by the sheer magnitude of its presence. Even today, INTA has probably the largest collection of data in the country; its potential to use these data to deal with issues related to the environment and climatic change is very large. However, since the 1990s INTA's leading role has been gradually substituted by the private sector and other public research institutions (universities, CONICET). Meanwhile, INTA has specialised in facilitating interactions with other public and private actors, particularly in the closer-to-market stages of the innovation process.

Figure 6.6. Human resources of INTA

Staff numbers by professional profile

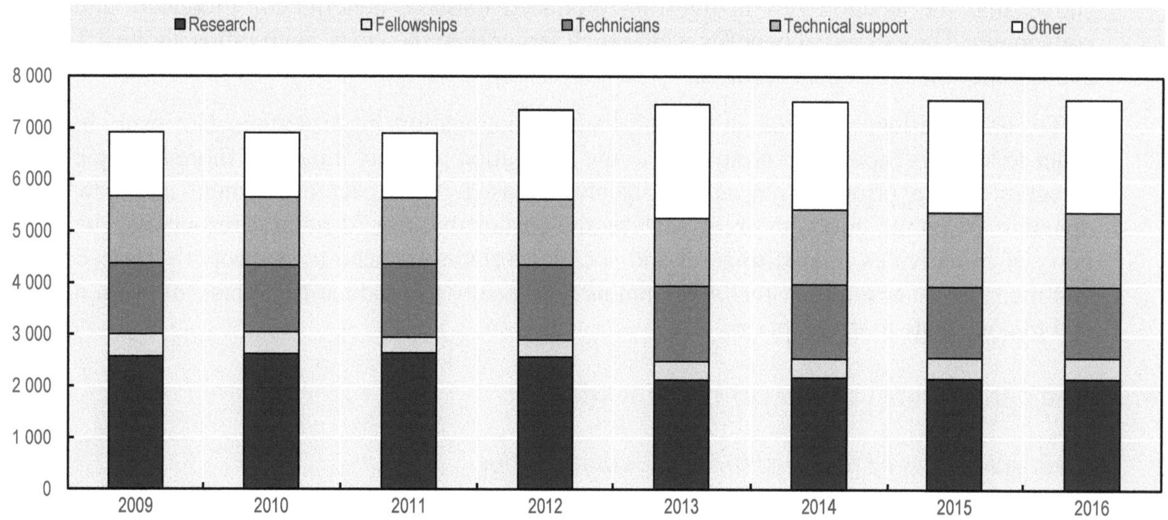

Source: (Trigo and Ciampi, 2018[55]) based on data from INTA.

StatLink https://doi.org/10.1787/888933908115

Despite these changes INTA's role may not be effectively fulfilled. The research planning structure goes directly from a list of general goals to hundreds of small projects in a bureaucratic process with little interaction with the different stakeholders. There is no effective priority-setting process and the research portfolio is basically led by supply. Additionally, ex-ante impact assessment is not required to submit a project for approval and funding. INTA's portfolio of projects is not the result of strategic decisions, but rather of the historical accumulation of lines of activities, with researchers' interests playing a determinant role in the decision (Trigo and Ciampi, 2018[16]).

INTA's portfolio of activities has also diversified to include the implementation of rural development support projects. During the last 10 to 15 years, INTA's extension component evolved from its initial focus on technology transfer to medium-size farmers to one increasingly including small farms and aiming more at social inclusion than at technological objectives. At the beginning, the new programmes were special projects, fully funded by the Ministries of Agriculture and Social Development and administered by the ArgenINTA Foundation. The justification for INTA implementing them was the institution's wide territorial coverage. However, after the 2001 crisis, these initiatives became a full component of the institution's programmatic structure, establishing strong competition for both its managerial and budgetary resources. This evolution represents a major change, moving the institution into segments of the agricultural sector where technology is not the main constraint.

There is no formal INTA-wide impact assessment. A list of the main achievements identified by INTA was recently published (INTA, 2017[38]). An internal document was commissioned to assess the impact of INTA for the 2002-11 period (Cap, 2012[39]). Only two technologies were the focus of the study: no-till practices and GM soybeans. There is consensus that these specific technological innovations would not have been possible without the long-standing work of the institution in generating the public good data. In the study, INTA's share of the credit for the reported economic benefits of adoption ranged from 10% (the lowest level of credit scenario) to 40% (the highest). The analysis shows that the technologies in question produced massive benefits for producers and consumers. The estimated benefits were much larger than the costs, with ratios above 4:1 even in the less favorable scenarios.

INTA has a history of leadership in agricultural innovation in Argentina. However, in order to keep its capacity to contribute to the innovation process, it needs a more strategic direction and a prioritisation of its objectives based on impact assessment and new demands of public goods in areas such as the sustainable use of natural resources. The new set of activities related to rural and social development need to be properly framed and managed to ensure that INTA maintains its capacity to produce first-class innovation and to contribute to its adoption.

6.6. Public and private investment in innovation

Characteristics of the general innovation system

Up to the early 1990s, ST&I activities were essentially funded through direct allocations to the institutions implementing R&D, and through public funds for specific projects. The private sector only participated to a minor extent. The funds managed by the decentralised agency ANPCYT (FONCYT, FONTAR and others) have become the backbone of the system and its main source of funding. These funds are managed through open and mostly competitive project-based mechanisms. FONTAR is particularly focused on innovation at firm level with the participation of the private sector. In 2015 Argentina dedicated 0.65% of its GDP to R&D activities, compared to an average of 2.36% for the OECD (OECD, 2018[40]; MINCYT, 2015[37]).

The bulk of funds come from public sources, 96% of the total in 2011-15, compared to 3.5% from the private sector and 0.5% from international sources. In terms of implementation, decentralised public institutions (such as CONICET, INTA, and INTI) represent almost 50% of the total, while public universities represent around 30% (MINCYT, 2015[37]). The group of decentralised public institutions brings together a very diverse set of data, but disaggregated data is not available. Expenditure on personnel represented 70% of all the expenditure on R&D activities. Almost half of all resources were destined to applied research, compared to 40% for basic research.

Figure 6.7 highlights the importance of agriculture and agriculture-related issues within the Argentinian innovation system. "Agricultural production and technology" alone represents the largest reported focus area for R&D investments in 2015. Furthermore, agriculture-related R&D objectives are included in a number of the other reported socieconomic objectives, such as "non-oriented research" (basic research), "structure and social relations", "control and protection of the environment", "land exploration and exploitation" and "production, distribution and rational use of energy". The share of total investments going into agricultural issues is difficult to estimate, but there is no doubt that it represents the largest area of focus.

Figure 6.7. Public R&D investments by socio-economic objective, 2015

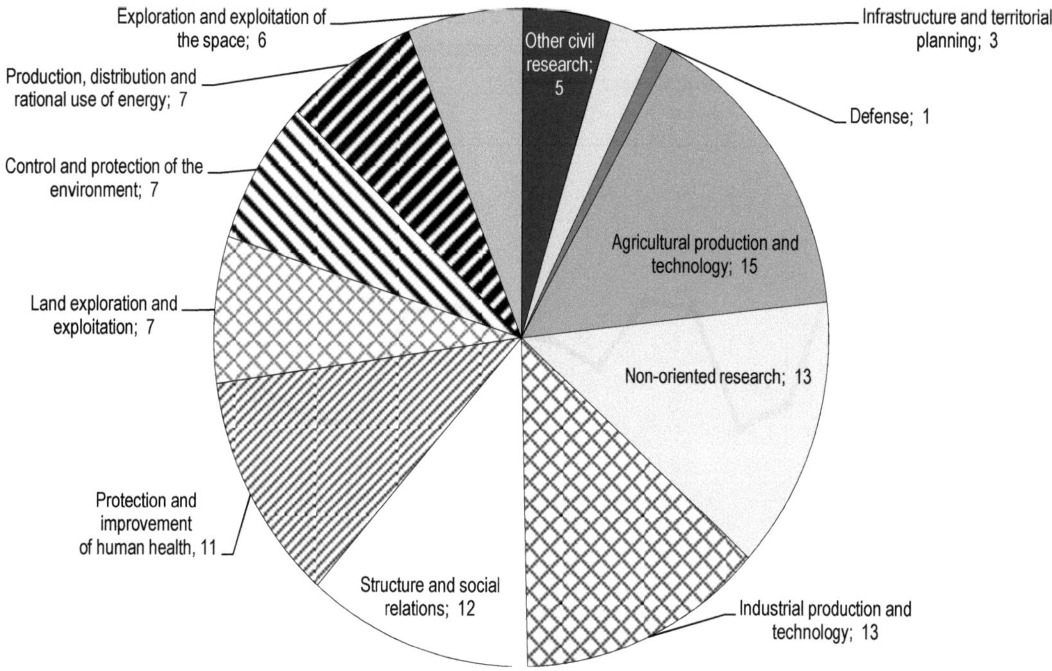

Source: (MINCYT, 2015[80])

StatLink https://doi.org/10.1787/888933908134

Public expenditure on agricultural research

Argentina's significant policy effort on its agricultural knowledge and information system is represented in the support indicators calculated by the OECD, in particular the General Service Support Estimate (GSSE). Most of agriculture policy expenditure focuses on general services, and even if the total amount is not large, more than half is spent on knowledge and innovation, including R&D, and extension services (Figure 6.8).

Figure 6.9 reports international comparisons for Argentina's agricultural R&D expenditure. Agricultural research intensity (measured as the percentage of public expenditure on value added) is higher than the economy-wide research intensity (measured as percentage of total R&D on GDP). The research intensity of agriculture is similar to that of Chile, but significantly lower than in the United States or Brazil (Figure 6.9). Furthermore, the research intensity of agriculture has fallen in the last two decades to 0.5% of the agricultural value added.

Figure 6.8. GSSE expenditures on agricultural knowledge and innovation system

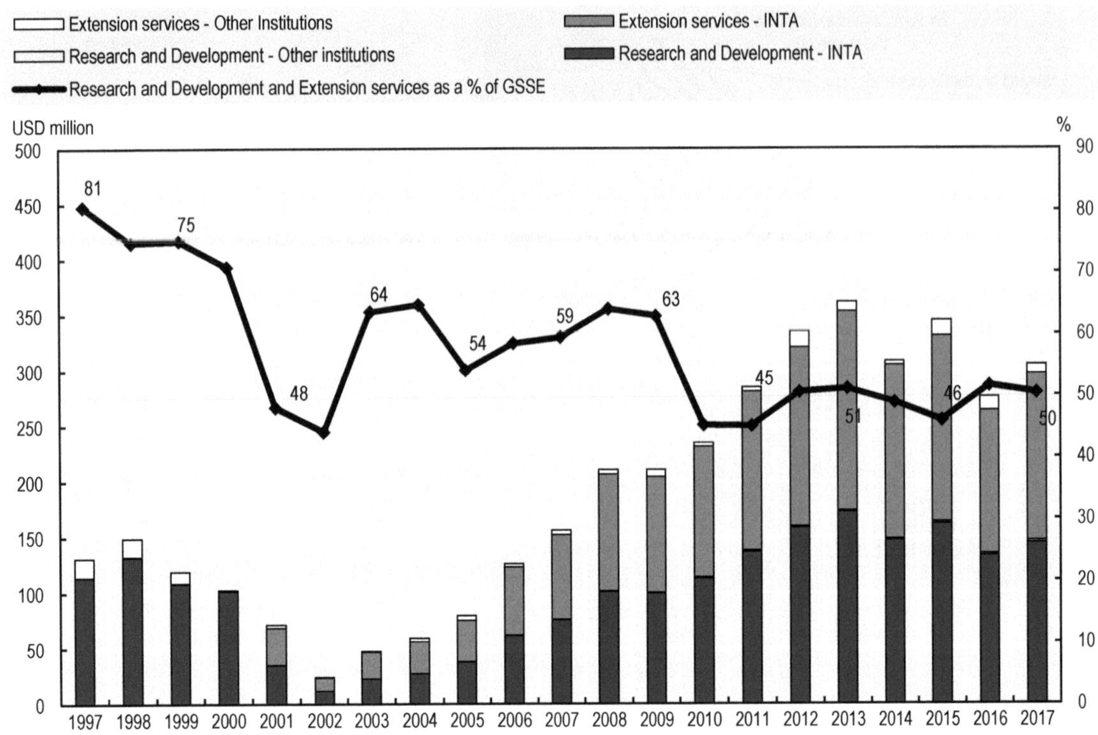

Source: OECD (2018), "Producer and Consumer Estimates", OECD Agriculture Statistics Database.
StatLink https://doi.org/10.1787/888933908153

Figure 6.9. Agriculture and economy-wide R&D intensity in selected countries

Government budget appropriations or outlays for research and development (GBAORD)

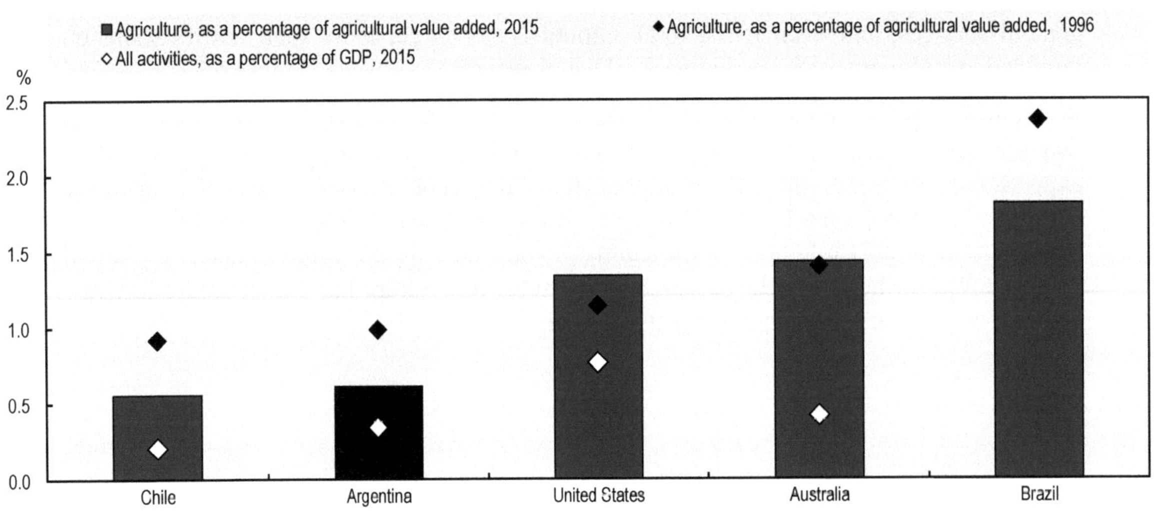

Note: 2015 and 1996 or closest available year.
Source: OECD estimates based on OECD (2018), "Research and Development Statistics" and "National Accounts", OECD Statistics (databases), http://stats.oecd.org/; For Brazil: ASTI (2018), Agricultural Science and Technology Indicators (database), https://asti.cgiar.org/data.

6.7. Knowledge flows: Extension and entrepreneurship

The Argentinian agricultural innovation system has a complex knowledge and technology flow mechanism which covers a wide range of activities and institutions, with strong national and international connections and public-private participation. INTA's agricultural extension system is the main technology transfer mechanism in the country. Very significant private initiatives also exist, such as AACREA and AAPRESID, which over the last three decades have pooled the efforts of farmers and industry to boost the adoption of innovations, in particular in the crop sector.

Agricultural extension is an integral component of INTA's institutional mandate, and its complex institutional framework recognises extension as an organisational objective on the same level as "research". This is reflected in the existence of a directorate for the co-ordination of technology transfer and a heavy training component with more than 330 extension agencies that hold operational responsibilities for field activities.

Since the 1990s, the orientation of extension activities started to evolve to include a broader rural development approach alongside the traditional extension methodologies. The emphasis has moved from education and technology transfer to an approach targeting agricultural development and social inclusion (Trigo and Ciampi, 2018[16]).The expanded focus aims to support the development of innovation capacities beyond the initial technology transfer and training focus, towards rural development, social inclusion, food security, and the sustainable management of natural resources. The main operational instrument is the "Federal Programme for the Support of Sustainable Rural Development" (PROFEDER), which supports the strengthening of producers' organisations, the most vulnerable groups and participatory consensus innovation-sharing networks. PROFEDER has currently 233 projects[4], with the participation of more than 9 500 producers.

INTA also executes related projects with the support of other public-sector institutions. The most prominent is ProHuerta, a large initiative working in peri-urban agriculture with the objective of improving self-consumption of fresh products from family gardens in targeted social groups'. This project has been implemented with support from the Ministry of Social Development for more than twenty years and is widely recognised as a successful high-impact social programme. The traditional extension activities also continue through the network of extension agencies located across the country.

One characteristic of the Argentinian AIS is the important role played by private associative initiatives to promote entrepreneurship and innovation, in particular AACREA and AAPRESID.

The Argentinean Association of Regional Consortia for Agricultural Experimentation (AACREA) is a farmer's organisation initiated in 1960 following the model of the French Consortia for Agricultural Technology Experimentation (CETA). It is a private organisation of agricultural entrepreneurs aiming at sharing experiences and knowledge to increase the profitability and sustainability of their farms. Comprising 226 groups, it includes more than 2 000 producers covering most agricultural activities and around 4 million hectares of land distributed across 18 regions. Each group has 10 to 12 members that meet monthly, led by a co-ordinator and advised by hired technicians. AACREA undertakes research and experimentation to find effective technologies to solve specific problems; it provides technical and business training, often also open to non-members; it transfers members' experience through the value chain; and it integrates results into the broader local community. In more recent years, its R&D activities have evolved from a heavy emphasis on experimentation towards a more formal programme of research.

The Argentinean Association of No-till Agriculture (AAPRESID) is a Non-Government Organization (NGO) that brings together agricultural producers and technicians in pursuit of sustainable agricultural principles and practices. Founded in 1989, it initially focused on the diffusion of no-till agriculture. Its mission is to promote the sustainable production of food, fibres, and energy through innovation, science, and knowledge networks. AAPRESID also strives to facilitate the development of sustainable production technologies. Its Certified Agriculture programme is an integral system of sustainable agriculture based on good agricultural practices and principles. Its Chacras System pursues experimentation and adaption of available knowledge to the production needs of specific territories. AAPRESID works with a wide range of public and private organisations, including INTA.

The co-operative system has a long history in Argentina and offers a diversified line of services to its members. Co-operatives are present in the grain and livestock sectors, where they supply agricultural inputs and services, most notably grain elevators, and technical advice including on animal nutrition. The centre of its activities in the grain sector are as grain elevators and suppliers of agricultural inputs and technical advice, both in agriculture and animal nutrition. Co-operatives are also present in the dairy sector and in some regional economies. In more recent times their presence has diminished.

Since the 1990s, policy instruments and public-private partnerships have been used to promote greater interactions between R&D institutions and the private sector. INTA, CONICET, and most public and private universities started institutional policies for researchers to become part of new start-ups created to benefit from their research results. In the 2000s, ANPCYT opened up competitions for funding the creation of new technology-based start-ups. This instrument complemented FONTAR, which has been quite effective in promoting interactions between already established firms to take advantage of R&D capacities. Within this context, during the last two decades, INTA has implemented hundreds of R&D, technical assistance and technology transfer agreements. This partnership approach is more recent but already growing in CONICET.

The national registry of business incubators lists more than 350 of these entities distributed throughout the country (http://www.produccion.gob.ar/incubar/). Business accelerators, a more recent development, share the objective of helping new ideas and projects survive the first stages and accelerating their consolidation. These accelerators take in projects that need a push to become profitable, offering services ranging from infrastructure (co-working spaces) to training, mentoring and networking opportunities. Incubators and accelerators are part of a continuum but, in general, the former are part of public institutions while the latter are private undertakings which take a management or capital stake (or both) in the new project in return for providing their services. A handful of incubators and accelerators have become quite visible over the last decade, with 200 projects in different stages of development. Several innovation competitions and prizes sponsored by large firms or institutions promote the process of innovation and its value to society, helping identify good investment opportunities for banks or large firms.

The Ministry of Production has recently set up a family of public-private co-investment funds aimed at supporting new firms throughout their development and consolidation process. These instruments fill gaps arising from weaknesses in the Argentine capital markets and target accelerators and funds for entrepreneurial development, and the creation of new high-impact firms (http://www.produccion.gob.ar/fondo-semilla/ and http://www.produccion.gob.ar/fondoexpansion/). The Acceleration Fund provides funds for already consolidated accelerators, while the Expansion Fund is a risk capital fund open to local and international investors. Their short history and lack of experience suggests that their success may depend on the success of the broader macroeconomic stabilisation programme.

6.8. Intellectual Property Rights and international co-operation

A secure system of Intellectual Property (IP) Rights is a primary asset for any Agricultural Information System. It creates incentives for research and development and should establish a secure balance between these incentives and the accessibility and adoption of innovations.

Argentina started discussing IP protection for plant varieties before the signing of the Agreement on Trade-Related Aspects of Intellectual Property Rights (TRIPS). The Law on Seeds and Phytogenetic (Act 20.247), approved in 1973, allows protection of plant varieties conferring plant breeders' rights (PBRs) for up to 20 years. Adherence to the TRIPS agreement since 1995 implied passing a new patent law, the ratification of the 1978 International Union for the Protection of New Varieties of Plants (UPOV) agreement and the adoption of a new confidentiality law (Law 24.766). The current legislation provides limitations to the monopoly power provided by the PBRs: first, the so-called farmers' exemption, allowing farmers to save part of the harvested grain to use it in their own land; second, the breeders' exemption, which enables a breeder to use any protected plant variety, without the owner's authorisation, to conduct research that could lead to the creation of a new plant variety.

Regarding patents, Argentinian legislation is rigorous with respect to patentability requirements, adopting wide exclusions to patentability and exceptions to the rights conferred by patents, with "balanced" precautionary measures (Trigo and Ciampi, 2018[16]).

The law adopts the UPOV 78 model to plant breeders' rights (rather than the 1991 one), without double protection and with wide exceptions. The existing framework has not supported many local developments in the agri-food sector, mainly because of the amplitude of the exceptions to the plant breeders' rights and the difficulties to obtain patent use exception in favor of plant breeders. These difficulties are also directly related to the large level of violation of seed regulations, which results in a weaker level of intellectual property protection than the Latin America average. Several projects to reform the legal framework of seeds have been presented, but an agreement acceptable to the different stakeholders has not been achieved.

Since the early 1990s there has been a significant evolution in the way R&D organisations handle IPRs. IP protection has become a legitimate strategy to protect results and researchers' right to participate in the benefits, independently from the origin of the resources. In the case of CONICET, intellectual property protection approved in 2007 establishes that up to 50% of the benefits could go to researchers and up to 60% to the research centre. This policy has been quite effective as from 2010 to 2015 there was a significant increase in the number of patents. In the case of INTA, the share received by researchers is 30%, another 30% for the research group, 20% for the research unit, and 20% for a technology valorisation fund that finances close-to-market developments.

Argentina has always had a significant presence in international co-operation on science and technology, which was enhanced and formalised with the creation of MINCYT in

2008. The objective is to promote scientific and technological regional integration within the MERCOSUR, to impel co-operation and exchange with science and technology excellence centres and to strengthen financial aid for basic research and its applications.

The number of specific initiatives is large: the Network of Argentine Researchers and Scientists Abroad (RAICES) programme facilitates engagement with Argentinian researchers living abroad; Argentina's most developed and complex partnership, the 1999 Cooperation Agreement in Science and Technology with the European Union, encourages and promotes Argentinian participation in the EU Framework Programmes; the Twinning Programme allows collaboration and sharing of results between Argentinian and European projects working in the same area of food, agriculture and fisheries, and biotechnology; the Biotecsur is a key joint effort implemented by the European Union, the MERCOSUR countries, and MINCYT for the development and use of biotechnology.

Argentina runs 34 binational research centres, nine of which are operated in co-operation with Brazil : the Argentinean–Brazilian Biotechnology Centre founded in 1987 promotes joint work on human resources training, support to scientific and technological research groups and intellectual property; the Argentinean Brazilian Nanotechnology Centre was created in 2005; other bilateral centres include the Binational Centre with Max Planck Society and the Spanish-Argentinian Binational Centre of Plant Genomics (CEBIGEVE).

6.9. Overall policy assessment and recommendations

Argentinian agriculture innovation was and is primarily privately driven by domestic and international economic incentives. However, the public sector has provided very valuable strategic support on specific knowledge inputs and their transmission to human resources for development and implementation, mainly from INTA and the entire ST&I system (Bisang, Anlló and Campi, 2015[8]). On the whole, the Argentinian AIS has been quite successful, as proved by aggregate cereal and oilseed production and productivity performance.

However, in regions outside the Pampas the dynamics of innovation has often been absent, with some specific exceptions. Export policies affecting Argentinians' principal food consumption products (such as beef, wheat and maize), including differentiated exports taxes and export permits for some crops, created relative incentives in favor of processed soybean that interacted with the innovation process on this crop.

The R&D system in Argentina has a very strong specialisation in agri-food research. As a result, 14% of all patents, 21% of scientific publications and 17% of citations refer to the agri-food sector. These shares are higher than in Brazil and in most OECD countries (Table 6.1). The share of these outputs that are co-authored is also high. However, the contribution of Argentina to worldwide R&D agri-food outcomes is modest.

The percentage of the national product going into ST&I activities in all sectors is modest but growing. Despite the organisational innovations that have provided new roles for new private actors, R&D expenditure is mainly public and more needs to be done to make the system more responsive to demand and less supply-driven. Investment levels on agricultural innovation policies are high relative to all agricultural support measures, with a high share in the General Support Estimate (GSSE) dedicated to agriculture knowledge and innovation system (mainly through INTA). These policies are and have been the core of the agricultural policy package in Argentina. However, the research intensity of the sector has fallen in the last two decades.

Table 6.1. R&D outcomes, 2006-11

	Argentina	Australia	Brazil	Chile	United States	OECD average	OECD total
Agri-food specialisation: agri-food as a share of country's total (%)							
Patents 1	14.3	7.4	11.0	21.6	6.8	5.6	..
Publications 2	21.5	10.5	19.4	15.4	6.7	7.6	..
Citations 2	16.8	11.0	16.0	12.5	6.4	7.5	..
Country's contribution to world agri-food output (%)							
Patents 1	0.1	1.6	0.7	0.2	35.9	2.6	92.3
Publications 2	1.1	3.3	4.7	0.5	18.2	1.9	68.9
Citations 2	0.8	3.9	2.5	0.4	22.8	2.2	80.7
Agri-food outputs with co-authors as a share of total agri-food outputs (%)							
Patents 1	44.3	23.1	29.7	27.7	14.3	20.5	..
Publications 2	37.5	47.3	22.3	50.4	36.4	50.7	..

1. Patents filed under the Patent Co-operation Treaty (PCT). Data refer to agri-food outputs for 2006-11.
2. Publications in scientific journals. For Collaboration, OECD average excludes Lithuania.
Source: OECD Patent Database, January 2014; SCImago. (2007). SJR – SCImago Journal & Country Rank. Retrieved March 19, 2014, from www.scimagojr.com.

The measurement of the Argentinian ST&I investment effort on agriculture and the monitoring of its results needs to be strengthened. No good measurement of the overall investment on AIS exists. The system needs to develop and institutionalise ways of measuring the innovation effort and of monitoring the performance of different initiatives and projects, in line with international initiatives. The overall evidence from sector performance is that support to innovation pays; however, the system should improve the monitoring and evaluation of the performance of different investments, in order to develop an information-based decision-making process.

A first important challenge for the Argentinean innovation system is the definition of a broader policy strategy focusing the use of public funds on sustainable development and environmental concerns that are not adequately tackled by the private innovation system. This should include the sustainable use of natural resources, the protection of the environment (covering soils, water, forest, and biodiversity), and the mitigation of and adaptation to climate change. In order to increase productivity and global agricultural production sustainably, it is essential to avoid the depletion of soils developing and adopting innovations that increase the rate of nutrient replenishment. The setting of AIS priorities needs to evolve towards the provision of public goods and long-term investments in sustainability.

The Argentinian AIS needs to better balance the innovation performance of agriculture in the Pampas with that outside it, where indicators on education, infrastructure, and investment lag alongside those for agriculture. The large differences in the structure of regional economies' agriculture systems and their insertion into the national and global markets affect innovation behavior and performance. A federal approach to innovation policy and capacities is needed, but the specific pathways go beyond agricultural innovation policies alone.

Argentina obtained significant economic benefits from exploiting genetic innovations – particularly glyphosate-tolerant soybeans – in very advantageous circumstances, but it is very unlikely that such situations will recur (Trigo, 2011[41]). IPRs, particularly with respect to seeds, is a key area for improvement by means of a secure and respected legal framework. Efforts are already underway to renew the legal framework and strengthen the operational capacities of the National Institute of Seeds (INASE) , but in order to reach consensus to provide both incentives to innovation and access to biological innovations in Argentina, a complex and diverse set of interests – such as those of small-scale farmers, medium and large agricultural producers, domestic breeding firms, multinational firms, and public institutions – need to be involved, and the economic, social and environmental impacts need to be evaluated.

The role of INTA as the most important component of the AIS needs to be better defined in the current context of its decreasing contribution to the main technologies and the diversification of its portfolio into rural and social development rather than R&D and innovation. A technical co-operation with IADB is being carried out during 2018 and 2019 to assess several aspects of INTA's activities: a quantitative assessment of the impact of R&D on agricultural technology on TFP, and a comparative study of the extension activities and scientific networks. Building on these and other existing assessment of INTA, it is recommended to undertake an open external analysis to evaluate and discuss the available alternatives for INTA and other institutional frames to tackle different policy areas more efficiently: innovation, R&D and extension activities; and broader social and community development objectives. The issue is beyond the political allocation of the budget to different policies. It is about an institutional design with the right management and operational structures for good priority setting, resource allocation, and human resources development, in both policy areas.

Such concerns were less pressing when the rural and social development programmes and projects were funded from external resources. However, they have become more pressing as these programmes and projects now compete for INTA’s and other institutions’ budgetary and managerial resources. The organisational needs, and the skills and incentives required for science and research activities significantly differ from those for implementation of rural development programmes. Today’s system is more diverse and the public goods for the next innovation cycle will also come from other actors such as universities and CONICET. The demand for public goods will grow as climate change and environmental sustainability increasingly become the focus for public investments in R&D.

References

Alapin, H. (2008), *Rastrojos y Algo Más: Historia de la Siembra Directa en Argentina*, Teseo. [13]

Albornoz, M. and A. Gordon (2010), *La política de ciencia y tecnología en Argentina desde la recuperación de la democracia 1983-2009*, Centro REDES. [32]

Anlló, G., R. Bisang and M. Campi (2013), *Claves para repensar el agro argentino*, Editorial Eudeba, https://www.eudeba.com.ar/Papel/9789502321967/Claves+para+repensar+el+agro+argentino (accessed on 09 May 2018). [5]

Barsky, O. and J. Gelman (2001), *Historia del Agro Argentino: Desde la Conquista Hasta Fines del Siglo XX*, Grijalbo Mondadori, https://books.google.fr/books/about/Historia_del_agro_argentino.html?hl=es&id=9Ei6AAAAIAAJ&redir_esc=y (accessed on 09 May 2018). [2]

Bisang, R. (2003), "Apertura económica, innovación y estructura productiva: La aplicación de biotecnología en la producción agrícola Pampeana Argentina", *Desarrollo Económico*, Vol. 43/171, pp. 413-442, http://www.jstor.org/stable/3455892. [17]

Bisang, R., G. Anlló and M. Campi (2015), "Políticas tecnológicas para la innovación: La producción agrícola argentina". [8]

Bisang, R., G. Anlló and M. Campi (2008), *Una Revolución (No Tan) Silenciosa. Claves para Repensar el Agro en Argentina*, Instituto de Desarrollo Económico y Social, http://dx.doi.org/10.2307/27667836. [10]

Bisang, R. and G. Gutman (2005), "Acumulacion y tramas agroalimentarias en América Latina", *Revista de la CEPAL*, Vol. 87, pp. 115-129. [33]

Bragachini, M. (2011), *Desarrollo Industrial de la Maquinaria Agrícola y Agropartes en Argentina. Impacto Económico y Social*, INTA, http://www.cosechaypostcosecha.org/data/articulos/maquinaria/DesarrolloIndustrialMaquinariAgricolaYAgropartes-2011-02.pdf. [29]

Cap, E. (2012), *Una rendición de cuentas a la sociedad: El impacto del INTA*. [39]

Consejo General Agropecuario (1995), *El Deterioro de las Tierras en la República Argentina: La Secretaría de Agricultura, Ganadería y Pesca y el Consejo Federal Agropecuario en Alerta Amarillo*, Secretaría de Agricultura, Ganadería y Pesca (Argentina), SAGyP, http://redbiblio.unne.edu.ar/opac/cgi-bin/pgopac.cgi?VDOC=43.41217 (accessed on 09 May 2018). [3]

Cruzate, G. and R. Casas (2012), "Extracción y balance de nutrientes en los suelos agrícolas de la Argentina", *Informaciones Agronómicas de Hispanoamérica*, Vol. 6, pp. 7-14. [28]

Dahlman, C. et al. (2003), *Beyond the Crisis: From the Old To the New Economy in Argentina*. [31]

Ekboir, J. (2002), *Developing no-till packages for small-scale farmers*, https://repository.cimmyt.org/xmlui/bitstream/handle/10883/1253/75824.pdf (accessed on 09 May 2018). [14]

Fuglie K., W. (ed.) (2012), *Productivity Growth and Technology Capital in the Global Agricultural Economy*, CAB International, Wallingford, UK. [1]

INASE (2018), *Catálogo Nacional de Cultivares*, https://www.inase.gov.ar/consultaGestion/gestiones (accessed on 09 May 2018). [25]

INTA (2017), *60° Aniversario. Instituto Nacional de Tecnología Agropecuaria, 1956-2016.* [38]

Lavado, R. and M. Taboada (2009), "The Argentinean Pampas: A key region with a negative nutrient balance and soil degradation needs better nutrient management and conservation programs to sustain its future viability as a world agroresource", *Journal of Soil and Water Conservation*, Vol. 64/5, pp. 150A-153A, http://dx.doi.org/10.2489/jswc.64.5.150A. [27]

Lódola, A. (2008), *Contratistas, Cambio Tecnológicos y Organizacionales en el Agro Argentina*, CEPAL. [30]

Lopez, A. (2010), *Intellectual Property Rights, Development, and Catch Up. An International Study*, Oxford. [20]

Marin, A. and L. Stubrin (2017), "Oportunidades y desafíos para convertirse en un innovador mundial en Recursos Naturales (RN). El caso de las empresas de semillas en Argentina", *Desarrollo Económico*, Vol. 56/220, pp. 471-497, https://dialnet.unirioja.es/servlet/articulo?codigo=6028816 (accessed on 09 May 2018). [24]

Mercado (1999), "Agroquímicos y fertilizantes. Tierra de fusiones", *Revista Mercado*. [26]

MINCYT (2015), *Indicadores de Ciencia y Tecnología argentina 2015*, Ministerio de Ciencia, Tecnología e Innovación Productiva, http://indicadorescti.mincyt.gob.ar/documentos/indicadores_2015.pdf. [37]

Ministerio de Agroindustria (2018), *Datos Agroindustriales - Estimaciones Agrícolas*, https://datos.agroindustria.gob.ar/dataset/estimaciones-agricolas (accessed on 09 May 2018). [6]

Ministerio de Agroindustria (2018), *El Contratista Rural*, https://www.agroindustria.gob.ar/sitio/areas/contratistas/contratista/ (accessed on 09 May 2018). [34]

Ministerio de Agroindustria (2018), *OGM Comerciales*, https://www.agroindustria.gob.ar/sitio/areas/biotecnologia/ogm/ (accessed on 09 May 2018). [18]

OECD (2018), *Main Science and Technology Indicators*, http://dx.doi.org/10.1787/2304277X. [40]

OECD (2013), *Agricultural Innovation Systems: A Framework for Analysing the Role of the Government*, OECD Publishing, Paris, http://dx.doi.org/10.1787/9789264200593-en. [42]

Posada, M. and M. Martínez de Ibarreta (1998), "Capital financiero y producción agrícola: Los "pools" de siembra en la región pampeana", *Realidad Económica*, Vol. 153, pp. 112-135. [35]

Qaim, M. and A. de Janvry (2003), "Genetically Modified Crops, Corporate Pricing Strategies, and Farmers' Adoption: The Case of Bt Cotton in Argentina", *American Journal of Agricultural Economics*, Vol. 85/4, pp. 814-828, http://dx.doi.org/10.1111/1467-8276.00490. [23]

Qaim, M. and G. Traxler (2005), "Roundup Ready soybeans in Argentina: farm level and aggregate welfare effects", *Agricultural Economics*, Vol. 32, pp. 73-86. [21]

Reca, L., D. Lema and C. Flood (2010), *El crecimiento de la agricultural argentina. Medio siglo de logros y desafíos*, Facultad de Agronomía de la UBA. [11]

Regúnaga, M. (2010), *Implications of the Organization of the Commodity Production and Processing Industry: The Soybean Chain in Argentina*, World Bank, Washington, DC, http://agris.fao.org/agris-search/search.do?recordID=US2014601274 (accessed on 09 May 2018). [7]

Rocha, P. and V. Villalobos (2013), *Soybean Cultivation. Genetically Modified and Conventional*, IICA. [9]

Senigagliesi, L. and S. Massoni (2002), *Transferencia de tecnología en Siembra Directa: Un análisis de lo realizado en el INTA*. [15]

Stads, G. et al. (2016), "Agricultural research in Latin America and the Caribbean: A cross-country analysis of institutions, Investment, and capacities". [36]

Traxler, G. (2006), "The GMO experience in North and South America", *Int. J. Technology and Globalisation*, Vol. 2/12, pp. 46-64. [22]

Trigo, E. (2016), *Veinte Años de Cultivos Genéticamente Modificados en la Agricultura Argentina*. [12]

Trigo, E. (2011), "Fifteen years of genetically modified crops in Argentine agriculture". [41]

Trigo, E., E. Cap and V. Malach (2009), "The case of zero-tillage technology in Argentina". [4]

Trigo, E. et al. (2004), *Los Transgénicos en América Latina y el Caribe: Un Debate Abierto*, CEPAL. [19]

Trigo, E. and M. Ciampi (2018), *Review of agricultural innovation policies in Argentina*, Background report for the OECD Review of Agricultural Policies in Argentina. [16]

Notes

[1] This chapter is based on the consultant background paper (Trigo and Ciampi, 2018[16]) which follows the OECD framework for analysing sustainable agricultural productivity growth (OECD, 2013[42]).

[2] (Trigo and Ciampi, 2018[16]) estimations based on data from COMTRADE: https://comtrade.un.org/

[3] The silo-bag consists of a relatively thick polyethylene sleeve of a diameter of between 1.4 and 2.2 metres, in which grains can be stored for a limited time – between 1 and 3 years. A specially designed machine – produced by a domestic firm – deposits the grain in the sleeves, closing them hermetically. The extraction can be done either manually or with extraction equipment.

[4] PROFEDER projects include: Minifundio, aiming to facilitate subsistence farmers' access to land and water, habitat and infrastructure, self-consumption production, and aggregating value; PROFAM, supporting family farms and their associations, management capacities and access to credit; Local Development Support Projects, working at local level with other public and private organisations; Cambio Rural II, assisting small and medium enterprises (SMEs) of the agro-industrial sector, the co-operative sector and family farmers on associative capacities.

Chapter 7. Sustainability of Argentina's agricultural transformation

Argentina's agriculture sector has transformed at an accelerated pace in recent years with new technologies and the expansion of the agricultural frontier. This has opened new opportunities for the sector but has increased environmental pressures. The trends in the agri-environmental indicators reveal that most of these pressures are still lower than in OECD countries. However, deforestation rates in Argentina are high and the use of pesticides per area of cropland has risen at rates well above the OECD average. In the context of reducing export taxes on the main exporting commodities, it is important to strengthen the Native Forest Law and good environmental practices on the use of pesticides and rotation, potentially incorporating targeted instruments to enhance the responsibility of producers in reducing negative agri-environmental externalities.

7.1. Potential environmental impacts of the technological package for crops

Argentina's agriculture sector has transformed rapidly since the 1990s from an extensive and semi-pastoral system to a more intensive one based on double cropping, genetically modified (GM) varieties and no-till (NT) practices. Comprehensively assessing the environmental impacts of this transformation is a complex task due to the diversity of elements in the technological package and of ecosystem and production patterns that vary continuously due to changes in market and weather conditions. This subsection attempts to assess these potential impacts based on available studies, including an overall assessment of the package, and a separate assessment of its two main components: GM and NT practices.

Overall assessment

Overall assessments for Argentina indicate both potential negative and positive environmental impacts of GM-NT adoption. Firstly, on deforestation: the package is associated with higher deforestation rates and higher greenhouse gas (GHG) emissions compared to non-GM technologies. The main channel is related to the high profitability of such package and the possibility to cultivate soybeans in dry areas (Zak et al., 2008[1]; Phélinas and Choumert, 2017[2]). Secondly, GM-NT is likely to increase pesticide use per unit of land, but lower pesticide risk due to the use of less hazardous substances. Thirdly, dissolved phosphorus runoffs are also likely to increase in the absence of good agricultural practices. Finally, positive impacts of GM-NT include reduced soil erosion, increased soil carbon content in shallow layers, and decreased particulate phosphorus runoff.

Vigglizo et al. (2011[3]) focused on the impacts of the overall transformation of Argentina's agriculture sector and concluded that, compared to the less intensive model prevalent in the 1960s, the new model presents larger net GHG emissions, higher habitat intervention, lower carbon (C) stocks, and lower nitrogen (N) and phosphorus (P) in soils. GHG emissions increased mainly due to higher deforestation and increased burning practices to manage grassland, despite a reduction of GHG emissions in the Pampas region due to no-till practices. The habitat intervention increased due to a higher expansion of the agricultural frontier. While C soil stocks tended to improve due to no-till practices mainly in the Pampa region, C stocks in biomass decrease with deforestation. Pesticides risk decreases due to a substitution of organo-chlorinated products by phosphorated ones and hypermetrines.

A comprehensive analysis of the long-term sustainability of the GM soybean specialisation system of Argentina (Phélinas and Choumert, 2017[2]) found environmental threats: water and air quality are compromised by pesticides, in particular, Endosulfan has been found in high concentrations in groundwater and air[1]. The adoption of the new technological package tended to increase productivity and, when not combined with good agricultural practices, deforestation and monocropping, potentially impacting GHG emissions, biodiversity, water availability and soil health.

Herbicide tolerant GM varieties

Meta-analysis as well as studies conducted in Argentina suggest that cultivating GM crops decreases the use of pesticides compared to non-GM varieties (Viglizzo et al., 2011[4]; Klümper and Qaim, 2014[5]). A global assessment of the differences between GM and non-GM crops on pesticide use, pesticide costs, yields and profits found that herbicide tolerant GM do not use more pesticide than non-GM crops, but tend to decrease costs and increase yields (Klümper and Qaim, 2014[5]). An empirical analysis based on interviews with farmers detected that GM soybean lead to higher number of herbicide applications but to lower toxicity of herbicide used compared to conventional soybean (Qaim and Traxler, 2005[6]). Increased applications are also related to the adoption of no-till practices, which contribute to the increase in pesticide use per hectare.

No-till practices

No-till has been shown to decrease particulate phosphorus (PP) runoff but can lead to higher dissolved phosphorus (DP) runoff (Dodd and Sharpley, 2016[7]); it is also associated with higher pesticide use due to a higher presence of weeds (Qaim and Traxler, 2005[6]). Wingeyer et al., (2015[8]) find that the adoption of NT is linked to reduced losses and sometimes increases in soil organic carbon (SOC) and particulate organic carbon (POC) in soil layers at 0–5 cm depth. At deeper levels no benefits of NT were found. Decreasing erosion rates, improved carbon content in soils and reduced surface runoff were detected in fields under NT compared to fields under conventional management (Casas, 2018[9]; Vázquez Amábile, Feiguin and Fritz, 2018[10]). Some authors highlight that no-till should in general not lead to higher chemical use but does so when used in monocropping systems (Friedrich and Kassam, 2012[11]). Inclusion of a 3-year pasture in the rotation after 7–8 years of grain crops could restore SOC and POC contents to levels before cropping (Wingeyer et al., 2015[8]).

7.2. Agri-environmental indicators reveal lower environmental pressures than in the OECD

Since 2004 agriculture production in Argentina has increased more rapidly than in other countries. Nevertheless, agriculture sector Total Factor Productivity (TFP) growth is lower than the world average, despite the good performance of the crop sector. Arable land has significantly expanded, by 41% since 2000. Even if the level of environmental pressure is lower than in other countries, it has increased during the last few decades of agricultural transformation.

On average, environmental pressures remain low compared to OECD countries but some risks are observed in terms of increased pesticide use. Nutrient balances, while positive, are still at low levels compared to OECD ones. Water use, direct on-farm energy consumption and GHG emissions levels (excluding land use, land use change and forestry [LULUCF]) are also still below OECD countries (Table 7.1). While pesticide sales per unit of agriculture land are lower than in OECD countries, their rate of growth is increasing.

Table 7.1. National agri-environmental performance compared to the OECD average

2012-14 averages or nearest available period

Indicator	Unit	Argentina	OECD
Agricultural production volume	Index (2004-06=100)	115	123
Nitrogen balance	kg per hectare	4.4	65.9
Phosphorus balance	kg per hectare	1.8	6.5
Pesticides sales	kg active of ingredients per ha	1.40	2.56
Direct on-farm energy consumption	tonnes of oil equivalent per ha	0.024	0.213
Water use	1 000 m^3 per ha	0.19	0.71
Greenhouse gas emissions	tonnes of CO2 equivalent per ha	0.64	3.12

Note: Argentina data for nutrient balances are preliminary. Argentina greenhouse gas emissions refer to 2012. The OECD figures of total factor productivity and agricultural production volume reflect world averages.
Source: OECD Agri-environmental Indicators database (2017).

Environmental pressures related to the intensification of Argentina's agriculture sector have increased at larger rates than in OECD countries. The increase in pesticide has surpassed the rate of growth of agricultural TFP, indicating no decoupling for this indicator. Pesticide sales, phosphorus balance and water-use intensity increased more than 1% annually in the period 2002-14. Particularly significant was the increase in pesticide sales. Greenhouse gas emissions (excluding LULUCF) slightly decreased in the period analysed (Figure 7.1).

Figure 7.1. Environmental pressures from agriculture are increasing in Argentina

Average annual per cent change 2002-04 to 2012-14, or nearest available period

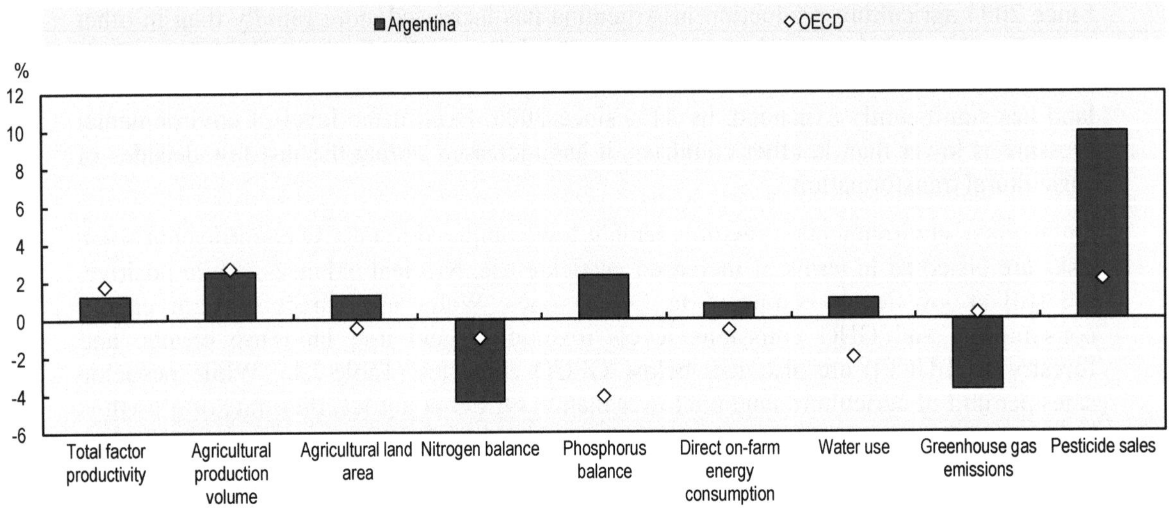

Note: Preliminary estimations are provided for Nitrogen and Phosphorus balance. Nutrient balances consider all agriculture land: pastures and cropland. Greenhouse gas emissions excludes LULUCF emissions. Nutrient balances, direct on-farm energy consumption, water use, greenhouse gas emissions and pesticide sales are calculated per unit of agriculture land. The OECD figures of total factor productivity and agricultural production volume reflect world annual growth rate averages. OECD average for pesticide use per ha excludes Denmark, Finland, Germany, the Slovak Republic, Sweden and Great Britain due to compatibility issues for data before 2010.
Source: OECD Agri-environmental Indicators database (2018). USDA Economic Research Service Agricultural Productivity Database for Total Factor Productivity. Pesticide sales for Argentina were retrieved from (FAO, 2018[12]) as a proxy for pesticide use.

StatLink https://doi.org/10.1787/888933908172

Fertiliser and pesticide use is on the rise

Fertiliser use has increased but remains low compared to regional and global levels. P fertiliser use could be increased to replace P deficit from increased P crop uptake, but care should be taken in terms of potential P runoff. Fertiliser sales per unit of cropland (excluding pastures) have increased from levels below 5 kg/ha in the 1990s to almost 15 kg/ha for P and19 kg/ha for N in 2014 (Figure 7.2). Such levels are still below those of Brazil, but already above the OECD average for P although some authors have stressed that P fertiliser applications in cropland (excluding pasture) have not been sufficient to replace fertiliser uptake by crops (Viglizzo et al., 2011[3]).

Figure 7.2. Fertiliser use shows a positive trend in Argentina

kg/ha of cropland

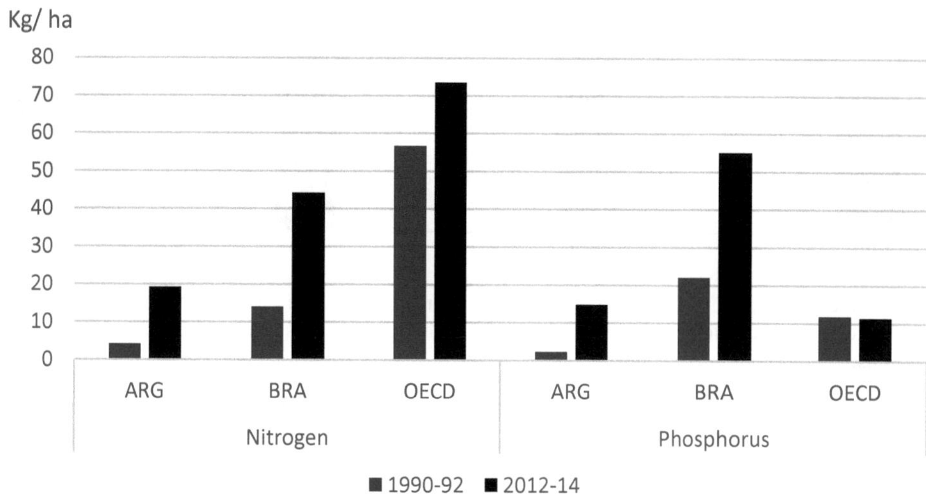

Source: OECD Agri-environmental Indicators database (2018).

StatLink https://doi.org/10.1787/888933908191

Excluding pastures, pesticide sales per unit of cropland are higher in Argentina than OECD countries and Brazil (Figure 7.3), although most common imported pesticides are only slightly or moderately hazardous.[2] As a result of the transformation of agriculture in Argentina, the importation of pesticides is on the rise.

Pesticide active substances imported are not among the most dangerous, and most of them are only slightly or moderately hazardous. In 2017, Atrazine represented nearly 7% of total imported pesticides (Table 7.2). This herbicide is widely used worldwide but is highly persistent, which poses potential human health risks in drinking water; it can also affect other vertebrates (Hayes et al., 2010[13]). Attention should be paid to monitoring Atrazine concentrations in water and, more in general, pesticide risks on human health and the environment. Used in excess, pesticides can lead to biodiversity loss and ecosystem degradation, as well as negative and severe effects on human health (OECD, 2019 forthcoming[14]). Pesticide active substance imports are dominated by glyfosate (55% of total imports), which is mainly used for soybean production (Table 7.2). While some studies have found few traces of pesticides concentration in groundwater in some basins (Vázquez Amábile, 2017[15]), additional monitoring efforts are needed to assess the risks of pesticides concentrations in water courses and groundwater sources and to identify hotspots.

Figure 7.3. Pesticide intensity in cropland is higher in Argentina than in other countries

Pesticide use per ha of cropland (kg of active ingredient/ha)

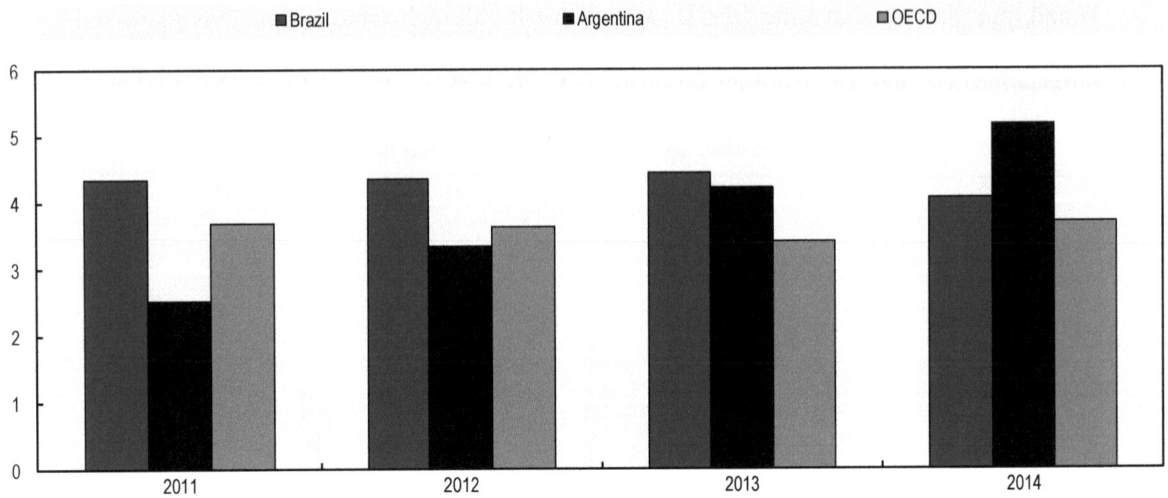

Source: Pesticide data for OECD countries comes from OECD Agri-environmental Indicators database (2018) and comprises pesticide sales. Data for Brazil and Argentina was retrieved from (FAO, 2018[12]) and indicates use.

StatLink https://doi.org/10.1787/888933908210

Table 7.2. Imports of pesticide active substance

Top 10 most imported formulated pesticides, 2017

Active substance	1 000 Tn	FOB million USD	WHO class	Share to total pesticides imports in Tn
Glyphosate	153.3	374.9	III	55.1%
Atrazine	18.7	92.8	III	6.7%
Paraquat	15.5	36.6	II	5.6%
2,4 D	8.9	18.9	II	3.2%
S-Metolachlore	8.7	47.1	III	3.1%
Metolachlore	6.9	26.3	III	2.5%
Clethodim	5.2	34.9	NA	1.9%
Mineral Oils	4.3	2.9	U	1.6%
Acetochlor	3.4	9.8	III	1.2%
Mancozeb	2.2	6.2	U	0.8%

Note: World Health Organisation (WHO) classification is Ia = Extremely hazardous; Ib = Highly hazardous; II = Moderately hazardous; III = slightly hazardous; U = Unlikely to present acute hazard in normal use; NA = Not available.
Source: Servicio Nacional de Sanidad y Calidad Agroalimentaria.

Deforestation and biodiversity have been affected

From 1990 to 2015 Argentina lost 77 000 km^2 of forests, or 22% of its forested area in 1990 (348 000 km^2) – an area equivalent to the size of San Luis province. Another study estimates that 40 000 km^2 of forested land were lost due to agriculture in the period

1990-2005 (De Sy et al., 2015[16]). Contrary to regional and global deforestation trends, Argentina has increased its deforestation rate in the last fifteen years: from 1990 to 2000 the annual deforestation rate was 0.8%, but from 2000 to 2015 it reached 1% – a rate three times higher than average deforestation rate in Latin America and nearly twelve times higher than the world average (Figure 7.4). According to the Ministry of the Environment (Ministerio de Ambiente y Desarrollo Sustentable, 2016[17]) deforestation rates have been declining since 2007 and in the period 2014-15, the deforestation rate was estimated to be 0.7%.

Deforestation has been mainly occurring in the regions of Santiago del Estero, Salta, Chaco y Formosa. In the period 2002-06, deforestation rates in the regions of Parque Chaqueño (which comprises the provinces of Formosa, Chaco, Santiago del Estero and parts of other neighbouring provinces) and Yungas reached 1.5% and 0.5% respectively (Ministerio de Ambiente y Desarrollo Sustentable, 2016[17]). Nearly 28% and 16% of the 1960 forested area in the Chaco and Yungas regions has been lost, respectively (Viglizzo et al., 2011[4]).

The main driver of deforestation rates in Argentina is agriculture. From 1990 to 2005 nearly 90% of forest loss was attributed to agriculture activities: half due to pasture and half due to commercial cropland (De Sy et al., 2015[16]; Fehlenberg et al., 2017[18]). Conversion from forest to cropland and grassland contributed to 35% of total GHG emissions from agriculture activities in 2014, including LULUCF emissions.

Figure 7.4. Annual deforestation rates in Argentina are high relative to the world and the Latin American region

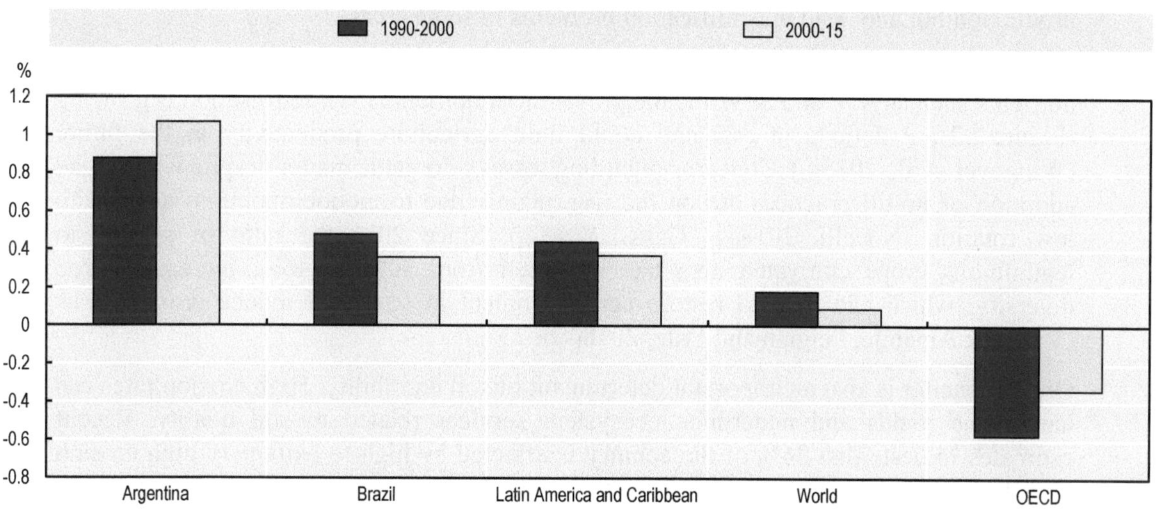

Source: WDI, World Bank (WDI, 2018[19]).

StatLink https://doi.org/10.1787/888933908229

Biodiversity has been affected by both the conversion of grassland and forest into cropland and the intensification of agriculture. Globally, pesticide use has contributed to reducing populations of birds, insects, amphibians and aquatic and soil communities, either through direct exposure or reduction in food and habitat availability (OECD, 2019 forthcoming[14]). The diversity of rodents, plants and crop-associated insects and, particularly, of birds and carnivores, in the Pampas region has been negatively affected by the expansion and intensification of agriculture (Medan et al., 2011[20]). Bird species richness and abundance has been found to be negatively correlated with crop density and positively correlated with grassland area (Cerezo, Conde and Poggio, 2011[21]; Medan et al., 2011[20]). Increased pesticide and fertiliser use and overgrazing associated to the intensification of agriculture have impacted small mammal populations and crop-associated insects (Medan et al., 2011[20]). Soil quality and erosion benefited from NT but monocropping is a risk

Soil characteristics affect a multiplicity of ecosystem services and outcomes: provision of food, raw materials, fresh water and water retention; carbon sequestration, water purification, climate and water regulation, erosion and flood control; nutrient cycling, soil formation and provision of habitat (Adhikari and Hartemink, 2016[22]; Wingeyer et al., 2015[8]).

Most of Argentina's agriculture is located in areas where mollisol soils dominate (Chaco-Pampas regions); such soil types are among the most fertile on Earth and are characterised by a dark topsoil rich with organic matter. Soil management and agriculture practices impact the quality and fertility of soils. Wingeyer et al. (2015[8]) assessed the extent to which the expansion of cropland in South America has impacted soil quality and concluded that three important indicators of soil quality – soil organic matter (SOM) content, aggregate stability and bulk density[3] – had 64%, 48% and 116% of the pristine values in areas with 10-20 years of continuous agriculture in Argentina (Wingeyer et al., 2015[8]). Organic carbon content in the Pampas region ranges between 5.5 and 38 g/kg and registered an average reduction of 30-52% compared to pristine soils (Sainz Rozas, Echeverria and Angelini, 2011[23]). PH levels ranged between 6 and 7.5, with an average of 6.3, which, according to the same authors, did not present risks for agriculture production but may lead to acidification problems in some areas.

Losses of organic matter in soils under cropping systems also yield reductions in other nutrients such as N, P and S. While the provision of nutrients from fertilisation is growing (Figure 7.2), P deficits in cropland could limit agriculture productivity in the future (Wingeyer et al., 2015[8]). Concerns regarding losses of organic matter despite widespread adoption of no-till practices are on the rise, mainly due to monocropping systems with low rotation (Nocelli, 2018[24]; Casas, 2018[9]). Since 2010 the ratio of grasses to leguminous crops cultivated area has increased from 30% to 46%, increasing crop diversity, which can help to restore carbon content in soils and reduce erosion risks (Vázquez Amábile, Feiguin and Fritz, 2018[10]).

Organic matter is also an important determinant of soil erodibility. High erosion rates can harm crop yields and undermine ecosystem services related to soil quality. Recent estimates indicate that 26% of the country is affected by high to extremely high erosion rates by water, with estimated soil losses of 50-200 tn/ha/year for high erosion areas and greater than 200 tn/ha/year for areas with extremely high erosion rates (Gaitán et al., 2017[25]). Erosion rates are higher than in 1990 mainly due to monocropping, deforestation and overgrazing (Casas, 2018[9]). Land with high erosion rates is located in steep and arid areas near the Cordillera and in the Patagonia region of the south. While in most of the central and the northeast regions, where agriculture activity concentrates, erosion rates are low (below 10 tn/ha/yr), steep regions within that area tend to be affected by moderate erosion levels (between 10 to 50 tn/ha/yr). Erosion rates in agriculture land is slightly below worldwide rates, which are estimated to be 12.7 tn/ha/yr (Borrelli et al., 2017[26]). No-till practices in Argentina have contributed to the country having the largest decrease in erosion rates worldwide: it is estimated that they have decreased 33% due to no-till (Borrelli et al., 2017[26]).

7.3. Potentially mild impacts of climate change on agriculture, but higher frequency of extreme events

Most climate models project increases in temperature due to climate change in all the Argentinian territory; more intense warming is expected in the north and west areas reaching increases up to 3.5°C and higher in the summer (Magrin et al., 2014[27]; Barros et al., 2015[28]). Precipitation is projected to increase in northern, central and eastern areas (between 17% and 20%) and decrease in the Patagonia and Mendoza regions (between -10% and -20%) (Magrin et al., 2014[27]; Barros et al., 2015[28]; Nuñez, 2018[29]). Temperature increases are projected to be in the 0.5-1.0°C range.

In the past, increases in temperature and precipitation, have improved yields in Argentina. While there are several uncertainties associated to projecting the impacts of climate change on agricultural production, the potential negative impacts of persistent and more pronounced climate change on yields may on average be mild, particularly in rain-fed areas of high productivity located in the central and eastern parts of the country. Higher CO2 concentrations in the atmosphere, which tend to improve photosynthesis and increase yields (Barros et al., 2015[28]; Murgida et al., 2014[30]), could more than compensate the potentially negative effects of hotter temperatures, particularly in the Pampas (Magrin et al., 2014[27]; Nuñez, 2018[29]). Regarding specific crops, climate change scenarios will likely favour soybeans over wheat and maize. Areas such as Mendoza which rely on irrigation for agriculture production (mainly viticulture) will be negatively affected by reduced water availability from lower snow in the mountains, the main source of river flow (Schwank et al., 2014[31]).

Notwithstanding potential average effects of temperature and precipitation, a source of risk for agricultural production may be increased interannual and decadal climate variability. Most common extreme weather events in Argentina include riverine floods, storms, wildfires, cold temperatures and storm surges (Nagy et al., 2018[32]). Even though, relative to other countries, droughts are not a common phenomenon in Argentina, their effects on agricultural production can be high as the 2018 drought has proven[4]. The frequency of floods are likely to maintain their observed growing trends, particularly in the south of La Plata basin (Barros, Garavaglia and Doyle, 2013[33]). Extreme high temperatures are also likely to increase (Barros et al., 2015[28]), which may exacerbate the frequency of extreme weather events.

7.4. Agri-environmental policies

This section presents a review of the main policies addressing the environmental impacts of agriculture, principally addressing whether they are aligned with the main environmental challenges identified through the agri-environmental indicators and whether they reflect key characteristics for being cost-effective.

Argentina has made progress in reducing some of the environmental pressures from agriculture, mainly those related to soil erosion and maintaining the soil quality. However, many pastoral and semi-pastoral production systems have been replaced by intensive soybean production systems dominated by double-cropping GM technological packages, and feedlots have an increasing role in cattle production. This transformation of the agriculture sector to intensive soybean production systems poses environmental challenges. Particular, increased deforestation and high and rising pesticide use per unit of land seem to be the major challenges, followed by the loss of organic matter and P content in soils when NT practices are not accompanied by good rotation practices.

The main agri-environmental policies in Argentina consist of incentives for good agriculture practices, and measures for natural resource conservation and protecting water quality (Figure 7.5). Since 1989, the province of Entre Rios has provided partial property tax exemptions for farmers undertaking soil conservation practices. More recently, in 2017, the province of Cordoba initiated a programme providing per hectare payments conditional on undertaking specific good agricultural practices in areas such as rotation, pasture, soils and fertilisation.

The National Plan of Agriculture Soils (Plan Nacional de Suelos Agropecuarios) was launched in 2018 in order to promote the conservation, sustainable management and restoration of soils to maximise their productivity and provision of ecosystem services in the context of climate change. The plan relies on six components: 1) the System of Soil Information of Argentina, based on the National Observatory of Agriculture Soils; 2) tools for promoting the sustainable management of soils; 3) training in soils management and knowledge; 4) strengthening of institutions and co-operation; 5) soil policy platform; and 6) support to research.

Other policies related to agriculture may affect the environment. The fertiliser VAT exemptions are unlikely to have significant impacts since they are not discriminated by fertiliser type, and they only affect farmers that are not able to deduct VAT, who are typically small producers. Bans on extremely and highly hazardous pesticides are also in place. Finally, commodity export taxes affect farmers' output prices and may affect the environment. To better assess the different policies, Table 7.3 displays each policy (in each row) and some of their key characteristics (in columns)[5].

Because Argentina is a federal republic, provinces have a high degree of autonomy to define policies and regulations. In many cases, regulations only apply in certain provinces, specifically those that tend to promote good agriculture practices and soil conservation. Most regulations are voluntary in nature and do not discriminate in terms of management unit (i.e. farmers are paid the same rates independently of the size of the operation). Regulations such as protected areas, protected wetlands and conservation of native forests rely on budgetary transfers for the management of these areas and or specific programmes with relevant communities and thus they cover not only farmers but other stakeholders.

The polluter pays principle (PPP) states that "the polluter should be held responsible for environmental damage caused and bear the expenses of carrying out pollution prevention measures or paying for damaging the state of the environment where the consumptive or productive activities causing the environmental damage are not covered by property rights" (OECD, 2001[34]). Advancing towards the application of the PPP requires strengthening the responsibility of farmers in reducing negative environmental externalities from agriculture.

Three main policy characteristics define the cost effectiveness of agri-environmental policies: environmental targeting, flexibility and budgetary/administrative costs (OECD, 2010[35]). Environmental targeting refers to the degree to which policy incentives are higher for those farmers whose actions are more likely to reduce environmental harm. A second fundamental characteristic that defines the effectiveness of any policy is the possibility to enforce it via monitoring and imposing sanctions to violators, as well as the recurrent assessment of the effectiveness of the regulations. Flexibility is related to the freedom of farmers to choose among different options to achieve a desired environmental outcome. A formal assessment of effectiveness is also desirable. Finally, budgetary and administrative costs define the monetary burden imposed on taxpayers to achieve certain goals.

Figure 7.6 summarises some of the relevant characteristics that influence the cost-effectiveness of policies in Argentina. Most regulations stipulate monitoring and sanctions guidelines.[6] There is room for improving policies by making them environmentally targeted, evaluating their effectiveness, and streamlining the costs that are involved to maintain the policy in place and ensure compliance. Regarding flexibility, the most flexible policies are those related to protected areas, wetland protected areas and conservation of native forests: all of these allow plenty of flexibility to local jurisdictions and private actors to ensure protection and conservation of natural assets.

Figure 7.5. Agri-environmental policies in Argentina

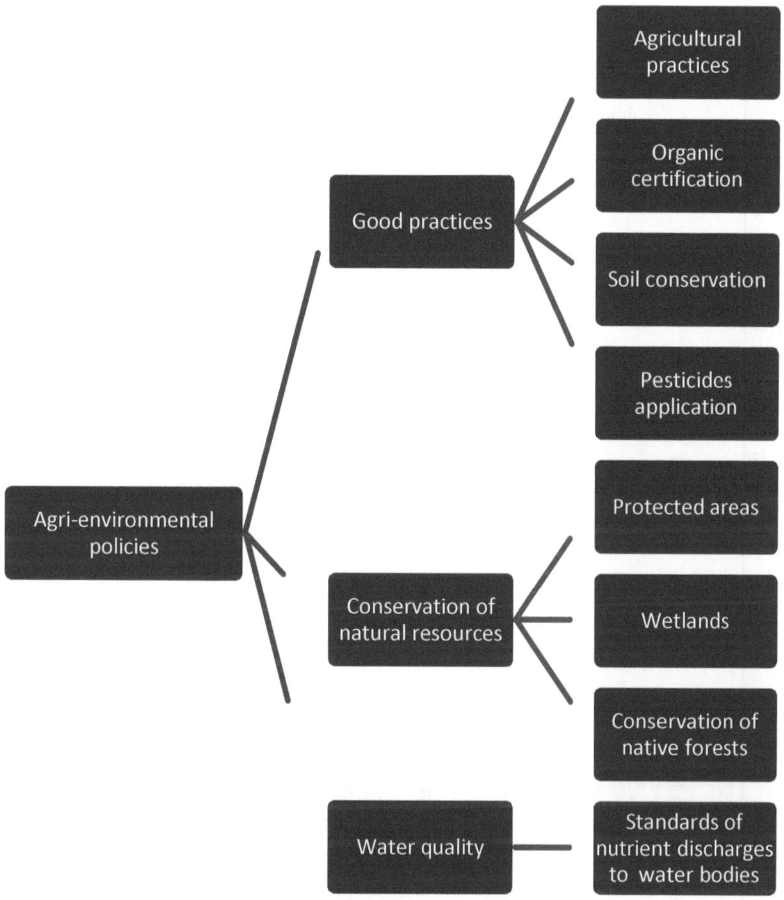

Source: Author's own work based on a country questionnaire.

Table 7.3. Characteristics of main agri-environmental policies in Argentina

	Main characteristics				Differentiation			Effectiveness				
Policy target/ Characteristics	Geographic scope	Mandatory/ Voluntary	Type of Support	Partial or total compensation of incurred costs	Differentiated by size of the management unit	Differentiated by geographic zone	Differentiated by crop	Environmental targeting	Monitoring	Fines	Effectiveness assessment	Budgetary cost assessment
Soil conservation practices	Provincial: Entre Rios	Voluntary	Property tax exemption	Yes	No	No	No	Yes	Yes	Yes	No	No
Good agricultural practices	Provincial: Cordoba	Voluntary	Payments based on current area, production required	Yes	No	No	No	No	Yes	Yes	No	Yes
Organic certification	National	Voluntary	n.a.	No	No	No	No	Yes	Yes	Yes	Yes	No
Good practices in the application of pesticides	National	Mandatory	n.a.	No	No	No	Fruits and vegetables	No	Yes	Yes	No	No
Standards of nutrient discharges to water bodies	Provincial	Mandatory	n.a.	No	No	No	n.a.	Yes	Yes	Yes	No	No
Protected areas	National/ Provincial/ Municipal	Voluntary: provinces need to cede the land	Budgetary	No	No	Yes	n.a.	Yes	Yes	Yes	Yes	Yes
Wetlands protected areas	National	Voluntary	Budgetary	No	No	Yes	n.a.	Yes	Yes	No	Yes	Yes
Conservation of native forests	National	Mandatory	Budgetary	Yes	Yes	Yes	n.a.	Yes	Yes	Yes	Yes	Yes
Other relevant policies												
Pesticide bans	National	Mandatory	n.a.	No	No	No	No	No	Yes	Yes	Yes	No
Fertiliser tax exemptions	National	Mandatory	50% of VAT	No	No	No	No	No	Yes	No	Yes	Yes
Commodity export tax	National	Mandatory	Export tax	No	No	No	Soybeans	No	Yes	Yes	n.a.	Yes

n.a.: Not applicable.
Source: Based on a country questionnaire and direct consultation to regulations and laws.

Figure 7.6. There is room for improving current agri-environmental regulations

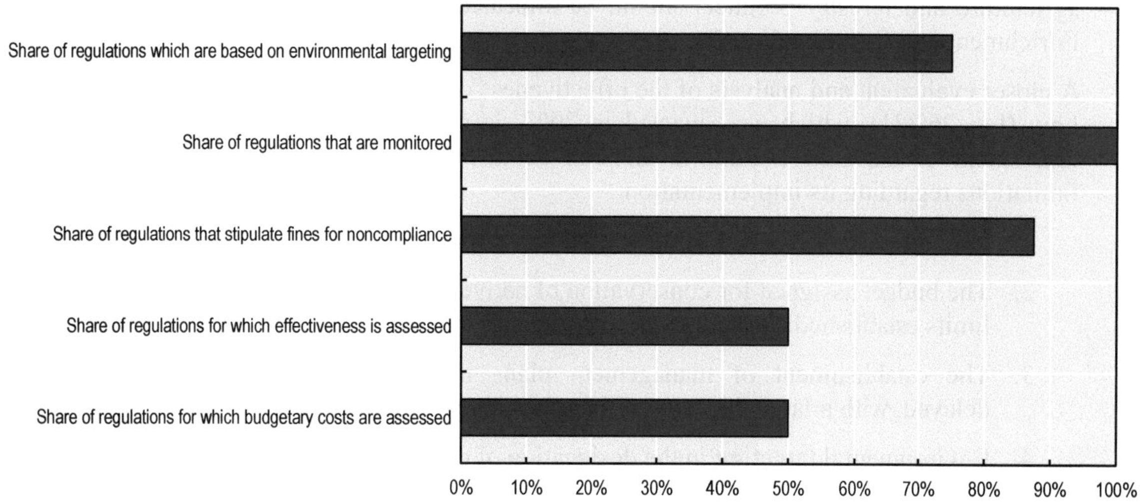

Source: Author's own work based on a country questionnaire and direct consultation to regulations and laws.

StatLink https://doi.org/10.1787/888933908248

Current policies are only partially aligned to the pressing environmental issues identified in previous sections. Deforestation is tackled mainly via the promotion of protected areas, including wetlands, and by the native forest conservation law. Increased pesticide sales per hectare are not particularly targeted by any policy. Increased loss of organic matter and P in soils is partially addressed by the promotion of good agriculture practices, although these are currently limited to certain jurisdictions.

Deforestation driven by the expansion of the agriculture frontier is a primary area of concern given the high deforestation rates experienced in the last decades. According to the mitigation actions submitted by Argentina in their Nationally Determined Contributions (NDC) as part of its commitment to the Paris Agreement to tackle climate change, combating deforestation and reducing emissions in the agriculture sector is a fundamental pillar, contributing to more than 20% of emissions reductions in the NDC (Ministerio de Ambiente y Desarrollo Sustentable, 2016$_{[17]}$). The key actions in those sectors related to curbing deforestation include: to develop conservation and use plans for forested areas to improve carbon sequestration in the Chaco and Selva Misionera areas, and increase afforestation. Other actions are related to promote crop rotation in order to increase cereal cultivated area and reducing soybeans cultivated area.

NDC from forestry are articulated around the Native Forest Law (Ley 26.331), which was enacted in 2007, and forest plantations. The Law specifies that provinces need to define forested land areas according to 3 categories: 1) red areas, which should be preserved due to their high ecological value; 2) yellow areas, which possess medium ecological value but can be subject to sustainable management; and 3) green areas, which have low ecological value and could be partially or totally transformed. The Law has several other dimensions: it defines a National Program for Native Forest Protection, whose purpose is to promote the sustainable management of yellow and green areas, taking into account local communities; it establishes that any forest clearance in green areas should be subjected to an environmental impact evaluation; it defines the sanctions that apply for illegal logging; and it creates the National Fund for Forest Enrichment and Conservation, which is intended to compensate those jurisdictions that conserve forests. According to the Law, at least 0.3% of the national budget and 2% of the revenue from export taxes to agriculture and forestry products should be allocated to The National Fund for Forest Enrichment and Conservation.

A closer evaluation and analysis of the effectiveness of the conservation of Native Forest Law (Ley 26.331), which was enacted in 2007, is necessary. A thorough government assessment of the Law (Auditoría General de la Nación, 2017[36]) identified several limitations regarding its implementation:

1. In practice, enforcement of the legislation is weak.
2. The budget assigned for conservation of native forests is well below the minimum limits established by the law.
3. The establishment of management plans in sensitive conservation areas is delayed, with a large majority of them lacking a management plan.
4. Environmental targeting in the designation of conservation areas is poor.
5. Public consultation for designing conservation areas is missing in most of them.

Finally, most agricultural policy can have impacts on the environment and any potential change in such regulations should consider these and the necessary legislation and measures to ensure that the polluter bears the cost of the negative environmental impacts (internalise externalities). For instance, export taxes on the main agricultural commodities including soybeans provide less incentive to expand agricultural activities, but they were removed or significantly reduced in 2015 and 2016. Such changes reduce market distortions and in the short term may stimulate crop diversification by eliminating taxes except for soybean, but they may also provide incentives to deforest and expand the agriculture frontier. Moreover, since part of the budget for the National Fund for Forest Enrichment comes from export taxes, once those are eliminated, the financial resources for the Fund could shrink. It is also becoming increasingly urgent to ensure that more targeted measures and regulations are effective to prevent potential damages to natural assets. This is particularly the case of the Native Forest Law and the rising use of pesticides. The promotion of crop rotation, including pasture rotation, is needed as a way to increase organic matter content in soils and ensuring the long term sustainability of the agriculture sector in Argentina. The incentives for a set of good practices could be strengthened, stressing rotation and P fertilisation but making sure runoff is avoided to prevent contamination of waterways.

There have been some recent agri-environmental policy developments in Argentina. Law 27.279, on integral management of empty plastic containers of agrochemicals, was approved in October 2016 and regulated in February 2018, extending liability regime for agrochemicals product registrants, establishing minimum requirements for the empty container management systems to be approved by the Provinces, and creating a national system for traceability of the containers. The Joint Resolution of the Ministries of Agribusiness and Environment and Sustainable Development of February 2018 established a national policy on good practices in the application of phyto-sanitary products. Finally, the Joint Resolution of the Ministry of Agribusiness and the Superintendence of Insurance of the Nation (SSN) 1/2018 creates the Environmental and Insurance Sustainability Program, a voluntary programme for insurance companies to contribute of 1% on automobiles policies to a trust administered by the SSN and designed to promote reforestation.

7.5. Policy assessment and recommendations

Argentina's agriculture sector has transformed in recent years at an accelerated pace. Many pastoral and semi-pastoral production systems have been replaced by intensive soybean production systems. While water use, nutrient balances and energy use are still relatively low compared to OECD countries, the principal concerns about the sustainability of the dominant agriculture system are related to high deforestation rates and relative high rates of pesticide use in cropland. Other potential risks are associated to loss of organic matter and insufficient P fertiliser applications to compensate the P uptake from crops. The application of the "Polluter pays principle" requires strengthening the responsibility of farmers in reducing negative agri-environmental externalities.

Deforestation rates are higher than regional and global figures. In a 25-year period, from 1990 to 2015, Argentina lost 22% of its forest mainly due to agriculture. Moreover, in the last 15 years, deforestation rates increased, contrary to regional and global trends. In spite of improvements and reductions in deforestation rates in recent years, they are still above regional and global averages. As a result, greenhouse gas emissions and the loss of biodiversity have increased, but water-related ecosystem services have also been on the rise.

While no-till practices are widespread and have reduced erosion rates and helped to maintain organic matter content in soils, monocropping and low rotation practices reduce organic matter content. Additionally, pesticide use is considerably larger than in OECD countries and there are some risks associated to the use of Atrazine due to its persistence and capacity to contaminate drinking-water sources.

The main agri-environmental policies in Argentina consist of 1) those stimulating good agriculture practices, 2) natural resource conservation and 3) protecting water quality. Current policies are hardly aligned to pressing issues but, given the current policy changes to reduce the tax burden of the main exporting commodities, it is recommended to strengthen the set of environmentally targeted policies and legislation which will also contribute to advancing the polluter-pays-principle. In particular:

- First, undertake an in-depth independent evaluation of the Native Forest Law to analyse its effectiveness in stemming deforestation. In particular, evaluate: the capacity of enforcement of the law in different provincial jurisdictions; the environmental targeting methods and procedures to identify conservation priorities; and the strength of the economic incentives to deforest, including sanctions for illegal logging, under the evolving agricultural technological package. The evaluation should include a realistic estimation of the budgetary allocations needed for compensation, implementation and potential decoupling of the allocations from the export tax. An independent evaluation of forest categorisations is needed to make sure highly valuable ecosystems are fully preserved.
- Second, establish a monitoring programme for pesticide residues in waterways, food and air. It is fundamental to define hotspots and areas which require immediate public intervention. Programmes to ensure the consistent application of best practices in the use of pesticides, such as Integrated Pest Management, via extension services should particularly focus on hotspots areas. A recent joint resolution (1/2018) of the Ministry of Agroindustry and the Ministry of Environment and Sustainable Development, which mandates the promotion of good practices in the application of pesticides, is a good first step in this direction.

Other measures such as taxes may be less effective in the short term, given that in general the price elasticity of pesticides is low. Some OECD countries have adopted pesticide taxes to complement command-and-control measures such as the ones proposed, but their effectiveness has proven to be in general limited, and measures targeted to properly identify hotspots are preferable.

- Third, strengthen the use of best environmental practices and information regarding their adoption. In this respect Argentina is well positioned in institutional terms and the Government can work in partnership with both private associations of farmers such as APRESID or AACREA and with the extension services of INTA. Advisory and information programmes run in collaboration between farmers associations and government agencies can be crucial to foster action and promote pro-environmental practices. Examples of such programmes can be found in Denmark, where farmers work jointly with government agencies to disseminate nutrient accounts and best practices to reduce nutrient loads (OECD, 2019 forthcoming[14]). Argentina has advanced on this regard by establishing the Network on Best Agriculture Practices (BAP), which gathers a broad range of private and public actors. A way forward is for the Network to strengthen the information on adoption rates and impacts of BAP engaging in a learning process. This may be particularly important to maintain soil productivity, prevent high erosion rates and contribute to the maintenance of carbon in soils.

To be able to attain the main environmental goals in the agriculture sector it is also recommended to:

1. Improve the environmental targeting of current policies.
2. Promote the adoption and implementation of good practices policies in jurisdictions where agriculture is prevalent and expanding.
3. Improve the enforcement of policies, including those currently in practice, defining goals in terms of inspections and sanctioning non-compliance.
4. Assess and evaluate the effectiveness, budgetary and administrative costs of the different policies.
5. Assess changes in other agriculture policies that can have direct impacts on the environment to identify if any potential negative environmental impacts arising from them can be mitigated or diminished by new or improved policies.

References

Adhikari, K. and A. Hartemink (2016), "Linking soils to ecosystem services - A global review", *Geoderma*, Vol. 262, pp. 101-111, http://dx.doi.org/10.1016/J.GEODERMA.2015.08.009. [22]

Auditoría General de la Nación (2017), *Informe de Auditoría: Implementación de la Ley 26.331 de Presupuestos Mínimos de Protección Ambiental de Bosques Nativos*, https://www.agn.gov.ar/files/informes/2017_230info.pdf (accessed on 05 June 2018). [36]

Barros, V. et al. (2015), "Climate change in Argentina: Trends, projections, impacts and adaptation", *Wiley Interdisciplinary Reviews: Climate Change*, Vol. 6/2, pp. 151-169, http://dx.doi.org/10.1002/wcc.316. [28]

Barros, V., C. Garavaglia and M. Doyle (2013), "Twenty-first century projections of extreme precipitations in the Plata Basin", *International Journal of River Basin Management*, Vol. 11/4, pp. 373-387, http://dx.doi.org/10.1080/15715124.2013.819358. [33]

Borrelli, P. et al. (2017), "An assessment of the global impact of 21st century land use change on soil erosion", *Nature Communications*, Vol. 8/1, p. 2013, http://dx.doi.org/10.1038/s41467-017-02142-7. [26]

Casas, R. (2018), *La conservación de suelo y la producción agropecuaria*, Asociación Argentina de Consorcios Regionales de Experimentación Agrícola - AACREA, G. Vázquez Amábile (Ed.). [9]

Cerezo, A., M. Conde and S. Poggio (2011), "Pasture area and landscape heterogeneity are key determinants of bird diversity in intensively managed farmland", *Biodiversity Conservation*, Vol. 20, pp. 2649-2667, http://dx.doi.org/10.1007/s10531-011-0096-y. [21]

De Sy, V. et al. (2015), "Land use patterns and related carbon losses following deforestation in South America", *Environmental Research Letters*, Vol. 10, http://iopscience.iop.org/article/10.1088/1748-9326/10/12/124004/pdf (accessed on 03 May 2018). [16]

Dodd, R. and A. Sharpley (2016), *Conservation Practice Effectiveness and Adoption: Unintended Consequences and Implications for Sustainable Phosphorus Management*, http://dx.doi.org/10.1007/s10705-015-9748-8. [7]

FAO (2018), *FAOSTAT*. [12]

Fehlenberg, V. et al. (2017), "The role of soybean production as an underlying driver of deforestation in the South American Chaco", *Global Environmental Change*, http://dx.doi.org/10.1016/j.gloenvcha.2017.05.001. [18]

Friedrich, T. and A. Kassam (2012), "No-till farming and the environment: Do no-till systems require more chemicals?", *Outlooks on Pest Management*, http://dx.doi.org/10.1564/23aug02. [11]

Gaitán, J. et al. (2017), *Estimación de la Pérdida de Suelo por Erosión Hídrica en la República Argentina*, INTA. [25]

Hayes, T. et al. (2010), "Atrazine induces complete feminization and chemical castration in male African clawed frogs (Xenopus laevis)", *PNAS*, Vol. 107/10, http://dx.doi.org/10.1073/pnas.0909519107. [13]

Klümper, W. and M. Qaim (2014), "A meta-analysis of the impacts of genetically modified crops", *PLoS ONE*, http://dx.doi.org/10.1371/journal.pone.0111629. [5]

Magrin, G. et al. (2014), *Central and South America.*, Cambridge University Press, Barros, V.R.; Field, C.B.; Dokken, D.J.; Mastrandrea, M.D.; Mach, K.J.; Bilir, T.E.; Chatterjee, M.; Ebi, K.L.; Estrada, Y.O.; Genova, R.C.; Girma, B.; Kissel, E.S.; Levy, A.N.; MacCracken, S.; Mastrandrea, P.R.; White, L .Eds.. [27]

Medan, D. et al. (2011), "Effects of agriculture expansion and intensification on the vertebrate and invertebrate diversity in the Pampas of Argentina", *Biodivers Conservation*, Vol. 20, pp. 3077-3100, http://dx.doi.org/10.1007/s10531-011-0118-9. [20]

Ministerio de Ambiente y Desarrollo Sustentable (2016), *Informe del Estado del Ambiente*. [17]

Murgida, A. et al. (2014), *Evaluación de impactos del cambio climático sobre la producción agrícola en la Argentina*, CEPAL, https://repositorio.cepal.org/bitstream/handle/11362/37197/1/LCL3770_es.pdf (accessed on 06 June 2018). [30]

Nagy, G. et al. (2018), "An Assessment of the Relationships between Extreme Weather Events, Vulnerability, and the Impacts on Human Wellbeing in Latin America", *International Journal of Environmental Research and Public Health*, Vol. 15/1802, http://dx.doi.org/10.3390/ijerph15091802. [32]

Nocelli, S. (2018), *Update! Evolution of no till adoption in Argentina*. [24]

Nuñez, M. (2018), *Escenarios esperados del cambio climático en la Argentina*, Asociación Argentina de Consorcios Regionales de Experimentación Agrícola - AACREA, al., Gabriel Vázquez Amábile Ed.. [29]

OECD (2010), *Guidelines for Cost-effective Agri-environmental Policy Measures*, OECD Publishing, Paris, http://dx.doi.org/10.1787/9789264086845-en. [35]

OECD (2001), *Improving the Environmental Performance of Agriculture: Policy options and market approaches*, OECD Publishing, Paris, http://dx.doi.org/10.1787/9789264033801-en. [34]

OECD (2019 forthcoming), *Biodiversity, Ecosystem Services and Agriculture*. [14]

Phélinas, P. and J. Choumert (2017), "Is GM soybean cultivation in Argentina sustainable?", *World Development*, http://dx.doi.org/10.1016/j.worlddev.2017.05.033. [2]

Qaim, M. and G. Traxler (2005), "Roundup Ready soybeans in Argentina: farm level and aggregate welfare effects", *Agricultural Economics*, Vol. 32, pp. 73-86. [6]

Sainz Rozas, H., H. Echeverria and H. Angelini (2011), "Niveles de carbono orgánico y ph en suelos agrícolas de las regiones pampeana y extrapampeana argentina", *Ciencia del Suelo*, Vol. 29/1, pp. 29-37, http://www.scielo.org.ar/scielo.php?script=sci_arttext&pid=S1850-20672011000100004 (accessed on 10 April 2018). [23]

Schwank, J. et al. (2014), "Modeling of the Mendoza river watershed as a tool to study climate change impacts on water availability", *Environmental Science & Policy*, Vol. 43, pp. 91-97, http://dx.doi.org/10.1016/J.ENVSCI.2014.01.002. [31]

Tejeda, R. et al. (2018), *Campaña 2017/18: Evaluación del Impacto Económico de la Sequía.* [37]

Vázquez Amábile, G. (2017), *Análisis de agroquímicos y nitratos en cursos y aguas subterráneas de cuencas rurales del Oeste y SE de Buenos Aires.* [15]

Vázquez Amábile, G. (ed.) (2018), "Impacto de la Agricultura sobre las propiedades edáficas en tierras de desmonte del norte argentino", *Gestión Ambiental: Desafíos para una Producción Sostenible*, pp. 27-34. [10]

Viglizzo, E. et al. (2011), "Ecological and environmental footprint of 50 years of agricultural expansion in Argentina", *Global Change Biology*, http://dx.doi.org/10.1111/j.1365-2486.2010.02293.x. [4]

Viglizzo, E. et al. (2011), "Assessing the cross-scale impact of 50 years of agricultural transformation in Argentina", *Field Crops Research*, http://dx.doi.org/10.1016/j.fcr.2011.05.014. [3]

WDI (2018), *World Development Indicators*, World Bank, Washington, DC. [19]

Wingeyer, A. et al. (2015), "Soil quality impacts of current South American agricultural practices", *Sustainability*, http://dx.doi.org/10.3390/su7022213. [8]

Zak, M. et al. (2008), "What drives accelerated land cover change in Central Argentina? Synergistic consequences of climatic, socioeconomic, and technological factors", *Environmental Management*, Vol. 42/2, pp. 181–189, http://dx.doi.org/10.1007/s00267-008-9101-y. [1]

Notes

[1] As of 2012, Endosulfan has been banned in Argentina and several countries in the world due to its high toxicity. More recent studies have found few traces of pesticides and nitrates residues in groundwater (Vázquez Amábile, 2017[15]).

[2] Since OECD data on pesticides indicates sales and data for Argentina and Brazil indicate use, if all were measured in terms of use, the gap between Brazil, Argentina and the OECD would be even higher as pesticides sales may over-represent use due to stocking.

[3] Soil organic matter consists of plant and animal residues, soil organisms, and other organic substances. Aggregate stability refers to the capacity of soil particles to resist external forces and keep its porosity. Bulk density is the weight of soil in a given volume; the higher the density the more difficult it is for roots to grow.

[4] The 2018 drought is estimated to have reduced GDP by 0.9% due to a reduction of 22% in maize production and 33% in soybeans (Tejeda et al., 2018[37]).

[5] The National Plan of Agriculture Soils was not included given that there are no specific policies yet derived from such Plan.

[6] Notice this assessment is based on what the regulation stipulates and not on what happens in reality.

Chapter 8. Managing agricultural risks in a volatile environment

Argentina has few policies oriented to risk management, mainly consisting of support derived from the Agricultural Emergencies Law and the plant and animal health services provided by SENASA. Several provinces have recently provided varying degrees of support to insurance. Disaster risk management policies are focused on ex-post assistance and could gain from refocusing on ex-ante prevention and preparedness. The significant policy and macroeconomic risk in Argentina and the underdevelopment of the financial sector creates a difficult environment for agricultural risk management. However, the focus of government policies on catastrophic risk has facilitated a remarkable development of technological innovations and market and contract strategies that have contributed to the resilience of the sector.

8.1. Introduction

The agricultural sector has always been exposed to production variability and price volatility[1]. This is partly due to the reliance of production on natural conditions and weather, and partly to the low demand elasticity of agricultural commodities, which can lead to sharp price reactions to changes in supply. Disease outbreaks and adverse weather events, such as floods and droughts, contribute to supply volatility and can negatively impact producer incomes, markets, trade and consumers. In Argentina, as in many other countries, climate change is likely to increase the frequency of extreme precipitation on one hand, and desertification on the other (Ministerio e Medio Ambiente y Desarollo Sustentable de Argentina, 2016[1]; Secretaria de Medio Ambiente y Desarrollo Sustentable, 2015[2]).

Risk management strategies need to be based on good information and risk assessment and follow a differentiated three-layer policy approach (OECD, 2009[3]; OECD, 2011[4]). Normal risk is frequent but not too damaging, and it is typically managed at the farm or household level, requiring no government policy. Catastrophic risks are infrequent but cause great damage for many farmers; the significant uncertainties associated with these events and the possibility of substantial systemic losses generate potential market failures that should be the focus of policy. Finally, between these two extremes, there is a category of risk that, because of its intermediate frequency of occurrence and magnitude of losses, is potentially insurable or transferable to other agents. The resilience capacity of farmers and the food system to manage agricultural risks crucially depends on their risk profiles, but also on the availability of a diversity of strategies and tools for the normal and market layers. A good policy-enabling environment, including agricultural risk management policies that cover only well-defined catastrophic risks, facilitates the development of these tools.

8.2. Risk assessment

Argentina's great climatic and regional heterogeneity over a large territorial expanse has given rise to different agricultural production systems. The territory stretches almost 4 000 kms in length, from subtropical to sub-Antarctic regions. It has a significant latitudinal variation (33° of latitude) and altitudinal differences, from 48 m below sea level in Salina Grande in Peninsula Valdes to 6 959 metres above sea level in Aconcagua mountain. Therefore, there are two gradients of physical variability: one north-south and the other east-west.

These gradients lead to a wide diversity of climates and land types that, at the same time, support a variety of biogeographical units (Bertonatti and Corcuera, 2000[5]; Burkart et al., 1999[6]). Two thirds of Argentina's total area is arid or semiarid and the remaining third comprises wetlands, woodlands or subtropical forests, rainforests and grasslands. Argentina's coastal area stretches along 4 725 kms from the mouth of the Río de la Plata river up to Tierra del Fuego (Bertonatti and Corcuera, 2000[5]). Figure 8.1 depicts the variability in precipitation and temperature.

Figure 8.1. Climatic map: Precipitation and temperature, average values (1981-2010)

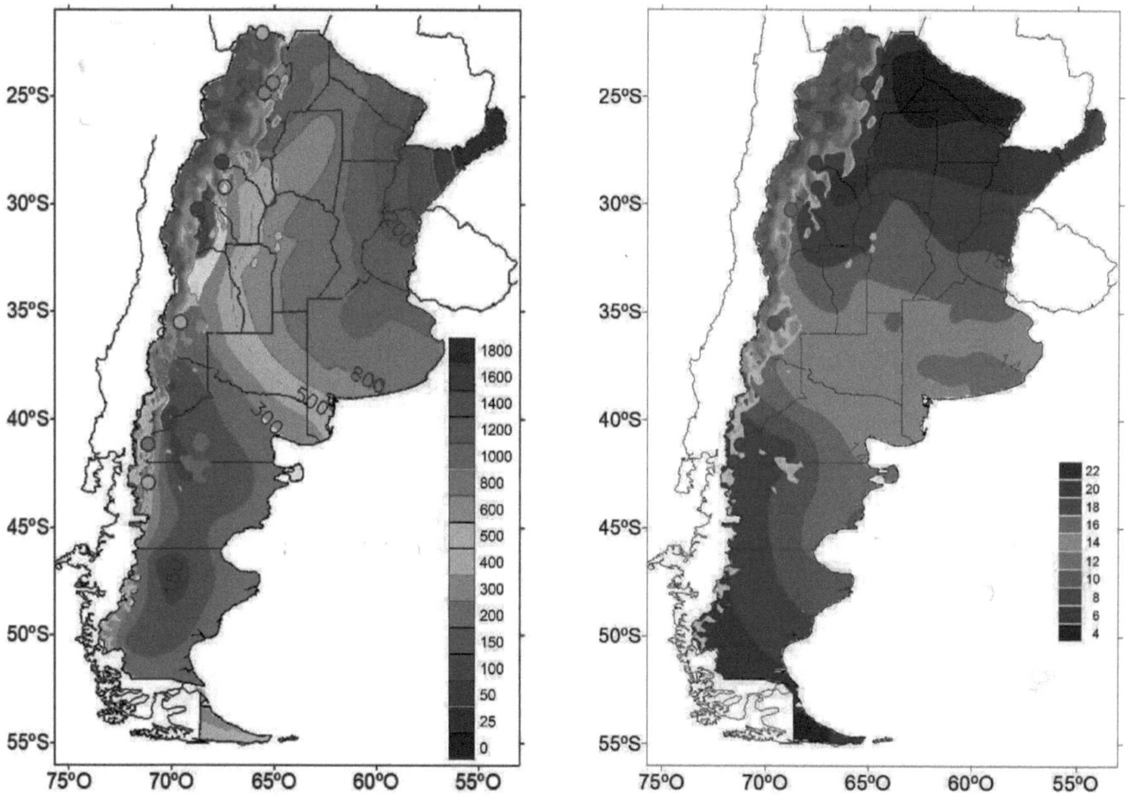

Note: The left figure shows annual precipitation in millimetres. The right figure shows annual temperatures in Celsius degrees.
Source: Servicio Meteorológico Nacional.

In Argentina, most of the annual crops and some perennial ones are produced in an open field and are rain-fed, making weather risks particularly significant (Fusco, 2012[7]). The variability of yields at national level in Argentina, as measured by the coefficient of variation, is higher than in many OECD countries such as the United States, Germany, Italy and United Kingdom, but below the variability in Australia (Fusco and Barelli, 2018[8]; OECD, 2011[4]).

Precipitation and temperature regimes are among the main climatic adversities affecting agricultural yield. In this regard, rain and temperature patterns in South America and in many regions around the world are influenced by *El Niño* Southern Oscillation (ENSO). This phenomenon arises from recurring changes in the temperature of the tropical Pacific Ocean and has two extreme phases: *El Niño*, characterised by the warming of temperatures, and *La Niña*, with water temperatures lower than usual.

In the case of the Pampas region, *El Niño* is associated with a rise above average in precipitation and eventually floods, and *La Niña* means precipitation being lower than usual and in the extreme case, droughts. (Bert et al., 2006[9]). There is significant correlation between ENSO and the variability in precipitation patterns in Argentina in general and in the Pampas region in particular (Aceituno, 1988[10]), and between weather variability and crop yields (Podestá et al., 1999[11]; Amissah- Arthur, Jagtap and Rosenzweig, 2002[12]). Podesta et al. (1999) have found a statistically significant relation between ENSO phases and crop yields in the Argentine Pampas region, even though it is not simple to deduce causality since there are multiple factors impacting yields (Ray et al., 2015[13]).

Sanitary risks are those risks which provoke a reduction in productivity due to plagues, diseases and epidemics in both animals and plants. These diseases or plagues can be of moderate or high impact as a result of either or both by a drop in production or by the closure of export markets. The Argentine beef sector is subject to several moderate-impact diseases that can be managed locally. Higher impact risks include foot-and-mouth disease (FMD), which affect bovine, ovine, caprine, porcine and bubaline production and exports. Since the outbreaks of 200/01, Argentina has significantly improved the control of the disease and since 2007 has been declared by the OIE free of FMD with vaccination in the Center North of the country and without vaccination in the Patagonia. Given the length and diversity of Argentinian borders (terrestrial and fluvial), the prevalence of sanitary risks in its neighbors, and the export orientation of production, sanitary risks are of primary importance.

Market risks can be measured by the variability of market prices. Argentina is an exporting country with most of its domestic markets fully integrated in world markets, and price volatility is linked to international price volatility. However, volatility in trade and domestic policies and macroeconomic instability has historically had a large incidence on price and revenue risk and uncertainty in Argentina. A main institutional and policy risk has been export taxes and restrictions, the levels of which have significantly changed with different administrations. Even if such measures were dismantled in 2016 (except for soybean) the risk of a future government reverting to them persists[2]. Another important institutional risk is derived from the weak implementation of the intellectual property regulations affecting plant seeds in particular (Trigo and Ciampi, 2018[14]; Fusco and Barelli, 2018[8]).

Macroeconomic and financial instability is an additional source of risk for the whole economy, not only the agro-food sector. It is particularly reflected in the inflation and exchange rates. Inflation was high for decades – often triple-digit – until it was contained during the peso-dollar parity in the 1990s. Inflation started to grow again at the end of the last decade and was still 26% in 2017. After a debt default in 2001 and restrictions on access to savings in the banks, the Argentinian peso started floating against other currencies in 2002. Since then the exchange rate with the dollar has depreciated significantly in different episodes from 1 peso per dollar in January 2002 to 28 in July 2018 and to 40 pesos per dollar in September 2018. Due to this recent history, the risk of macroeconomic and financial volatility is perceived as potentially highly relevant. Both institutional and policy risks and macroeconomic and financial instability contribute to Argentina's poor ranking of 92nd position in the World Economic Forum Global Competitiveness index in 2017, behind other countries in the region like Brazil, Uruguay, Peru and Chile.

8.3. Farmers' strategies and retention of risks at farm level

Farmer and other actors in the Argentinian agricultural risk management system have access to significant information to manage their risks. Public and private institutions generate and develop information, such as the Servicio Meteorológico Nacional on weather and climate, the provincial grain exchanges and other private associations on prices, the National Institute for Agricultural Technology (INTA), the Secretariat of Agroindustry and the universities. Although the volume and quality of information is significant, it is not currently systematised and unified, and there is no information on risk profiles at farm level.

Table 8.1. Main risk management strategies reported by farmers in Argentina

Source of risks	On farm retention	Risk transfer: Market / community
Production	Most spread and adopted: - Activity diversification. - No-till system. - Use of improved vegetable materials both for grain and fodder. - Changes in sowing dates; late sowing of corn. - Forage reserve by using silo bags and rolls. - Sanitary plan for livestock (basic). - Check climatic information. To a lesser extent and subject to restrictions: - Geographical diversification. - Incorporation of genetics through the purchase of male breeders and artificial insemination. - Per hour or rotative grazing (meat and dairy livestock). - Food supplements for livestock. - Strategic confinement (for cattle when finishing fattening phase).	- Professional consultancy, both agricultural (through inputs/services supplier companies) and veterinary (mainly feedlots and dairy farms). - Technical plan and input level of the technological package according to the climate year, market and crop field, to a lesser degree due to institutional/macroeconomic risk. - Irrigated crops and complementary irrigation. - Insurance crop coverage and service.
Market	- Use of silo bag for grain stocking (schedule sales). - Crop rotation (portfolio diversification)	- Futures contracts (mainly OTC), through a trade agent/stocking, or directly through exports/industry. - Integration for joint supply purchasing (mainly producers that are members of co-operative businesses). - Contract farming
Institutional / macroeconomic		- Participation in unions.
Financial & other		- Use of bank services, mainly the instruments for working capital (agricultural cards in local currency, cheque exchange and, to a lesser degree, financing in dollars, principally in agriculture) - Pools and associations: one participant provides capital and the other, labour; or both provide a portion of each. Co-operatives and mutual funds also provide risk management services. - Use of financial services from service companies (sale and/or exchange of supplies, stocking, among other) and co-operative businesses.

Source: (Fusco and Barelli, 2018[8]) and interviews with farmers and experts.

Argentinian farmers implement a large diversity of risk management strategies based on this information. Table 8.1 presents the results of a set of interviews with farmers and experts and a literature review (Fusco and Barelli, 2018[8]), both of which show the diversity of strategies employed. These strategies include several on-farm practices such as diversification, or the use of silo bags for grain storage. But there are also a variety of instruments to transfer risk through markets or other institutional or co-operative agreements, such as contracts with other actors in the value chain, future markets or more comprehensive contracts and farming pools. Many Argentinian farmers, particularly in the Pampas region, manage their risk in an entrepreneurial manner.

Since the 1990s, investment and innovation have transformed Argentinian agriculture with a significant impact on producers' management of risks. The technological package of no-till farming and GM seeds improves chemical, physical and biological soil conditions, increasing their resilience. These high-productive crops are tolerant and resistant to an active principle, disease/plague or abiotic factors. As a result, larger surfaces were destined to agriculture and less to cattle breeding, and one crop, soybeans, increased participation in crop rotation. These movements implied a reduction in diversification activities in producers' portfolio, affecting the resilience of farms that reduce their diversification that helps agricultural producers and cattle breeders to cope with risks (Barbieri and Mahoney, 2009[15]).

However, crop diversification continues to be a leading risk management strategy in Argentina (Table 8.1). Winter (wheat and barley) and summer (principally sunflower, corn, soybean and sorghum) crops are rotated with each other and with fodder (winter grass and summer forage crop and pastures) to manage risks and the sustainability of soils. But diversification activities in Argentina also include non-traditional crops and agricultural practices such as organic or free-range pastures. Farmers also diversify their economic activities off-farm, for instance, providing contract services to other farmers or through adding value by processing and packaging agricultural products.

Figure 8.2. Intensity and frequency of not reaching the breakeven yield

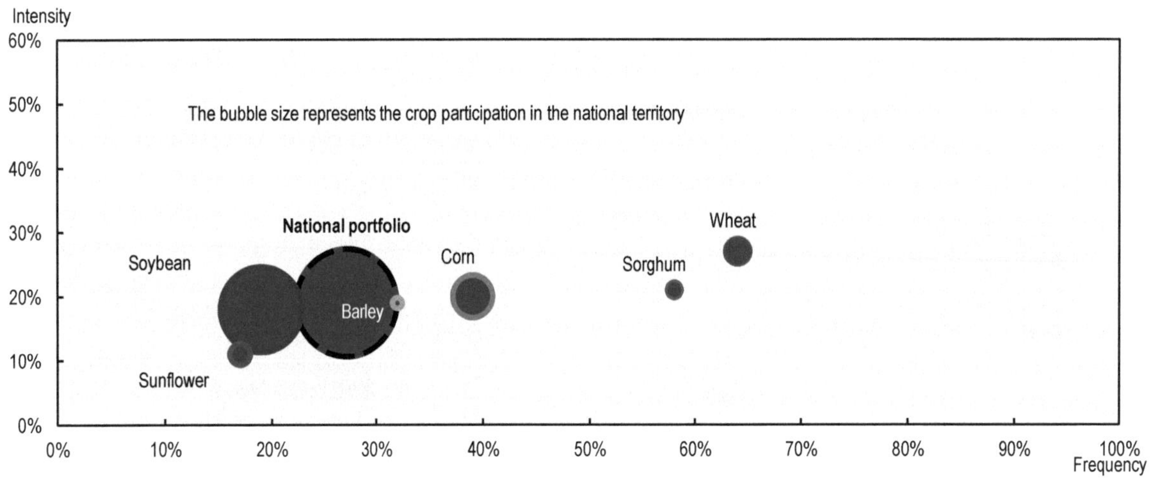

Source: (CREA, 2017[16]) and (Fusco and Barelli, 2018[8]).

StatLink https://doi.org/10.1787/888933908267

The analysis of the variability of prices, yields and income from different crops in Argentina shows that the production of soybeans experiences lower levels of risk than other commodities, particularly corn and wheat (Fusco and Barelli, 2018[8]). Another perspective to measure the risk of different crops and the potential for diversification is to observe the relation between the crops' average yield and the breakeven yield. The indicator of frequency F in Figure 8.2 conveys the percentage of years in which a crop's average yield was lower than the expected breakeven yield, while the indicator of intensity I expresses the difference between the expected breakeven yield and the average yield in those years.

The calculations from data for the period 2004/05 to 2015/16[3] show that wheat presented the highest risks, with a negative frequency of 64% and an intensity of 27%. That is, in 64% of the years, the average yield was below the calculated breakeven yield by 27% on average. At almost the other extreme, soybean and sunflower had both frequency and intensity indicators below 20%. The combination of different crops diminishes the risk, although never below the soybean and sunflower option. Soybean is the least risky crop, which may have contributed to the expansion of its production.

The presence of cereals (wheat, sorghum, corn and barley) in the portfolio provides benefits that are not quantified in Figure 8.2. It allows grasses to be incorporated in the rotation, thus providing a higher degree of carbon fixation to the soil and a better vegetable coverage, which reduces wind and water erosion. This plays a crucial role in improving the resilience of the agricultural systems to external shocks (biotic and abiotic).

8.4. Risk transfer and pooling through markets and private arrangements

Argentina's history of macroeconomic instability that has impacted the strength and dynamics of the local financial system. Countries with solid financial systems allow the economy in general and the agricultural sector in particular to generate and transfer funds inter-temporally through formal secure savings and credit. Argentina's financial system did not evolve as consistently as in OECD or other Latin American countries. In OECD countries, the average ratio of domestic credit over GDP increased from 120% to 176% in the period 2000-16 (Figure 8.3). Mexico, Brazil and Chile also experienced increases up to 42%, 70% and 184% respectively. Meanwhile the ratio in Argentina fell from 37% to 18% and experienced minimum values around 10% in 2004. Bank deposits have also decreased as a share of GDP to 18% in Argentina, well below the OECD average and that of other Latin American countries like Brazil, Chile, Mexico or Colombia.

Disaggregating by activity, cereals and oilseeds production account for 36.1% of the debt stock of the agricultural sector. Other relevant actors are beef, agricultural services and industrial farming (such as grapes, tobacco, cotton and sugar cane), which account for 17%, 10.8% and 18.1% respectively. According to the central bank (BCRA), the remaining 18% is distributed among other activities such as dairy (2.3%), vegetables (2.4) or fruits (1.7%). Furthermore, the Argentinian rural sector is also financed with credit in other currencies, particularly dollars, adding exchange rate risk to the use of finance.

The absence of well-developed financial markets, is a handicap to financing agricultural investment and working capital and to using basic banking services to manage agricultural risks. Argentinian farmers often finance working capital through input and service providers rather than banks. Transferring funds over time through the banking system is a very efficient way of managing agricultural risks from different sources, but it is not a fully available strategy in Argentina.

The Secretariat of Agroindustry provides credit to producers at preferential conditions through FINAGRO. Support from the Secretariat compensates banks for the extra cost of keeping preferential financial conditions to producers of different commodities. It amounted to ARS 156 million in 2017. In 2017 a new fund, FONDAGRO, was created to provide credit to producers, in particular for regional economies (agricultural production systems outside of the Pampas region). It was initially funded with a maximum of ARS 1 700 million, but by the end of 2017 had a portfolio of ARS 750 million in credit (Ministerio de Agroindustria, 2017[17]).

In 2016, agricultural insurance in Argentina was provided by 25 insurance companies across the country: 22 offered coverage for cereals and oilseeds, 1 for tobacco, 1 for vegetables and 1 for fruits. As regards the type of coverage, 23 companies offered hail damage insurance, 22 offered hail and an additional type, and 4 offered multi-crop peril insurance. The market share of three agricultural-insurance companies with the highest sales (Segunda, Allianz and Sancor Seguros) represented 57% of the total (Superintendencia de Seguros de la Nación, 2017[18]).

The total volume of premiums in real terms and the number of insured hectares almost doubled in the period 2003-16, to cover almost 20 million hectares in 2014-16. Hail insurance is the most frequent, but the producer might opt for contracting hail and additional insurance, such as strong winds, frost, or lack of land as a result of excess rain. Multi-peril crop insurance is offered by few insurance companies and includes other weather risks such as droughts and floods. An increasing share of the insured hectares is being covered by hail insurance, reaching 83% in 2016, compared with 17% for hail and other damage and 0.5% for multi-peril.

Figure 8.3. Financial markets are hardly developed

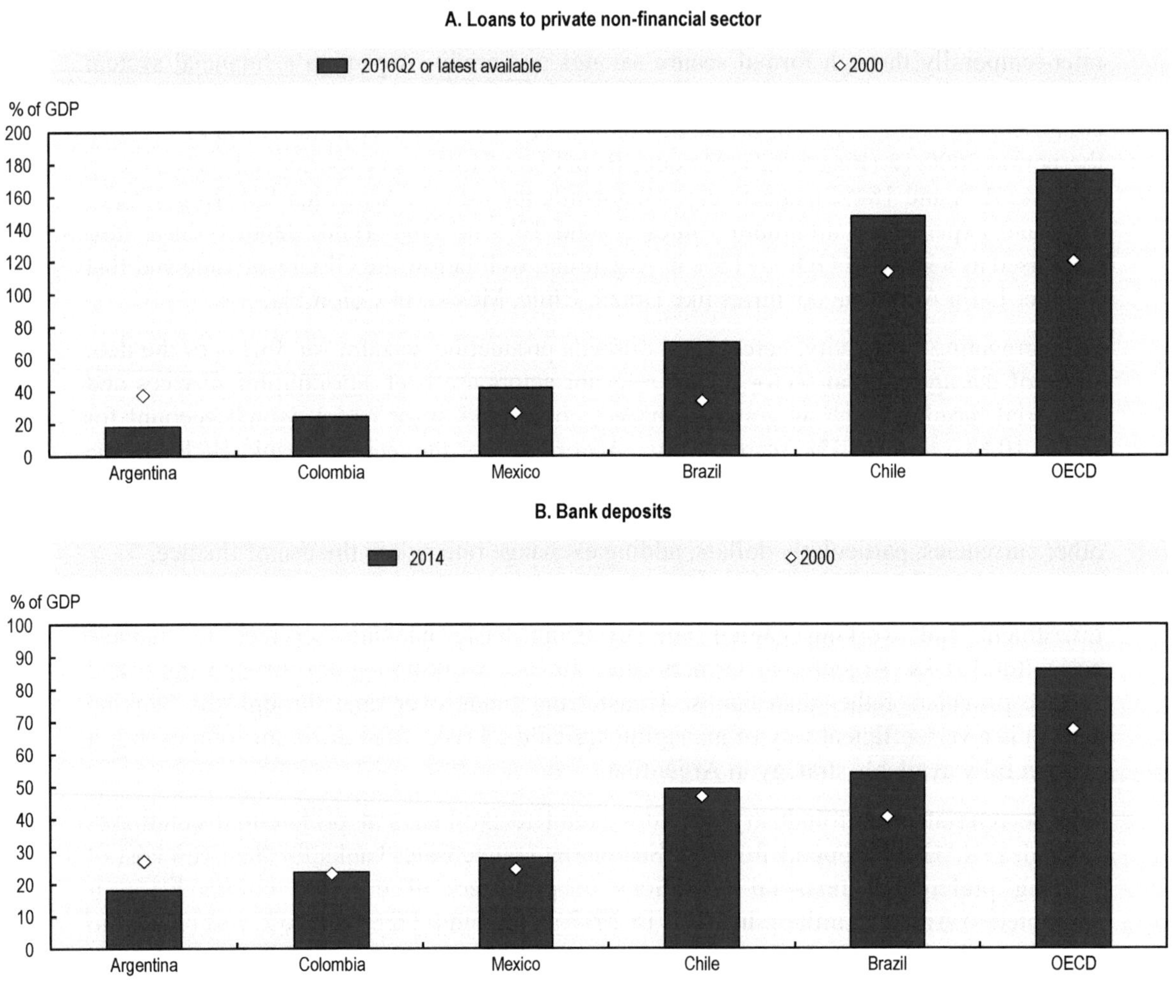

Source: Bank of International Settlements; World Bank Financial Development and Structure Dataset; and (OECD, 2017[19]).

StatLink https://doi.org/10.1787/888933908286

In terms of commodities, 92% of the volume of premiums corresponded to cereals and oilseeds in 2003-16, mainly soybean, corn, wheat, sunflower and barley. In relative terms, insurance penetration is calculated as the share of sowed hectares in the country that are insured (Figure 8.4). For the period 2014-16, the insured hectares over sowed area was on average: soybean 54.2%, wheat 59.1%, sunflower 67.3%, corn 33.7%, sorghum 11%, rice 32% and barley 58.8%. All insurance companies involved are fully private, and the ratio of claims paid over premiums was on average 83% in the period 2003-16.

In recent years, support programmes for the development of insurance for crops of strategic local importance have been undertaken in some provinces: Mendoza, Corrientes, Santa Fe, Jujuy, Río Negro and Neuquén. Most of these programmes are in the design or pilot phase. Some provinces are creating specific funds to provide assistance in the case of an extreme climatic events, others are subsidising the insurance premiums. Mendoza has designed insurance for the season 2017/18 as a public-private partnership; it covers frost and hail for grapevine, fruits, vegetables and fodder. This province also has an "Agricultural Compensation Fund" whose aim is to compensate producers and contractors participating in the programme for damages caused by climate contingencies, but the objective is to replace this fund with the insurance programme. Among the other provinces, Corrientes and Santa Fe have subsidised insurance for greenhouse horticulture since 2016.

Figure 8.4. Insurance penetration by crop

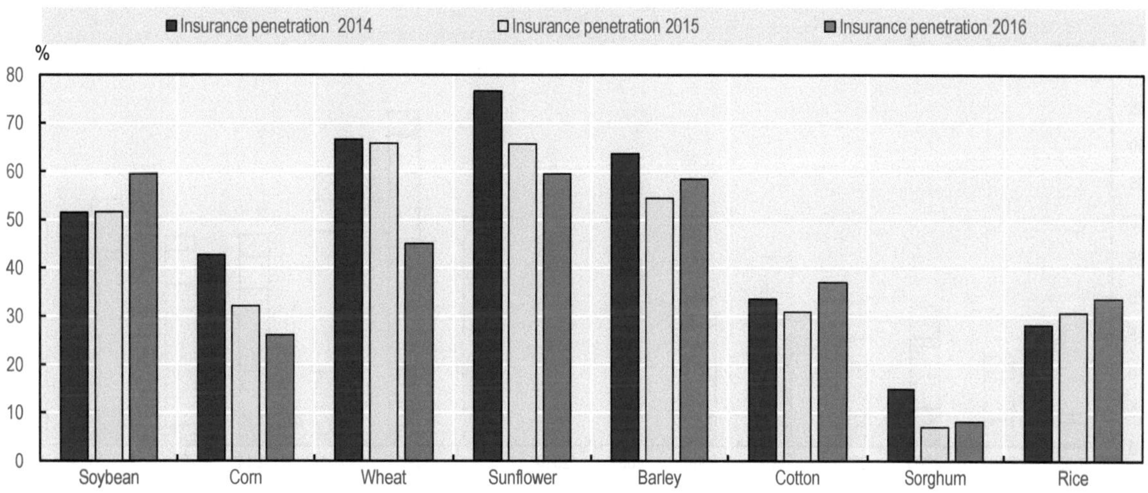

Source: (Fusco and Barelli, 2018[124]) based on Secretariat of Agroindustry and (Superintendencia de Seguros de la Nación, 2017[133]).

StatLink https://doi.org/10.1787/888933908305

Some studies analyse the correlation between crops and different indexes, such as the average area yield index (cotton – Chaco province), Normalised Difference Vegetation Index (NDVI – Buenos Aires Southwest region) and precipitation index (corn – Entre Ríos and Santa Fe provinces). However, up to now none of these analyses have led to commercially available index insurance nor to index-based government or provincial programmes. Recently a market of climatic derivatives has started to develop based on the Normalized difference Vegetation Index (NDVI), allowing "over the counter" (OTC) operations to cover for drought and flood events. This product was developed by a private company and operates through the ROFEX derivatives market (see https://s4agtech.com/en/create/#s4-go). In 2018 the derivative reached USD 81 million of coverage, USD 55 million for drought and USD 27 million for floodings.

Well-developed institutionalised markets exist in Argentina. These include both spot markets, like the Bolsa de Comercio de Rosario, and futures and options markets, like the Mercado a Término de Buenos Aires (Matba) and Mercado a Término de Rosario (Rofex). Matba represents the highest share of the volume traded of agricultural products (Figure 8.5), while Rofex operates agricultural and livestock contracts, but is focused on financial derivatives. Matba has 13 different agricultural contracts.[4]

For its three main products (soybean, corn and wheat), Matba has an average volume of trade of 26% of the national harvest of soybeans for the seasons 2015/16 and 2016/17, 25% for wheat and 13% for corn (Fusco and Barelli, 2018[8]). Rofex, on the other hand, presents eight agricultural derivatives[5]. Through different initiatives, both entities are exploring their trade platforms' interconnections in order to increase the amounts they operate in the market. Finally, a "Unified System of Compulsory Information of Grain Trade Operations" (SIO-Granos) is conducted in the Argentine physical market to register and share grain purchase and sale operations, which constitutes valuable information for producers and relevant participants in grain commercialisation.

Figure 8.5. Volume traded in Argentinian futures markets

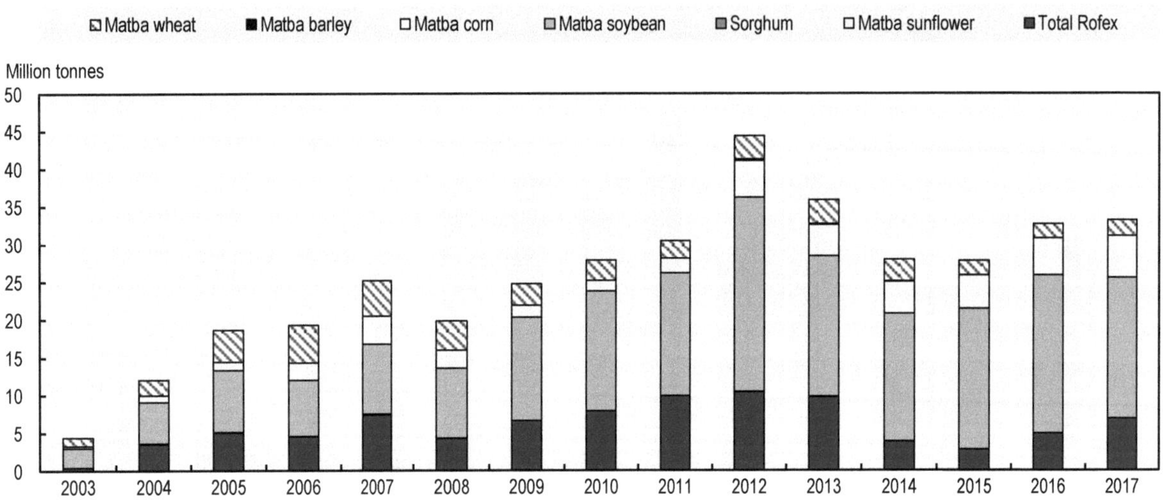

Source: (Fusco and Barelli, 2018[8]) based on Matba and Rofex.

StatLink https://doi.org/10.1787/888933908324

The Liniers market, located in the Autonomous City of Buenos Aires, concentrates beef cattle activities and is a reference for consumption. For the commercialisation of breeding, rearing and fattening cattle, there are several auctions in trade fairs, both in venues or remotely via the television or Internet (Rosgan and Meganar, among others) and through direct sales. Currently, the livestock producer counts on two instruments offered in the institutionalised markets (Rosgan calf index contracts and live steer contracts developed by Rofex) and diverse modalities of contracts for future delivery. SIO-Carnes is a unified information system for sales of livestock for meat, based on fiscal information from AFIP crossed with sanitary information from SENASA. For milk production, the main existent tool is the Integrated System for Milk Production Management in Argentina SIGLeA). This is a platform for information exchange between every link in the chain, and it allows, among other things, to know and compare the basic price per fat kg and protein kg. To date, there are no future price coverage tools for milk in institutionalised markets, and supply and price agreement contracts are not usual.

Producers also use alternative routes to the institutionalised markets (physical and futures, and options) through different types of contracts in order to commercialise and obtain coverage from price risk. Contract farming is and has been widely implemented within the Argentine agricultural sector so that the industry can assure the supply of goods. The principal sectors are aviculture, nuts, citric, berry fruits, horticulture, speciality crops (for instance popcorn), differentiated oilseeds production (shelled sunflower seeds), grains and selected bovine meat production. The following modalities of commercialisation contracts stand out in agriculture: payment on delivery operations (the parties establish the price and agree on the payment being made after the goods are delivered), advance payment operations and informal futures through forward business.

Pools are a way of organising the production which allows producers to share risks with their partners. Technically, pools are formal or informal associations where participants agree to contribute with different goods (seeds, capital, land, and supplies) or labour. At the end of the production process, benefits and risks are distributed according to the agreement. This methodology is widespread in Argentina as it allows production to be separated from ownership and facilitates access to finance, but there is no official data to quantify its importance. Pools in Argentina are not necessarily large investments – small and medium-sized contractors also exist. In Argentina the figure of "rural contractor" has been widely adopted as the owner of agricultural machinery (sowing, pulverisation, harvesting, etc.) and supplier of services. Producers do not need either to finance or buy the machinery.

According to data from the National Agricultural Information Network (RIAN), the national territory under lease was 34% of the surface and 4% in sharecropping (Barsky and Gelman, 2009[20]). Three forms of land leasing exist: paying a fixed value, a production percentage, or a combination of the two. The latter two options allow for the transfer of risk. Another form for reducing exposure to climate risk is leasing geographically diverse land, which reduces exposure to non-systemic risks.

Co-operatives and associations allows producers and businessmen from the agricultural sector to reduce risk exposure, to lower costs through economies of scale and to link their activities with the value chain. Joint actions such as input purchasing and product sales increase bargaining power. Some regional co-operatives like La Riojana offer insurance to their members. Co-operatives also offer financing of inputs, training, counselling and access to information. Co-operatives contain approximately 120 000 agricultural producers, representing 30% of Argentine producers. It is estimated that 91% of producers who are members of a co-operative have less than 500 hectares (Ressel, Silva and Martí, 2008[21]). Co-operatives are more relevant within regional productions where there are no institutionalised markets. Some important co-operatives are: the *Agricultores Federados Argentinos* (AFA), a first-level agricultural co-operative of 36 000 producers; the *Asociación de Cooperativas Argentinas* (ACA), a second-level co-operative formed by 155 co-operative businesses; and the "*Confederación Intercooperativa Agropecuaria*" (CONINAGRO), a third-level institution formed by co-operative federations (see Annex A for more details).

Due to the macroeconomic context and particularly the institutional conditions for this sector, farmers unions have also become important, in particular the Argentine Rural Society (SRA), the Argentine Rural Confederation, CONINAGRO, and the Argentine Farming Federation (FAA).

8.5. Coping with catastrophic risks

The Agricultural Emergency National Law 26,509 of 2009 defines the procedures for declaration of agricultural emergencies and disasters due to "climatic, meteorological, telluric, biological or physical factors which affect agricultural production significantly and/or the capacity of production, putting at risk the continuity of familiar or corporate exploitations affecting directly or indirectly rural communities". The National Emergency and Agricultural Disaster Commission is composed of representatives from different Ministries including Finance, the Interior, Public Works and Agroindustry, and from the National Meteorological Service (SMN), INTA, the development public bank Banco Nación (BN), the central bank (BCRA), the Fiscal Agency (AFIP), the national agricultural sector and the provinces.

According to this law, the provinces take the initiative for an agricultural emergency or disaster request to the National Commission, after a provincial resolution defining the adverse effects of the event, the affected area, the start and end date, and the benefits that the declaration will bring about for the province. If the request is accepted, the Commission will propose to the national government through the Secretariat of Agroindustry a declaration of emergency for the area, defining the period of time during which the emergency will be in effect. The eligible producers will receive a certification after verification of damage by the province.

The law makes a distinction between emergency (losses of production capacity of more than 50%) and disaster or catastrophe (losses of more than 80%). The creation of a single registry of producers was foreseen to obtain detailed and specific information of producers, geographical location and impact of the catastrophe, but has not yet been created. The law creates an annual national fund for agricultural emergency and disaster mitigation (FONEDA) of ARS 500 million that cannot be cumulated from one year to the next. This amount of money has not been updated since the law's promulgation in August 2009 and has lost significant real value. However, the total provisions of the fund were not exhausted in any of the years 2009-17 (Table 8.2). The law enables other ad hoc contributions from the national budget, but there is no record of such contributions.

Disaster assistance can include financial and tax benefits. Financial benefits are: special direct assistance to affected producers; debt consolidation with banks, 90-day suspension of trials and administrative procedures; credit lines with grace periods and reduction or preferential interest rates, 25% reduction for emergencies and 50% for disasters[6]; and payments and technical assistance sent from the Secretariat of Agroindustry to the provinces or local councils that will distribute the funds among producers. Tax benefits include extension for existing tax deadlines and full income tax deductions for benefits from forced liquidation of the farm and for duties on animals sold coming from areas declared under emergency or disaster.

In the period August 2009 to December 2017, there were 269 emergency and/or disaster resolutions, with several emergency resolutions per year often in a single province. The province of Buenos Aires accounts for the highest number of declarations (38), followed by Cordoba (24) and Rio Negro (21). While agricultural emergencies in Buenos Aires and Córdoba impact mainly on extensive agriculture and livestock (wheat, soybean, corn, sunflower, pasture), in Río Negro and Mendoza the affected productions are olive, grapevine, fruit production and ovine and caprine livestock. Table 8.2 shows that the most frequent events are droughts (38% of declarations) and floods (28%), followed by frost (12%) and hail (11%). The international database EM-DAT (www.emdat.be) records a drought in 2003 and a flood in 1998 as the main disasters in Argentina, with estimated impacts of more than USD 1 000 million each.

There is little correlation between large negative deviations of average yields with respect to trend, and the number of declared events or the expenditure by FONEDA (Fusco and Barelli, 2018[8]). This could be due to delays in the bureaucratic process, or to the incidence of non-systemic events that are not reflected in average yields, such as hail or frost and, to a lesser extent, floods.

Table 8.2. Emergency resolutions by year

Event	2009	2010	2011	2012	2013	2014	2015	2016	2017	Total
Biologic	1	3								4
Volcanic ash			6	1			1			8
Hail	3	6	2	3	2	4	1	5	4	30
Frost	2	5	6	2	3	7		4	3	32
Fire	1		1			1			4	7
Flood	1	6	4	3		20	5	19	18	76
Snow									1	1
Drought	26	16	30	9	10	7	2	1	2	103
Strong winds	1	1	2		1	1	1		1	8
Total	35	37	51	18	16	40	10	29	33	269
Expenditure by FONEDA (ARS million)	146	426	436	73	147	212	326	437	399	2 601

Source: (Fusco and Barelli, 2018[8]) based on Secretariat of Agroindustry and on National resolutions of agricultural emergencies.

8.6. Managing plant and animal health

The National Service for Agro-food Health and Quality (SENASA) is a decentralised agency of the Argentine government, with economic-financial and technical-administrative independence, and its own legal personality (see Chapter 3 for more details). It is in charge of implementing national policies on food safety, on animal and plant health, and on input control, verifying that producers take care of their responsibilities in plant and animal health and comply with in-force regulations. Since 2010 SENASA is organised in 14 regional centres that implement zoological and phytosanitary programmes in accordance with national protocols.

SENASA performs border controls through 131 border checkpoints (terrestrial, maritime, fluvial and aerial) and 69 port terminals where commercial cargo, passengers and luggage are controlled. Likewise, Argentina has zoological and phytosanitary controls in strategic locations, with 71 internal checkpoints where SENASA controls access to these zones. SENASA has an active role in prevention, contention, elimination and emergencies associated with plant and animal pests and diseases. It has more than 5 000 staff to implement its technical functions.

SENASA is funded from the national budget and from the fees that are charged on the services it provides to the sector. A 0.5% of the CIF value of imports is assigned by the budget to SENASA, and additional contributions could be provided by the Treasury if this revenue (together with the fees) were not enough to cover costs. SENASA expenditure represented almost 30% of all the general services provided to agriculture in Argentina in 2015-17 (Figure 8.6).

Figure 8.6. GSSE expenditures on inspection and control

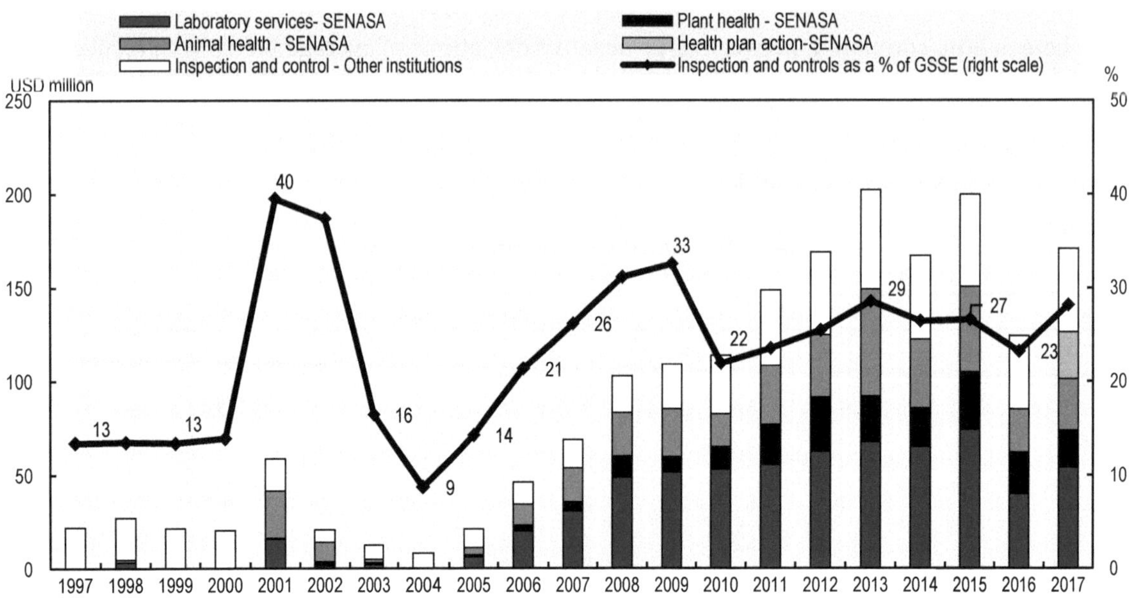

Source: OECD (2018), "Producer and Consumer Estimates", OECD Agriculture Statistics Database.

StatLink https://doi.org/10.1787/888933908343

8.7. Assessment and recommendations

The Argentinian agricultural risk management system has significant strengths, in particular regarding the institutions and the organisation of the sector. Most Argentinian farms are commercial entities with an entrepreneurial approach to farming, including the assessment and management of agricultural risks. They are organised in associations and co-operatives, or though the value chain by means of private contracts and pooling agreements. Agricultural spot and future markets are dynamic in Argentina. There are also strong public institutions providing research (INTA) and managing plant and animal health (SENASA). Information about market and weather risks is available and accessible.

Argentina's production growth and innovation in the last decades has been very much focused on a single commodity, soybean. Soybean has increased its share of the Argentine production and export portfolio, displacing winter and summer crops. Its growth has conditioned and limited cattle breeding and milk production activities. This strong orientation towards a single crop has produced over time a decrease in diversification of farming activities, which may threaten the sustainability of productive systems and may increase exposure to different sources of production and market risk.

The main weaknesses of the Argentinian agricultural risk management system lie beyond the agricultural sector. One significant source of risk is policy and macroeconomic volatility. Improvements in policy predictability and the strengthening of the financial sector, in particular for agriculture and rural activities, could improve the management of agricultural risks. The underdevelopment of Argentinian financial markets is a major limitation to developing efficient strategies to manage agricultural risk, including basic tools which are widely used in other countries, such as secure and accessible saving accounts and credit. The weakness of the market for financial services is also a barrier for the further growth of more diverse insurance and derivatives products. The existing programmes for preferential credit to specific projects provided by the Secretariat of Agroindustry cannot substitute private credit and do not tackle the structural economy-wide deficiencies of the financial system.

Despite these difficulties, Argentina already has a well-developed private market for agricultural insurance, though one restricted to few risks and commodities. Insurance penetration reaches more than 50% of all agricultural land. The insurance sector still has the opportunity to explore the potentialities of index insurance and digital technologies to expand agricultural insurance. Index insurance can reduce the administration cost of insurance and eradicate moral hazard and adverse selection. These indexes can use meteorological, sensor and satellite information and digital technologies. If appropriate research and knowledge is developed to reduce basis risk, index insurance could be an option to increase insurance coverage and extend it to more commodities and locations.

The government has a limited role in managing agricultural risks in Argentina. The relatively low funding for the Agricultural Emergencies Law and existence of disaster declaration requirements prevents the crowding out of market instruments. This is reflected in the alignment of policies and strategies in Argentina with the best practices in risk layering (Figure 8.7). Improvements in the disaster assistance programmes should focus on increasing the predictability of their outcomes, the traceability of the beneficiaries and the measurement of its effectiveness.

Three measures may contribute to this end. First, developing a register of farmers (or at least a single database of beneficiaries) to follow up and monitor the reception of this support. Second, innovative ideas such as index-linking could be used to define the triggers of emergency and disaster declaration in areas affected by droughts or floods. These mechanisms can contribute to an efficient delivery through reducing the processing time for declarations and improving the predictability and transparency of the indemnities. Finally, FONEDA should be able to work with multiyear budgets; this would allow it to create incentives to save and spend the disaster assistance budget according to effective damage. This mechanism would allow the accumulation of emergency funds during the years in which there is no high-impact risk, and reserve them for years with high claims.

Disaster risk management policies in Argentina are focused on ex-post assistance. More policy effort should be concentrated on ex-ante risk management and prevention. One area for improvement would be in the diffusion of technologies and strategies to limit exposure to production risks. Policies could provide training on holistic risk management approaches, emphasising information and preparedness, adaptation to climate change and new risk environments, diversification of the risk portfolio and use of appropriate technologies. The Project on Integrated Management of Agro-industrial and Rural Risks (GIRSAR) announced in January 2018 is an attempt to move towards a more holistic approach that includes training, strengthening information systems, investing on risk reduction and improving disaster assistance.

There are private and public entities in Argentina (INTA, CONICEF, Universities, AACREA, AAPRESID, CRA, SRA, CONINAGRO and FAA) that could collaborate in partnerships and play an important role when increasing practices that allow the producer to incorporate risk management and sustainability strategies, focusing on technology adoption. Information will be crucial to develop preparedness strategies and practices, and information systems that are being developed for the sector (such as the census or surveys) should consider collecting individual characteristics and risks of farmers to improve risk assessment.

Figure 8.7. Main agricultural risk management strategies and policies

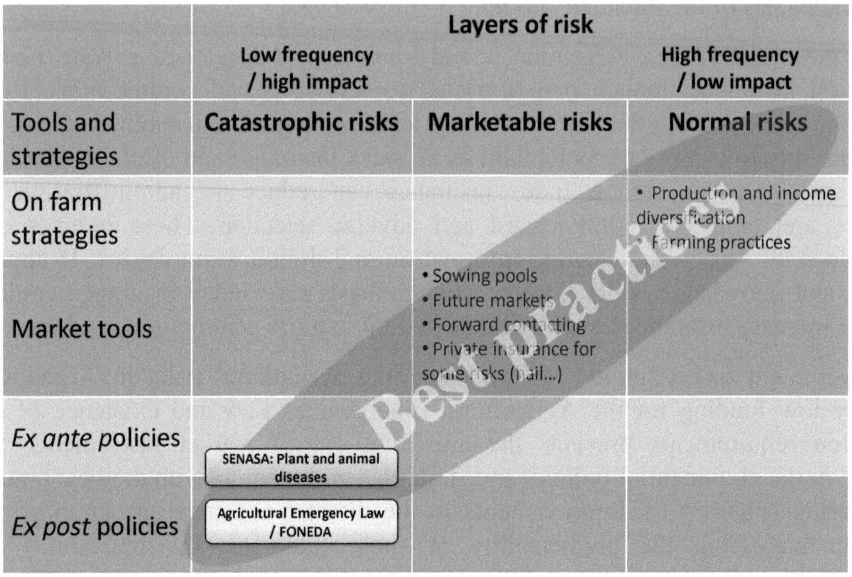

Note: This graph follows the holistic approach to risk layering in (OECD, 2009[3]).
Source: Adaptation by the authors.

References

Aceituno, P. (1988), "On the functioning of the Southern Oscillation in the South American sector, Part I: Surface climate", *Monthly Weather Review*, Vol. 116, pp. 505-524. [10]

Amissah- Arthur, A., S. Jagtap and C. Rosenzweig (2002), "Spatio- temporal effects of El Niño events on rainfall and maize yield in Kenya", *International Journal of Climatology*, Vol. 22, pp. 1849-1860. [12]

Barbieri, C. and E. Mahoney (2009), "Why is diversification an attractive farm adjustment strategy? Insights from Texas farmers and ranchers", *Journal of Rural Studies*, Vol. 25, pp. 58-66. [15]

Barsky, O. and J. Gelman (2009), *Historia del Agro Argentino: Desde la Conquista Hasta Comienzos del Siglo XXI*, Sudamericana. [20]

Bert, F. et al. (2006), "Climatic information and decision-making in maize crop production systems of the Argentinean Pampas", *Agricultural Systems*, Vol. 88, pp. 180-204. [9]

Bertonatti, C. and J. Corcuera (2000), *2000. Situación ambiental Argentina 2000.* [5]

Burkart, R. et al. (1999), *Eco-regiones de la Argentina.* [6]

CREA (2017), "Agricultura: Riesgo de actividad agrícola", *Informe-Microeconomico* 52. [16]

Fusco, M. (2012), *Riesgo Agropecuario: Gestión y Percepción del Productor e Incentivos Gubernamentales a Través de Políticas Públicas.* [7]

Fusco, M. and E. Barelli (2018), *Agricultural risk managment in Argentina*, Background report for the OECD Review of Agricultural Policies in Argentina. [8]

Ministerio de Agroindustria (2017), *Descripción del Sistema Financiero del Sector Agropecuario.* [17]

Ministerio e Medio Ambiente y Desarollo Sustentable de Argentina (2016), *Informe del Estado del Ambiente 2016.* [1]

OECD (2017), *OECD Economic Surveys: Argentina 2017: Multi-dimensional Economic Survey*, OECD Publishing, Paris, http://dx.doi.org/10.1787/eco_surveys-arg-2017-en. [19]

OECD (2011), *Managing Risk in Agriculture: Policy Assessment and Design*, OECD Publishing, Paris, http://dx.doi.org/10.1787/9789264116146-en. [4]

OECD (2009), *Managing Risk in Agriculture: A Holistic Approach*, OECD Publishing, Paris, http://dx.doi.org/10.1787/9789264075313-en. [3]

Podestá, G. et al. (1999), "Associations between grain crop yields in central-eastern Argentina and El Niño–Southern Oscillation", *Journal of Applied Meteorology*, Vol. 38, pp. 1488-1498. [11]

Ray, D. et al. (2015), "Climate variation explains a third of global crop yield variability", *Nature communications*, Vol. 6, pp. 59-89. [13]

Ressel, A., N. Silva and J. Martí (2008), *Estudio de las Cooperativas Agrarias en Argentina.* [21]

Secretaria de Medio Ambiente y Desarrollo Sustentable (2015), *Tercera Comunicación Nacional de la República Argentina a la Convención Marco de las Naciones Unidas sobre el Cambio Climático*, Presidencia de la Nación Argentina. [2]

Superintendencia de Seguros de la Nación (2017), *Los seguros en el sector agropecuario y forestal 2016.* [18]

Trigo, E. and M. Ciampi (2018), *Review of agricultural innovation policies in Argentina*, Background report for the OECD Review of Agricultural Policies in Argentina. [14]

Notes

1 This chapter is based on the consultant background paper (Fusco and Barelli, 2018[8]) which follows the OECD holistic approach for Agricultural Risk Management (OECD, 2009[3]; OECD, 2011[4]).

2 A temporary tax on all exports was introduced in September 2018 in order to raise revenue and reduce the fiscal deficit.

3 See the results in (Fusco and Barelli, 2018[8]) based on representative regional economic models developed by Agricultural Radar from the Argentine Association of Regional Consortiums for Agricultural Experimentation (AACREA). The national frequency and intensity indicators observed, disaggregated by crop and also calculated at national portfolio, are formed by the participating share that each crop shows in the season.

4 Matba currently offers: wheat contract and Chicago wheat, corn contract and Chicago corn, soybean contract and Chicago soybean, sorghum contract, sunflower contract, barley contract, and soybean oil contract.

5 Rofex currently offers: standard condition soybean contract, factory condition soybean, wheat contract, corn contract, Rosafé soybean index contract, Chicago soybean contract, Chicago corn contract and futures-based contracts.

6 For instance, the convention with Banco Nacion (BNA) and with Provincial Bank of Buenos Aires (BAPRO).

Chapter 9. Value chains in Argentina: Apples and pears, and viticulture

Structural duality is an important characteristic of Argentina's agriculture and is reflected in the differences between the Pampas region and those that surround it. In the Pampas region, most of the grains, oilseeds and beef is produced by large-scale, export-oriented producers. This agriculture is highly productive, with well-developed value chains linked to international markets. Oher regions ("the regional economies") produce fruits and vegetables and agro-industrial products like wine, tobacco, cotton or sugar. Some of these products, like apples, pears and wine, are exported in competitive world markets but have an internal duality. In the apple-and-pear value chain farms which are fully integrated into global markets (usually large and medium size) coexist with less integrated farms (mostly small-scale). These small-scale farms have several difficulties, particular the low use of technology, deficient pest control, old orchards, and in general, very limited investments at farm level. Meanwhile, the viticulture value chain has had significant investments since 1990s by both foreign and local investors attracted by deregulation and relatively low-price, good-quality land. Nonetheless, it still faces several constraints, particularly related to limited research and development, training and extension services.

9.1. Introduction

Argentine agriculture has experienced substantial changes over the last five decades[1]. These include significant increases in output as well as in the Total Factor Productivity (TFP) of most commodities. Shifts in resource use include the dramatic rise in soybean production, increased use of fertilisers and other modern inputs, and increased use of farm machinery, with corresponding decreases in the amount of labour employed in the sector. This led to a structural adjustment, with a fall in the number of small-scale farms and an increase in average farm size in most regions. However, this success story has not taken place with equal intensity in all regions and all production activities (Lema and Gallacher, 2018$_{[1]}$).

A characteristic of Argentina's agriculture it is the duality of its structure, reflected in the differences between the Pampas region and those surrounding it. The Pampas region accounts for the production of most of the country's grains, oilseeds and beef. It is characterised by large-scale, highly productive, export-oriented agriculture with well-developed value chains linked to international markets. As discussed in chapter 2, it has important forward linkage to domestic and global value chains (GVCs). The remaining regions in the country – those surrounding the Pampas and called "*the regional economies*" – produce fruits and vegetables and other agro-industrial products like wine, tobacco, cotton or sugar. These regional economies have relatively low levels of productivity and less dynamic value chains.

In terms of agricultural policy, there has been a distinction between the Pampas region and the regional economies. For the Pampas, in general, a policy of negative support has been a common denominator over the years. The regional economies have not been similarly burdened. On the contrary, some support has been given to farmers producing specific like tobacco; however, key problems in these regions have not been widely addressed by public policy, and public investment on agricultural infrastructure, R&D, extension services, and technical assistance has been limited. This chapter explores two value chains situated in the regional economies: apples and pears, and wine.

The principal apple and pear producing region of the country comprises the provinces of Rio Negro and Neuquén. Total area of fruit production in this region is 56 000 irrigated hectares, of which more than 80% is planted with apples and pears. The apple-and-pear value chain in Argentina has a duality within its structure, whereby farms fully integrated into it (usually large and medium size ones) coexist with less integrated farms (mostly small-scale ones).

The viticulture value chain includes a set of productive linkages oriented to the production of wine and must. The total area of grapevine production is 224 706 hectares, distributed in more than 25 000 vineyards with an average area per vineyard of 9 hectares. Around 92% of vineyards are for wine production, the rest is consumed as table grapes. During the 1990s, along with the deregulation of the industry, significant investments in the viticulture sector took place, and Argentina's exports grew alongside an improvement in quality and of average export prices.

9.2. The apple-and-pear value chain

Description of the value chain

Production

A standardised agricultural value chain connects farmers with the commercialisation of their products. The main stages include inputs provision, producers, middlemen/wholesalers, distributors and retailers. Depending on the commodity, additional stages can include industrial processors, and exporters. Figure 9.1. shows the value chain of apples and pears in Argentina.

The apple-and-pear value chain is organised around a significant infrastructure of orchards, irrigation facilities, packing and cold-storage plants, logistic and transport services, and a modern export port facility. The industry also has access to significant R&D expertise from INTA and local university resources. Heterogeneity of firm size exists, ranging from large, vertically integrated export-oriented multinational firms, medium-sized firms specialising in production linked via contracts to marketing channels, and small-medium independent farms (Leskovar, 2016[2]).

Argentine apples and pears are produced in several areas of the country; however, Rio Negro and Neuquén provinces account for most of the country's production, with 70% of the total planted area of the country. The rest is mostly in the provinces of Mendoza and San Juan. For this assessment, only Rio Negro and Neuquén provinces are considered. Apple and pear production is irrigated, with 24 179 hectares to apples and 22 585 to pears. The total number of apple and pear farmers in the region is 2 266, making an average size of 18.7 hectares (Ministerio de Hacienda, 2016[3]).

In terms of land structure for apple- and pear-producing farms, Table 9.1. suggests that nearly 80% of farms are less than 20 hectares. Some structural change can be observed in this subsector from 2007 to 2016, where small-scale farms (less than 10 hectares) lost an important number of operations. Possible variables explaining this adjustment are labour costs, mechanisation, difficulty to access international markets, as well as relatively higher regulatory costs (Ministerio de Hacienda, 2016[3]).

Technology used by apple and pear farmers range from very low to medium. Nearly half of producers in the Rio Negro and Neuquén provinces are characterised by low or very low technology, with orchards older than 26 years, and relatively small production units of less than 10 hectares. This type of farmer accounts for nearly 30% of area planted with apples and pears in the Río Negro valley. High technology farms are those with more than 30 hectares and with orchards between 14 and 20 years old. These large farms also tend to use other technologies; for example, 70% use sprinkler irrigation for frost protection versus only 15% of small-scale farms (those with less than 10 hectares).

Yields in Argentina are relatively far below the yields of the main producing countries (Table 9.2). Argentina has a better relative positioning of average yield per hectare in pear production than in apple production (Ministerio de Hacienda, 2016[3]).

Figure 9.1. Argentina's apple-and-pear value chain

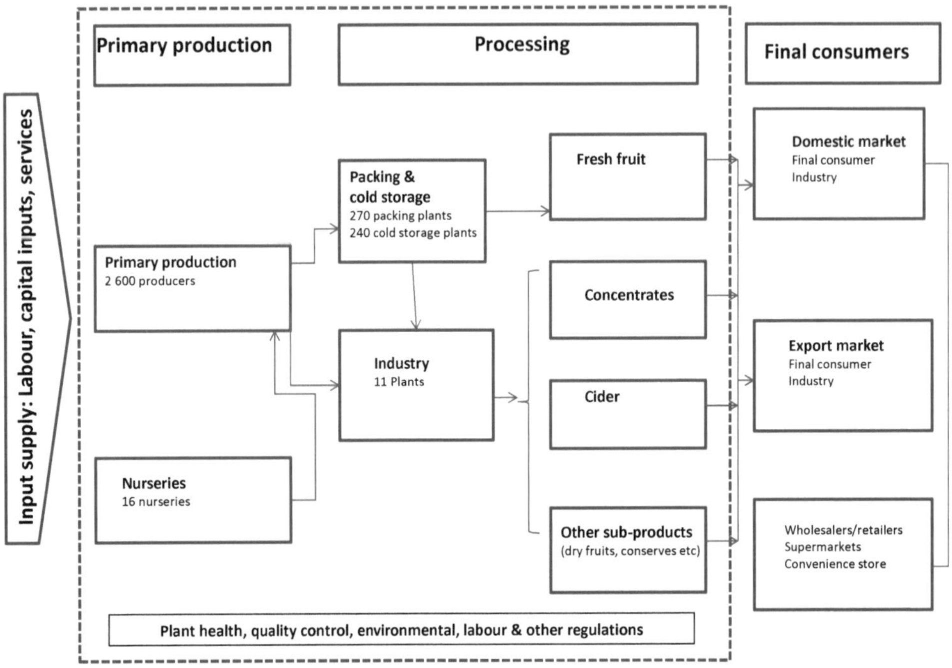

Source: Ministerio de Hacienda, 2017.

Table 9.1. Size distribution of producers and number of apple and pear producers

Size range (ha)	2007	2016	2016/07
0 - 10	1 380	1 201	0.87
10 - 20	606	568	0.94
20 - 30	213	219	1.03
30 - 40	113	115	1.02
40 - 50	47	43	0.91
50 - 100	89	73	0.82
> 100	48	47	0.98
Total	2 496	2 266	0.91

Source: (Ministerio de Hacienda, 2016[3])

Table 9.2. Average yields 2002-12, selected countries

Apples		Pears	
Country	Yield (tonnes/ha)	Country	Yield (tonnes/ha)
New Zealand	49.5	New Zealand	43.4
Chile	43.3	Chile	28.9
South Africa	35.2	South Africa	28.7
Average	33.1	Argentina	27.1
Brazil	32.9	Average	26.1
Argentina	24.6	Australia	17.3
Australia	13.2	Brazil	11.4

Source: Ministerio de Hacienda, 2017.

In apple and pear production, labour is a significant input, representing between 45% and 50% of total costs. Output per unit of land is not necessarily the crucial metric for profitability, and output per labour-hour is more correlated with profitability.

In 2016, the total production was 594 000 tonnes of pears and 550 000 of apples (Leskovar, 2016[2]). Around 56% of these fruits are sold in the domestic market; the remainder is for export. Approximately 72% of aggregate output of both apples and pears is consumed fresh, with the remaining 28% sent to agroindustry. Around 60% of production for fresh consumption is exported, and 35% is consumed domestically. Pear exports represent 80% of fresh output and apples only 35%. The variety of apples most consumed in Argentina is Red Delicious (80%), and those of pears are Williams (61%) and Packham's (35%). The national per-capita consumption of apples is around 7 kg and only 2.2 kg for pears (Ministerio de Hacienda, 2017).

As a system, the apple-and-pear value chain is governed by both formal and informal organisations, and numerous linkages among them. Formal organisations can be public, private or of a non-governmental, non-profit type. Public institutions include INTA, SENASA, the Secretariat of Agroindustry, public banks and universities. Private organisations are formed by fruit producers, packers and storage plants, transport and general logistics firms, input suppliers including agricultural professional services, and private audit/certification services. Non-profit organisations and NGOs also play a role at the producer, packer and transport stages. Such organisations include producer associations, producer and processing co-operatives, chamber of commerce, committees of plant health, and trade unions. Informal organisations include input and output markets at all levels of the value chain, informal information exchange networks, and lobbying efforts by private agents.

At the primary level, co-ordination along the value chain involves interaction of some 2 400 producers, with more than 300 packers, industrial processing plants, transport networks, wholesalers, and exporters, input suppliers, workers and financial institutions. The organisational problem faced by this value chain is not different from other contexts: potential conflict has to be converted into co-operation, resources have to be mobilised and effort has to be co-ordinated. These activities take place among individuals whose preferences, information, knowledge and interests differ (Lema and Gallacher, 2018[1]).

Conventional producer co-operatives have made modest inroads in the apple-and-pear value chain of Argentina's main producing area (Río Negro province). The first fruit co-operative was created in the late 1930s, and it currently has only 50 members. The interest in co-operatives has not translated into new effective start-ups or growth of existing co-operatives (Hak, 2009[4]). This situation of low horizontal integration contrasts with other countries, where agricultural co-operatives play a significant role. In the United States, for example, there are 167 fruit and vegetable co-operatives, with 32 200 members and a volume of sales of USD 7.6 billion per year (USDA, 2011[5]).

Although the potential exists for improving producer profitability through co-operative marketing arrangements, significant well-known co-operative challenges remain: the dispersion of authority, partial non-alienability of individual property rights over resources, absence of the profit motivation, and free rider problems all conspire against co-operative survival in a competitive marketplace.

Packing/processing and retailing

Leskovar et al. (2016[2]) describe marketing channels for domestic consumption of pears and apples in Argentina:

- Integrated producer (orchard + packing) with the following variants:
  - selling directly in the central market
    - from central market to self-service retailers
    - from central market to hyper-supermarkets
  - selling directly to purchasing unit of hyper-super markets
  - selling to wholesaler operating in central market
    - from large wholesaler to smaller wholesaler and then to groceries
    - from wholesaler to fresh produce groceries.
- Non-integrated producer contracts out classification, packing and cold storage.
- Non-integrated producer sells output to packing plant.

In general terms, small-scale producers (those with less than 15 hectares), tend to be non-integrated and thus contract out the marketing work or sell their output to the packing plant, while large-scale farms use the first integrated channel Although a large number of producers are organised around channels 2 and 3, a substantial portion of output uses channels where some degree of integration exists. In the Rio Negro region, there are around 300 packing/processing plants of different sizes, suggesting a relatively high degree of competition in this link of the chain.

For producers of apples and grapes, two marketing channels can be distinguished: the city of Buenos Aires and the rest of the country. The Buenos Aires market is the largest channel where vertically integrated producers sell to the main wholesale market of the country (the *Mercado Central de Buenos Aires*) and from this wholesale market to retailers. This channel is followed in importance by supermarket chains purchasing directly from integrated producers, and in third place by integrated producers selling directly to retailers. For the rest of the country, supermarkets are less significant than small and medium traditional retailers, who tend to buy from non-integrated farmers (Lema and Gallacher, 2018[1]).

As in many other countries, important changes have taken place in the retail process in Argentina during the last half-century. The shift from small specialised stores (e.g. butchers, fruit stalls, dry goods stores) to large, diversified and self-service retailers (supermarkets) started in the early 1960s and has grown steadily since then. Carrefour (France), Walmart (US), CENCOSUD (Chile), and Groupe Casino (France) are some of the main companies in the country. By 2012, around 10 large supermarket chains (foreign and local) were operating in the country (Lema and Gallacher, 2018[1]).

Ablin (2012[6]) provides information on the degree of market power of the retailer sector in Argentina. According to the author, the eight largest supermarket chains account for 15% of supermarket points-of-sale (POS) (1 300 of a total of 8 700). Around 32% of POS belong to firms with two or more POS, and the remaining 68% belong to firms with only one POS. About 80% of firms with only one POS are owned by individuals of Asian origin, mostly Korean or Chinese. The market shares of the principal supermarket and self-service retail channels break down as follows: hypermarkets 34%; supermarkets

29%; self-service stores of Asian origin 25%; other self-service stores 8%; and discount stores 3% (Ablin, 2012[6]).

Price differentials between various stages of the value chain result from associated cost differentials in transforming/transporting/selling products along successive stages. Table 9.3 shows prices along the value chain. The last two columns show price differentials between value chain stages: i.e. between the producer and packer, and between wholesaler and retailer. Under competitive conditions, these price differentials approximate the cost involved in each value chain stage. The wholesale-retail process involves considerably higher costs than the producer-packer stage. This situation reveals the importance of efficiency in the transformation process from the orchard to packing warehouse, and eventually the wholesale to retail sale. As can be calculated from the table, these strictly agribusiness costs (farm-warehouse plus warehouse-wholesale stages) represent between 40% and 45% of the total cost of transferring products from farm to consumer (Leskovar, 2015[7]).

Table 9.3. Apple and pear prices along the value chain (USD/kg), 2015

Fruit	Producer FOB packing plant	Exit packing plant	Wholesaler exit central market	Retailer	Producer-packer difference	Wholesaler-retailer difference
Williams pear Buenos Aires market	0.26	0.64	0.80	1.61	0.38	0.81
Red Delicious apple Buenos Aires market	0.31	0.94	1.25	2.39	0.63	1.14

Source: Leskovar et al. (2015[7]).

Exports and competitiveness

Future expansion of the Argentine apple and pear sector depends on access to international markets. The reason is that domestic markets are not expected to absorb large increases in production without a significant drop in prices (i.e. demand for most foods, including fruits, is generally price-inelastic). Access to international markets depends on the structure and nature of tariff and non-tariff barriers, as well as on the functioning of the value chain from the farm gate, through export ports and subsequent linkages up to the final consumer in the importing country (Lema and Gallacher, 2018[1]).

Table 9.4 shows the structure of the apple-and-pear export subsector. Four firms account for 40.4% of exports. The next four account for another 17.6%, and the rest of the exporters account for 42%. There is a reasonable degree of competition as the Herfindhal-Hirshman index[2] suggests a number of 600, corresponding to an un-concentrated industry. Notwithstanding, attention is warranted on the characteristics of price transmission in the value chain due to the heterogeneous and perishable characteristic of the product, and the possibility that significant information asymmetries exist among market participants (Leskovar, 2015[7]).

Table 9.4. Apple and pear export firms in Argentina, 2015

Order	Firm	Pear (%)	Apple (%)	Total (%) apple and pear
1	Patagonian Fruit Trade SA	11.2	13.4	11.8
2	Univeg Expofrut	9.9	17.2	11.7
3	Moño Azul SA	9.6	8.6	9.4
4	PAI SA	7.5	7.6	7.5
5	Ecofrut SA	6.3	3.8	5.7
6	Kleppe SA	4.2	5.9	4.6
7	Montever SA	3.8	4.3	3.9
8	Tres Ases SA	3.5	2.9	3.4
9	Estándar Fruit Arg. SA	3.6	0.0	2.7
10	Salentein Fruit SA	2.3	2.8	2.4
11	Mario Cervi e Hijos SA	2.2	5.4	3.0
12	Carbajo V	1.9	0.6	1.6
13	Via Frutta SA	1.8	0.5	1.5
14	Martínez R.	1.2	1.6	1.3
15	Others (pears 116, apples 91)	30.8	25.6	29.5
	Total	100.0	100.0	100.0

Source: Leskovar et al., (2015[7]).

Leskovar et al., (2015[7]) present a detailed analysis of marketing channels in the export markets for apples and pears, as well as of prices in different stages of the value chain. The authors identify different organisational forms in the apple-and-pear export value chain: large and medium-scale integrated producer-exporters; and small and medium-scale non-integrated producers. In the case of overseas shipments (mostly to Europe) the chain includes exporter, importer, distributor, supermarkets and consumers. Importers can also link directly to wholesalers, then to medium retailers and finally to consumers. Significant economies in the cost of information transfer (including quality control) are achieved by large-volume players, and frequency on transactions is crucial in facilitating exchanges (Leskovar, 2015[7]).

The Argentine agricultural sector is characterised by a strong competitive export position in oilseeds, cereals, beef, poultry and dairy products, despite export taxes. This success story contrasts with performance of the apple-and-pear value chain, where Argentina appears to have lagged behind (Lema and Gallacher, 2018[1]).

Under the standard assumption of reasonably competitive conditions, cost minimisation and resulting efficiency should prevail. However, these conditions may apply only partially due to low levels of farmer education, risk aversion, severe financial constraints, information asymmetry, government regulations, positive or negative externalities, or below-optimum provision of public goods. For example, inadequate monitoring of pesticide applications by producers selling in the domestic market may reduce the prospects of pear and apple producers aiming at the international markets: pesticide residues in irrigation water, or the presence of plant diseases require not only orchard-specific but area-wide compliance of production practices (Lema and Gallacher, 2018[1]).

Comparing competitiveness of participants in apple and pear international markets show interesting results for Argentina. In the World Apple and World Pear reviews produced by Belrose,[3] factors of competitiveness are classified as: (a) orchard-level production efficiency, (b) industrial infrastructure and inputs and (c) financing and markets[4] (Villareal, 2011[8]). Table 9.5 summarises results for four Southern Hemisphere countries that compete for the same market niche: the off-season in the Northern Hemisphere: Chile, New Zealand, South Africa and Argentina. Some of these countries are middle-income economies that may face similar overall constraints for the development of an export-based industry.

In terms of overall competitiveness, Chile is ranked first out of a sample of twenty-nine countries, both for apples and pears. New Zealand ranks high for apples, and somewhat lower for pears. Argentina shows a poor overall ranking for apples, below South Africa and New Zealand, but a better one for pears, for which it is above both countries. Why is Argentina more competitive in pears than in apples?

Further insights are provided by rankings in the three competitiveness factors considered in Table 9.5. Infrastructure and input provision does not seem to be the most severe constraint in Argentina: it is ranked fifth for both apples and pears, slightly below New Zealand, which ranks third. Again, Chile leads the ranking for this dimension. Infrastructure and inputs include irrigation facilities, access to inputs (fertiliser, pesticides, and machinery services) as well as access to packing, logistics, marketing and export services. The medium to high ranking for Argentina in this dimension suggests that port-facilities are efficient and reasonably priced, roads are operable year-round, and packing and classification plants are numerous and competitive (Lema and Gallacher, 2018$_{[1]}$).

Table 9.5. Competitiveness in apple and pear production, ranking, 2010

Country	Overall	Production	Infrastructure and inputs	Financing and markets
Apples				
		Competitiveness dimension		
Chile	1	2	1	4
New Zealand	5	5	3	8
South Africa	13	6	9	21
Argentina	16	14	5	24
Pears				
Chile	1	11	1	13
New Zealand	9	14	3	6
South Africa	11	2	8	17
Argentina	8	1	5	16

Source: Villareal, (2011$_{[8]}$) based on Belrose, World Apple Review, World Pear Review.

However, Argentina performs poorly for both apples and pears in the financing and markets dimension. Argentina's high interest rates and high and variable inflation has led to financial constraints and difficulties in business planning beyond the fruits subsector, or indeed the whole agricultural sector (Chapter 7). Additionally, the property rights variable is also included in the financing and markets dimension, and Argentina's litigation system involves significant levels of red tape. Inflation, coupled with weak property rights, possibly explains the reluctance of banks to extend mortgage-backed credit to producers (Lema and Gallacher, 2018$_{[1]}$).

The main factor explaining the different competitiveness ranking of pears and apples in Argentina is production efficiency at the orchard level, where significant differences are observed between the two fruits. For pears, the country produces high quality high demand varieties and ranks first, while Chile, an otherwise strong competitor, is in 11th place; for apples, Argentina occupies 14th place, far below the other countries (Table 9.5).

To recap, two points emerge from an analysis of Argentina's apple and pear subsector. First, Argentina is characterised by significant lags in the financing/markets dimension, which in relative terms is more significant than infrastructure and input deficiencies. Secondly, as compared to other countries such as Chile, Argentina shows a significantly higher orchard-level production efficiency in pears, but not in apples, where it ranks poorly; this advantage in the primary production of pears partially compensates for other weaknesses that affect both pears and apples, positioning Argentina in the top ten competitive pear exporters.

SWOT analysis and challenges of the value chain

Several problems are faced by the Argentine apple-and-pear value chain, suggesting that the subsector has performed below its full potential. At the production stage and despite the better performance of pears, a significant portion of production units in both value chains are characterised by small-scale size and low capitalisation. There are partially abandoned or sub-managed orchards, which constitute breeding grounds for pests (in particular the codling moth). These orchards generate a negative plant health risk for modern, export-oriented production units. There are deficiencies at orchard-level management and agronomic practices such as non-adoption of risk-mitigation alternatives, low level of R&D and technology transfer, particularly for small-scale farms. High volatility of net incomes results in financial constraints and reduced incentives along the value chain (Sturzenegger, 2017[9]).

The strengths, weaknesses, opportunities and threats (SWOT) of the apple-and-pear value chain in Argentina are summarised in Table 9.6. The principle strengths are public institutions such as INTA and SENASA, and the long history of production and comparative advantage. The principle weaknesses relate to Argentinian macroeconomic conditions and markets, in particular financial and labour markets. Labour input costs are most significant, adding up to 50% of total costs. An important threat is the variability of the real exchange rate (RER) that has the determinant role of income volatility throughout the value chain (Sturzenegger, 2017[9]). Fluctuations in the RER (a product of macroeconomic instability) pose a threat to exporters, particularly those operating in a sector where non-tradeable inputs comprise a substantial portion of total costs. Moreover, labour markets in Argentina are highly regulated and pose risks for entrepreneurs, in particularly small and medium SMEs. For example, there is heavy red tape in the litigation processes.

In contrast with extensive grain production, fruit output can be of widely varying quality, and productivity measures should take into account the ratio of quality-adjusted output to input. The fact that fruit is exported puts a premium on environmental practices and food safety and quality attributes. The fresh fruit value chain is highly complex, and both entry into it and success are difficult for firms lacking experience, technology and scale. Furthermore, food safety, environmental, labour and other standards are a critical aspect in international trade of agricultural products. These standards are of particular importance for fresh produce, whose perishable and physical characteristics require specialised transport, storage and handling procedures. Sanitary conditions for fruit are also critical to access export markets. The increased importance of private standards in international trade is an important aspect to consider within public policy, and in particular how such standards benefit larger and more integrated producers to a greater extent than small-scale producers, who may need technical assistance to adapt.

Perspectives for further insertion of Argentine fresh fruits in the international markets will be closely linked to macro developments, political stability and the rule of law, the stability and development of domestic financial services, and labour legislation which reduces litigation and non-salary labour costs. Further insertion will also be linked to infrastructure developments (roads, ports, and communications). Improvements in these dimensions increase the rate of return to foreign direct investment and facilitate the transition of firms to world-wide player status, a necessary condition for competing in the highly complex environment of the fresh fruit markets (Table 9.6 and Lema and Gallacher (2018[11])).

Table 9.6. SWOT analysis of the apples and pears value chain, 2018

Strengths	Weaknesses	Opportunities	Threats
Availability of land.	Macroeconomic fluctuations (exchange rate).	Export markets seem to be growing.	Increased productivity and efficiency in other southern hemisphere producers.
Availability of water and irrigation infrastructure.	Relatively high economic and political risk.	Possible increased FDI in Argentina.	Possible biotech innovations reducing cost of fruit storage (delayed maturation) thus reducing advantages of SH production.
Long history of apple and pear production. General community resources.	Inflexible labour markets. High labour costs due to competition from high-revenue industries (in particular energy).	Presence of some large, multinational producers and exporters.	Possibility of entrance of exotic plant diseases.
Potential contribution of Public Institutions (INTA and SENASA). Availability of general agronomic, accounting and engineering expertise.	High cost of capital, credit/capital availability. High costs of inputs due to high taxes. Time and possible red tape delays for importing inputs.	Possibility of upgrading technical and market know-how. Increased quality with use of IT for production, marketing, storage and exports.	Variability of the real exchange rate.
General managerial capabilities.	Availability of technical know-how in some specific areas.		
Absence of serious political threats (wars).	Thin market co-ordination/information conditions faced by some producers.	Possibility of improving climate forecasts thus reducing damage from wind, frost and hail.	
	Inefficient value-chain channels for domestic consumption.		
Reasonably competitive domestic wholesale and export sector.	Lack of research on determinants of firm-level management and production efficiency.	Possibility of improving organisation of medium producers through consortium type enterprises.	
	Possible below-average size of numerous firms.		
	Production risks: high winds or hail (damage).		
	Logistics costs both for domestic and export markets.		

Source: Lema and Gallacher (2018[11]).

9.3. The viticulture value chain

Description of the value chain

Production

In Argentina the viticulture value chain includes a set of productive linkages oriented mainly to the production of wine and must. It spreads from grapevine farmers, farmer co-operatives, winemaking companies, winemaking co-operatives, private wineries and retailers to consumers. The principal producing regions are in the provinces of Mendoza and San Juan in the west of the country, where most of the production is concentrated, together with provinces of La Rioja, Salta, Catamarca, Neuquén and Río Negro. Mendoza province accounts for 71% of the area planted with grapevine and 76% of the production of wines, and San Juan province represents 22% and 18%, respectively. In these two main producing provinces, the value chain has an important economic role, both in terms of share of the total production value and employment (Lema and Gallacher (2018[1]) and Table 9.7).

Table 9.7. Vineyards and planted area, 2015

Province	Number of vineyards	Planted area	Percentage of total planted area
Mendoza	16 510	159 649	71.05%
San Juan	5 119	47 394	21.09%
La Rioja	1 237	7 449	3.32%
Salta	267	3 144	1.40%
Catamarca	1 251	2 678	1.19%
Neuquén	90	1 751	0.78%
Rio Negro	269	1 676	0.75%
Córdoba	127	278	0.12%
La Pampa	14	243	0.11%
Other provinces	165	443.7	0.20%
Total	25 049	224 706	100%

Source: Ministerio de Hacienda, 2016.

The land structure of grapevine production suggests that 60% of farms have less than five hectares but only represent 14% of total vineyard land, while only 8% of total vineyards have more than 25 hectares and represent 45% of the total land destined to vines (Table 9.8). Regarding the age of plantations, 36% of the planted area is less than 15 years old, while more than 42% exceeds 25 years.

Table 9.8. Grapevine farms structure, 2016

Hectares	Number of vineyards (%)	Area (%)
less than 5 ha	60	0.14
5-15 ha	25	0.25
15-25 ha	7	0.16
25-50 ha	5	0.18
50-100 ha	2	0.14
more than 100 ha	1	0.13

Source: Ministerio de Hacienda, 2016.

Grape varieties for wine production predominate in vineyards, with approximately 92% of the total planted area in year 2015. Grapes for fresh consumption represent 6%, and raisins 2%. Red varieties are the most significant (54%) in the total area planted with grapes for wine, followed by pink (26%) and white (20%). Since the mid-nineties the production of varietal high-quality wines expanded, and red varieties increased the planted area by 61% between the years 2000 and 2015. Pink and white varieties decreased their participation by 22% and 19%, respectively, during the same period.

In 2015, approximately 67% of the area planted with wine grapes were varieties of high quality wine, totalising 139 000 hectares. Vineyards of high-quality varieties usually have lower yields and higher prices. Malbec is the largest high-quality red variety in Argentina; it is followed in importance by Cabernet Sauvignon and Syrah. The Malbec variety covers the largest number of hectares, and the planted area has increased 141% since 2000 (Ministerio de Hacienda, 2016[10]).

The total planted area has remained approximately constant at 224 000 hectares in the last 15 years, and the variability of grape production is mostly due to climatic issues. Variability in production of grapevine was relatively large in the period 2005-16, with the highest production of 3 million tonnes obtained in 2007, and the lowest level due to frosts, hail and rains in 2016 – less than 1.8 million tonnes (Ministerio de Hacienda, 2016[10]).

In 2016, a total of 12.7 million hectolitres of wine and must were produced. Figure 9.2 shows that on average, 75% of the total production correspond to wine production and 25% to must production. The production of must has been increasing in the last decades, driven by external demand. Around 85% of must production is exported as concentrated must; by contrast, 20% of wine production is exported and 80% is consumed domestically.

Figure 9.2. Grapes, wine and must production

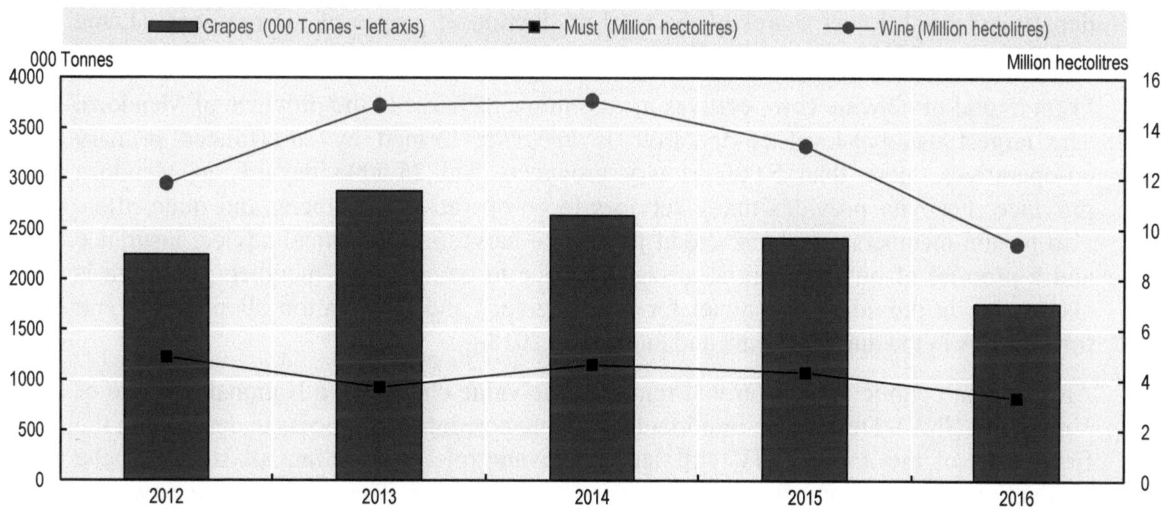

Source: Ministerio de Hacienda, 2016.

StatLink https://doi.org/10.1787/888933908362

Even though the local practices, on average, are lagging relative to international standards, the technological environment of grapevine production has undergone a radical transformation in the last twenty years, regarding adoption of modern technologies and the diffusion of agricultural practices. Relevant innovations were related to greater professionalisation of agriculture, adoption of high-quality varieties, the use of the anti-hail systems, drip irrigation and the introduction of modern training systems for canopy management (Lema and Gallacher, 2018[1]).

The most important technological change in the last two decades was the introduction of grape varieties with a high oenological quality, mostly imported from Europe. This is part of a change in the production strategy from high yields per hectare and low quality, to low yields and high quality (and prices) of grapes and wine. The expansion of the planted area with Malbec varieties is a clear example of this strategy. The total planted area of this variety was, on average of 9 000 hectares in Mendoza and 1 000 hectares in the rest of the country between 1993 and 1999 (4.8% of the total planted area). In 2013 these figures were 31 000 and 4 800 respectively, covering 16% of the total planted area. High-quality oenological varieties increased from 52% of the total area in 2002 to 67% in 2015.

Despite its rapid adoption, pressurised irrigation such as sprinkler and drip systems still represents a small percentage in the main production provinces of Mendoza and San Juan, where it is used in 19% and 16% of the planted area respectively. Its use, however, is higher in other provinces, reaching 45% in La Rioja, 57% in Salta and up to 94% in Neuquén (Ministerio de Hacienda, 2016[10]).

Many producers do not have access to technological improvements because the scale of their vineyards determines high unit costs. In addition, the wine industry increasingly relies on exports and the sector is more vulnerable to changes in foreign markets, consumption and production. In response to these challenges, some small-scale producers are organised in co-operatives. Co-operatives have been important players in the wine industry since the 1950s and wine is the second agro-industrial co-operative sector in terms of value of production after the dairy. Usually, co-operatives are present in the departments with lower shares of the total production of grapes of the province. (Lema and Gallacher, 2018[1]).

From a total of 62 wine co-operatives in Argentina, 82% are in the province of Mendoza. The largest national-level co-operative is *Fecovita,* formed by 29 affiliated primary co-operatives, more than 5 000 primary producers and 25 000 vineyards in Mendoza province. Fecovita provides many services to co-operatives members, and quite often, also to non-members suppliers: credit to finance harvesting, technical advice, insurance and a promise of buying wine at an agreed price to co-operative members. Fecovita is also active in providing a channel for selling grapes and information about prices and transactions in the market (Lema and Gallacher, 2018[1]).

An important public institution that regulates the value chain is the National Institute of Viticulture (INV). Despite the important economic deregulation process undertaken in the first years of the 1990s, INV still has a relevant role, controlling all stages of the production process from primary production to marketing. The INV has the power to impose regulations that range from requiring quality attributes (e.g. alcoholic content of wines), marketing rules (authorising or temporarily limiting the quantities of wine allocated to the domestic market), labelling and varietal identification rules.

Regulation has had a greater impact in the provinces of Mendoza and San Juan with an agreement that was reached through twin provincial laws in 1994. According to these laws, the wineries must allocate to the elaboration of musts a mandatory percentage of total grapevine production. The percentage is determined by the government of San Juan and Mendoza provinces on an annual basis, depending on the total vine production. The objective is to regulate the total production of wine and to support prices. In recent years, with the rising importance of noble varieties such as Malbec and Cabernet, the regulatory system based on quantities has begun to be publicly debated. For example, one proposal was a modification of the quantitative regulation to a quality model with more detailed harvest forecasts, based on specific data by regions and varieties (Ministerio de Hacienda, 2016[10]).

In 2004, another institution, the Argentine Viticulture Corporation (COVIAR), was created by a national law as a non-state public institution, with the participation of the national government, provincial governments and science and technology organisations with the aim of implement a Strategic Viticulture Plan (PEVI) that co-ordinates actions and policies along the value chain.

Packing/processing and retailing

There are approximately 700 wine-making firms in Argentina, of which 62% are oriented primarily to the domestic market, and 38% are export-oriented. Most of the exporting firms are in the province of Mendoza, where 88% of the wineries with export profiles are concentrated. In this province a large part of firms are small or medium enterprises, some 90% of the total of firms, counting for 8% to 5% of the total production. On the other hand, a mere three firms with an export profile and fifteen oriented to the domestic market account for more than 70% of total production.

In recent years, big wineries have gradually increased their role as drivers of the sector. The structure of the wine industry is characterised by some concentration in the processing stage. Few buyers and processors may have market power to determine price and marketing conditions for small and dispersed producers. In terms of its geographical location, consistent with the distribution of the vineyards, there is a high degree of concentration in the provinces of Mendoza and San Juan. Together, these provinces account for approximately 90% of a total of 1 000 wineries, with Mendoza's share consistently above 70% (CEPAL, 2014[11]).

The processing of wine consists of two separate stages: elaboration and fractionation. Grapes are the basic input for wine, although they are part of other production activities such as for musts and juices. Wine is the main product and explains most of the economic results of the chain. The first industrial transformation begins with obtaining the juice of the grapes. This juice goes to the stage of alcoholic fermentation and, in the case of red wines, maceration. After maceration, the liquid is drained and separated from the solids. This concludes the basic process of winemaking. The second stage of industrial transformation involves the fractioning, bottling and packaging of wine (Figure 9.3 and Figure 9.4).

Both stages can be carried out in independent firms or in fully integrated wineries. Approximately 43% of Mendoza wineries are involved only in the first stage, selling the wine in the bulk market; the equivalent figure for the province of San Juan is 63%, and 61% for La Rioja. Some wineries (36% in Mendoza and 21% in San Juan) concentrate their activities exclusively in the second stage of the industrial transformation: bottling and marketing. The remaining wineries are vertically integrated, performing both stages of industrial transformation. The share of integrated wineries is significantly higher in the remaining provinces due to specific geographic and market conditions (CEPAL, 2014[11]).

The main characteristic of the wine industry is the great heterogeneity between firms in terms of scale, products, technology and strategy. There are winemaking firms that combine different structures of ownership (family, transnational, investment fund, national companies), activities (production and fractionation of wine, bulk sales, diversification or specialisation in high quality wine) and distribution channels (domestic or external markets) (CEPAL, 2014[11]). Despite this heterogeneity, it is possible to identify two large groups within the industry: wineries that produce *table wines;* and wineries focused on *fine wines*. These two sub-markets are characterised as much by their respective business models as by the type of product: one is based on large quantities (table wines), the other in quality differentiation.

The *table wines* are those with low prices and low unit margins, and economies of scale are the key factor in the production stage, with high concentration of sales in the market. Six large companies (*Fecovita, Peñaflor, Baggio, Balbo, Orfila and Garbin*) account for 80% of the market, while the remaining 20% is distributed among 30 wineries that sell wines, almost exclusively, in their regional area. The low margin strategy is replicated in the different stages of the table wine value chain, and the leading companies show different productive strategies and different degrees and forms of vertical integration. Figure 9.3 shows the actors of the table wines.

Figure 9.3. Value chain of table wines

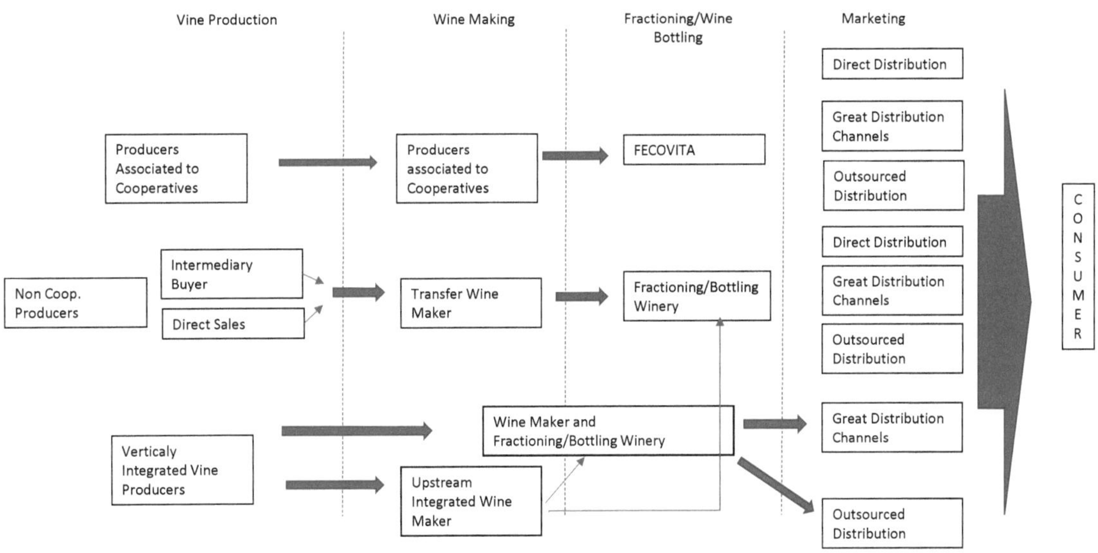

Source: Lema and Gallacher (2018[1]) based on CEPAL, 2014.

Table winemaking is based on two main strategies: on one hand, the *Peñaflor* and *Fecovita* wineries are vertically integrated wineries that process, fraction and market their wines. They sometimes produce wine for small grapevine producers, using their grapes, in exchange for a percentage of the price. On the other hand, both *Baggio* and *Garbin* are firms without vineyards; they buy wine from wineries and sell the bottled (or packaged) wine in the wholesale and retail market. They market for small or medium wineries, accumulate stocks in their own warehouses and then sell the wine in the wholesale and retail market (Lema and Gallacher, 2018[1]).

Fine wine can be separated in two sub-groups. The first one produces low-priced fine wines, which are commercially known as "*Seleccion*". This segment increased participation in the domestic market, attracting much of the demand from previous consumers of table wines. The strategy and competition of firms in this segment is similar to that in the table wine market: it based on low costs and high volumes, although quality is also a factor in the marketing strategy. Mergers and acquisitions during the 1990s created a large part of the current market structure, and the main players in this segment are the same leaders as among table wines, plus some traditional wineries (e.g. *Finca Flichman* or *Viñas de Balbo*) and some 30 medium-sized wineries. Figure 9.4 shows the value chain of this type of wine.

Figure 9.4. Value chain of fine wines

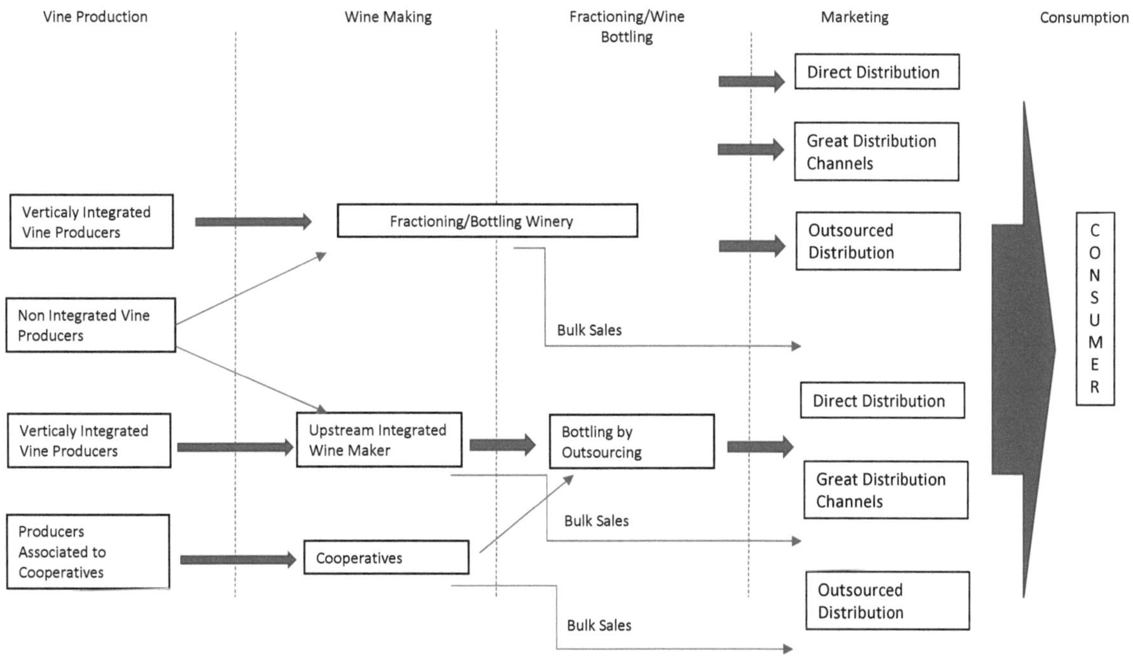

Source: Lema and Gallacher (2018[1]) based on CEPAL, 2014.

The second type of *fine wines* wineries focus on high price wines, the "*Premiums*" or the most expensive in the market. Large specialist companies dominate this segment, where a wide variety of price and quality strategies co-exist. The fine wines market is not driven by costs or volumes, but quality and product differentiation. Product differentiation strategies include advertising, using labels with the name and sometimes image of the winery, the variety of grape and the location. Given the importance of reputation and the specificity of assets involved, vertical integration plays a key role in this segment.

Forty-five companies produce fine wines for the domestic and export markets, showing a high degree of vertical integration. Some 33% of the grapes used by the fine wine wineries are from their own vineyards, while the rest is provided by implicit contracts with long term relationships. Two wine makers are relevant, by size and reputation, in this market, The *Catena Group* and *Chandon* wineries.

The growing importance of wineries with an export profile is a result of the modernisation and opening-up process that Argentine viticulture went through in the last two decades. However, the historical importance of the domestic market remains, accounting for almost 80% of total sales. With a clear focal point in the province of Mendoza, the growing internationalisation of the sector is gradually extending to the rest of the country, with a dual structure in terms of the size of the wine firms. Despite the large number of firms, there is some concentration in terms of volume. The two leading fine wine companies account for more than 40% of production, the twelve biggest firms account for 70% of the market and with the remaining 30% divided among 700 small wineries.

Exports and competitiveness

Until 1990, Argentina's wine exports were occasional and focused on non-varietal wine and must. Rather than being the driver of the business, they were a way to sell the surplus of the wine industry. The deregulation process of the 1990s radically shifted the focus of the industry and boosted investment. The industry and primary producers started to look at the international markets, which demanded high-quality products. To achieve these higher standards, technological improvements and investments were introduced along the value chain.

Foreign investors in the wine sector were attracted by the relatively low price and good quality of land, while local investors were attracted by its promising perspectives in terms of high quality wine exports. Both groups had a wide range of investment options, from buying existing wineries or building new ones to acquiring land or vineyards.

Argentine exports grew both in volume and value (Figure 9.5). The high increase in values suggests an improvement in both price and quality of the wine sold in international markets. Exports of varietal wine have increased steadily in terms of quantity and price per litre, but this is not always the case for non-varietal wine. Both non-varietal wine and must behave as commodities, with low margins and profitability linked to high exported volumes (Ruíz, 2011[12]).

Figure 9.5. Argentina wine exports

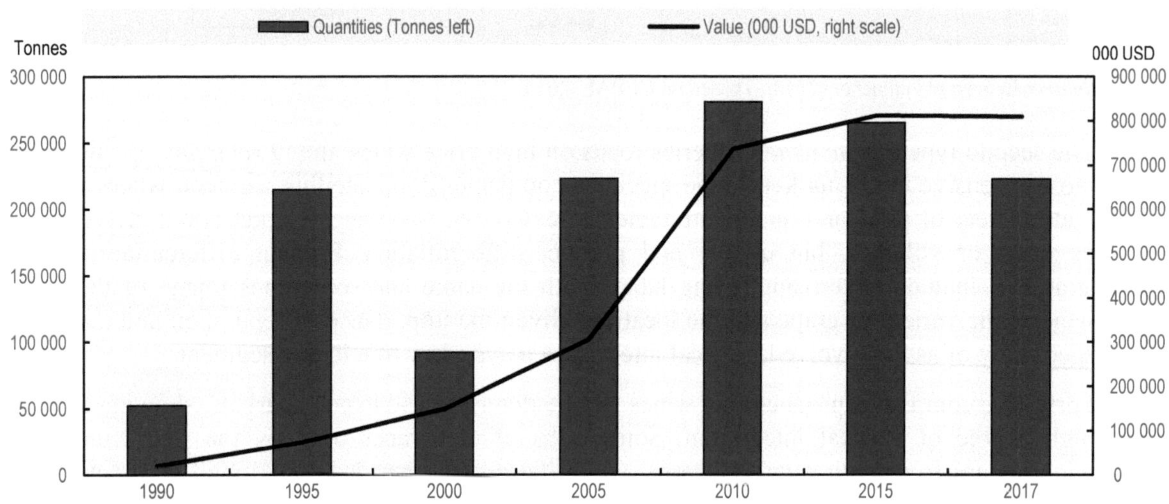

Source: Ministerio de Hacienda, 2016.

StatLink https://doi.org/10.1787/888933908381

The price received for Argentine wines as a proportion of the best-rated French wines can be used as an approximation to the average improvement in their quality and to explain the increase in export values. Figure 9.6 therefore shows how the ratio of

Argentine/French wines improved considerably from 1990 to 2013. Several Argentine winegrowers and investors innovated and succeeded in producing world-class wines locally, driven by the economic and institutional changes of the 1990s. A variety of investments on frontier technology and equipment and innovation paths were undertaken by industry participants in the process of internationalisation of Argentine wines (Elías and Ferro, 2018[13]).

Figure 9.6. Wine export price as a proportion of French wine export prices

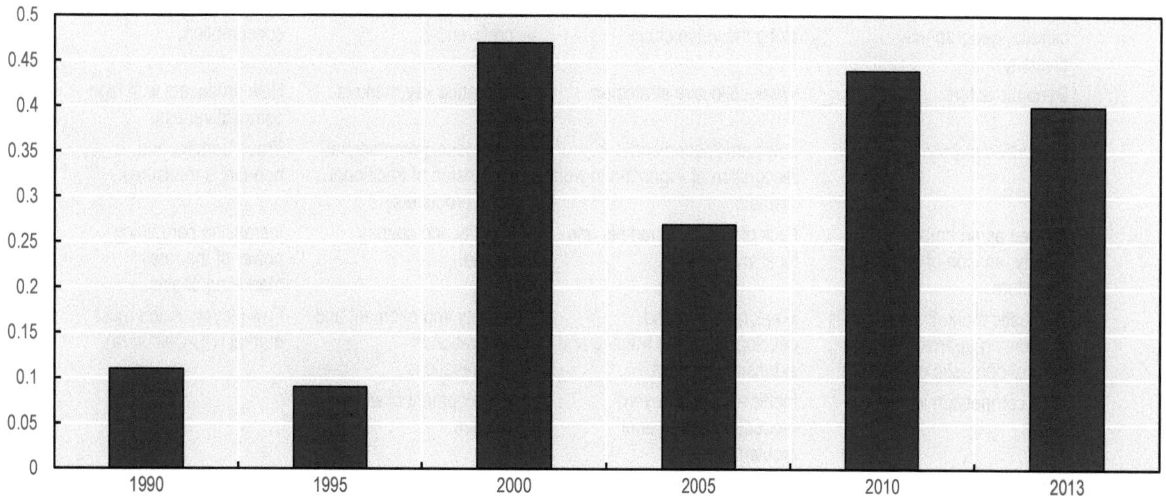

Source: Elías and Ferro (2018[13]).

StatLink https://doi.org/10.1787/888933908400

SWOT analysis and challenges for the value chain

Argentina has environmental conditions that allow high-quality production of grapes and wines, giving it a comparative advantage over other producers. In addition, the country's geographical diversity allows the production of wines that are differentiated by production areas, varieties and styles. Dynamic actors from primary producers to foreign companies installed during the nineties add to Argentina's strengths. The presence of these dynamic actors is essential both to take advantage of the new conditions of global demand and to overcome the threats facing the wine value chain (see SWOT analysis in Table 9.9).

Argentina has a long tradition of wine co-operatives among small and medium-scale producers. Approximately 20% of its table wine is produced by co-operatives. This has helped the subsector to generate volumes and obtain bargaining power by obliging it to co-ordinate a diversified supply. At the same time, it has ensured a very broad export portfolio, with different grapes, wines, qualities and prices, which is an advantage. Products other than wine such as must, concentrated juices, table grapes and raisins also contribute to the value chain.

Argentina's Malbec variety is emblematic of the country's viticulture, and its international recognition contributes both to the country's brand and to that of its wines. Malbec aside, Argentine wines have not yet developed an internationally consolidated image, nor does the country have recognised brands in the world market. The diversification in export destinations for its wines does not allow it to achieve a significant share in target markets. The development and communication of an identity and a country image is a key element for consumer preference. To this end, continuous work toward the construction of the "Argentine wines" brand is required, as is boosting the international recognition of certain wineries, wine-producing regions and high-end wines.

Table 9.9. SWOT analysis of the viticulture value chain, 2018

Strengths	Weaknesses	Opportunities	Threats
Comparatively advantageous climate, geographical diversity.	Insufficient internal linkages along the value chain.	Changing consumer preferences.	Decrease in local wine consumption.
Dynamic actors.	Weak collective strategies.	Targeting key markets.	New producers with high competitiveness.
Diversified supply.	Low participation and recognition of Argentina in world markets.	Decreasing commercial expansion of traditional wine producers.	Trade barriers and non-tariffs measures.
Malbec as an emblematic variety, an icon of national viticulture.	Lack of financial markets and local investments.	Identity and country image.	Increasing bargaining power of the retail marketing chains.
Domestic market: Argentina is consuming approximately 75% of domestic production.	Weak research and development, and training and extension services.	Quality improvement and innovation in organisations.	Few players in the must market (US-California).
High competition in fine wines.	Inefficiency in vineyard production managerial problems.	Development of wine tourism.	
Long tradition of producer co-operatives.	Insufficient adaptation to changing markets, to market demands.	Increase of wine sales in supermarkets.	
	Negative perception of Argentina as a reliable supplier in international markets.		
	High cost of glass for bottles, domestic suppliers with oligopolistic power and high tariff protection.		

Source: (Lema and Gallacher, 2018[1]).

The viticulture value chain faces several challenges, insufficient internal linkages being among them. For instance, a lack of co-ordination exists between primary producers and wineries. The dominant position held by the wineries allows them to transfer market instability and unpredictability to the primary producers, who are already exposed to significant weather risks. Meanwhile, a lack of horizontal integration among small primary producers inhibits co-ordination and reduces their bargaining power. A need for greater co-ordination between the productive sector and other components of the value chain, such as suppliers of related industries, also exists. The country lacks organisations, institutions and collective strategies that work towards strengthening both the internal market and the export market (Lema and Gallacher, 2018[1]).

Market concentration in industry and potential market power is an issue in the table-wine market. Greater competition is observed as the quality of the wine increases. Independent wine producers appear to be the weakest link in the chain. Some 5 000 small and medium producers are co-operative associated in the secondary co-operative *Fecovita*, which takes advantage of the volume integration, producing approximately 20% of all table wine.

Argentina has limited financial markets and local investors. The influx of foreign capital to the country during the 1990s was largely responsible for the important restructuring that viticulture went through in the last twenty years. Currently, the absence of alternative financing mechanisms to commercial banks limits investment and innovation. As a consequence, research and development (R&D) and training and extension on wine is weak. These shortcomings have led to inefficiency in vineyard production that is transformed into low quality grapes in certain regions. Argentina has also limited adaptability to changing markets. In spite of the varietal reconversion that took place in the 1990s, there is still insufficient adaptation to market demands. This is manifest in a shortage of high-quality red varieties and an excess of pink grapes.

9.4. Policy assessment and recommendations on value chains

During the last decades, growth and innovation in Argentinian agriculture has focused on grain production in the Pampas region. The value chains of the other regions (the "regional economies") suffer from low productivity and lack of dynamism. But this is not unique to the pear-and-apple and wine subsectors analysed in this chapter. Key bottlenecks in the regional economies have not been widely addressed by public policy, and public investment on agricultural infrastructure, R&D, extension and technical assistance, for example, has been limited. This is particularly the case for small producers and for production located in economically poor regions, such as tobacco.

Argentina's apple-and-pear value chain contains a duality in its structure, whereby farms which are fully integrated into value chains (usually large and medium-size ones) coexist with less integrated farms (mostly small-scale ones). Small-scale farms of apples and pears have several difficulties, particular the low use of technology, deficient pest control, old orchards, and in general, very limited investments at the farm level. In terms of agricultural policy, the apple-and-pear value chain has received limited support over the years. Orchard renewal is a crucial factor for the improvement of fruit quality, as is reduction in pest control and labour costs. More recent orchards are generally planted with varieties better adapted to current market conditions. These are characterised by plant densities, plant size and plant arrangements that allow improvements of land and labour productivity. Pear production is slightly more competitive than that of apples.

Until the 1990s, Argentina's *viticulture* value chain was oriented to the domestic market, with occasional exports focused on non-varietal wine and must. During the 1990s, along with the deregulation of the industry, significant investments took place. Foreign and local investors were attracted to the wine sector by the relatively low price and good quality of land, and the promising perspectives in terms of high quality wine exports. Investors developed a wide range of strategies: buying existing wineries, building new ones, acquiring land with existing vineyards and planting in new areas. Argentine exports grew with an increase in the prices and qualities of the wine sold in international markets.

Key public goods in the areas of knowledge and plant health and food safety are provided by public agencies such as INTA and SENASA. However, the innovation system and the public provision of R&D have delivered its main outcomes in the grain sector. The regional economies outside the Pampas region have not been the focus of INTA. INTA's knowledge and technical assistance for these productions could be strengthened by a system of technical assistance by value chain, focused on R&D, extension services to small-scale producers, and pest control.

The future of some small-scale farmers may not lie in agriculture, and non-farm economic alternatives should be explored for a gradual re-allocation of resources such as labour, land and irrigation, and as part of technical and business advice. This could be achieved, for instance, through an increased emphasis on understanding the economics of fruit production, markets, industrialisation and logistics. Areas of knowledge to be analysed and transferred include: production efficiency and technology adoption, returns from orchard renewal and irrigation, managerial decision-making, risk management, marketing and negotiation in the production/processing interface, financial constraints, economies of size/scope, water economics, use of geographical information and monitoring systems, and the regional labour market and its impact on pear and apple production (Lema and Gallacher, 2018[1]).

The survival of small-scale producers of pears and apples is linked to the possible emergence of organisational forms that allow them to participate directly in the benefits accrued through the value chain. Additionally, as co-operatives have limited popularity, new emerging alternatives for organisational structures for improving access to markets by small and medium-sized farmers could be explored. Different types of alliances and forms of integration between the different links in the value chain may successfully compete with larger, multinational operations. A small joint private-public group could analyse and identify alternative organisational forms for the sector.

Two governance structures in the wine production chain coexist. Quality varietal wines are predominantly produced with grapes from own production and through vertical integration. Meanwhile, the production of common or table wines is co-ordinated through the market, with transformation services predominating and low vertical integration. There is a lack of co-ordination between primary producers and wineries for better management of the problems the former face: market instability, unpredictability and climatic risk. Small primary producers could improve their horizontal integration, which would enhance co-ordination and increase bargaining power. Finally, there is a need for greater co-ordination between production and other components of the value chain, such as suppliers of related industries. This is particularly so for the provision of public goods and services such as market information, climatic services and technical support for risk management, all of which would contribute significantly to governance of the value chain.

Viticulture is among the most regulated sectors of the Argentine economy, through the National Institute of Viticulture (INV). Despite the deregulation of the 1990s, the state has some control of all stages of production; public regulation can complement private standards and enhance both public and private efficiency. Potential improvements in regulations include the simplification of procedures and mechanisms of command and control in wine production and export, the distinction between table and fine wines, and the improvement in forecast systems for primary production.

A limiting factor in the viticulture value chain has been the absence of a specialised institution to orient its innovation and transformation processes within a long-term plan, despite COVIAR's attempt to develop a Strategic Viticulture Plan (PEVI). For instance, sector-wide quality improvement and innovation in organisations allows increases in quality and competitiveness to be achieved. Organisational innovation in the industry would help to build networks of knowledge and experience, to comply with appropriate standards and export specialisation, to co-ordinate within the value chain from primary producers to wineries, to improve distribution and marketing systems and to boost R&D, extension and training in new technologies.

Increased participation in export markets is a necessary condition for growth of the apple-and-pear and viticulture value chains. Argentina's domestic demand for food can be expected to increase primarily as a function of (relatively low) population growth, and only secondarily as a result of per-capita income growth. A search for new markets is crucial. The government could develop agricultural promotion offices to facilitate information and access to main importing countries.

References

Ablin, A. (2012), *El Supermercadismo Argentino. Alimentos Argentinos*, Ministerio de Agroindustria, http://www.alimentosargentinos.gob.ar/contenido/sectores/niveldeactividad/08Ago_2012_supermercado.pdf. [6]

CEPAL (2014), *Estudios de las estructuras de mercado de complejos agroindustriales. Cadena vitivinícola*, Documento nº 3 - parte 7, Comisión Económica para América Latina y el Caribe (CEPAL), Buenos Aires. [11]

Elías, J. and G. Ferro (2018), "Understanding innovations and the diffusion of knowledge in new world wines: Conceptual and experimental innovations in Argentina", *Working Paper UCEMA*. [13]

Hak, L. (2009), "Frutícolas retornan a las cooperativas para salvar negocio", *Ámbito Financiero* July 24, 2009. [4]

Lema, D. and M. Gallacher (2018), *Apple, pears and viticulture production in Argentina*, Background report for the OECD Review of Agricultural Policies in Argentina. [1]

Leskovar, E. (2016), *La cadena de valor de manzanas y peras de Río Negro y Neuquén para Mercado Interno*, Asociación Argentina de Economía Agraria. Reunión Anual, Septiembre 2016. [2]

Leskovar, E. (2015), *Comercialización externa de manzanas y peras de río Negro y Neuquén: Aproximación a la identificación de canales relevantes*, Asociación Argentina de Economía Agraria, Reunión Anual, Septiembre 2015. [7]

Ministerio de Hacienda (2016), *Informes de Cadenas de Valor: Frutícola - Manazana y Pera*, Subsecretaría de Programación Microeconómica, Ministerio de Hacienda y Finanzas Públicas Presidencia de la Nación. [3]

Ministerio de Hacienda (2016), *Informes de Cadenas de Valor: Vitivinicultura*, Sud Secretaria de Programación MicroeconómicaMinisterio de Hacienda y Finanzas Públicas Presidencia de la Nación Ministro de Hacienda y Finanzas Públicas. [10]

Ruíz, A. (2011), *Prospectiva y estrategia: El caso del plan estratégico vitivinícola 2020 (PEVI)*. [12]

Sturzenegger, A. (2017), *Producción de peras y manzanas en el Valle de Río Negro. Un programa de acción*, Ministerio de Agroindustria (Argentina). [9]

USDA (2011), "Understanding cooperatives: Farmer cooperative statistics", *Cooperative Information Report* 45, Section 13. [5]

Villareal (2011), *Balance frutícola 2009-2010. Manzanas y peras*, Secretaría de Fruticultura de Río Negro. [8]

Notes

[1] This section is based on the consultant background paper (Lema and Gallacher, 2018[1]).

[2] The Herfindhal-Hirshman index is a measure of the size of firms in relation to the industry and an indicator of the amount of competition among them. A number below 0.01 (or 100) indicates a highly competitive industry. A result below 0.15 (or 1 500) indicates an un-concentrated industry. A number between 0.15 to 0.25 (or 1 500 to 2 500) indicates moderate concentration. And an index above 0.25 (above 2 500) indicates high concentration.

[3] Belrose is a market intelligence firm located in the state of Washington, United States.

[4] Production efficiency includes output growth, output variability, area of abandoned orchards, percentage of new varieties. Infrastructure: plant capacity and age, marketing system, irrigation availability, labour availability. Financing and markets: interest rates, inflation rates, property rights, distance to markets.

Annex A. Main agro-industrial organisations in Argentina

Agricultores Federados Argentinos (AFA). AFA was created in 1932 and is the main agricultural first level co-operative in Argentina and one of the largest in Latin America. AFA is formed by 36 000 member producers, 1 600 permanent employees in 26 Primary Centres, which together with the Sub-Centres, Offices and Representations have a presence in 130 locations in nine Argentine provinces: Santa Fe, Buenos Aires, Córdoba, Entre Rios, Santiago del Estero, Chaco, Salta, Tucumán and San Luis. AFA stockpiles around 5 million tonnes of agricultural production per year, has a storage capacity of 3 million tonnes and more than 220 trucks. It also provides a diverse range of services throughout the year and to its members. In recent years, it has supported projects aimed at adding value to primary production, deepening processes of industrialisation of raw materials and agro-inputs, as well as generating new services for collection and commercialisation. http://afa.afascl.coop/index.php

Asociación Argentina de Consorcios Regionales de Experimentación Agrícola (AACREA). AACREA was founded in 1957 by a small group of agricultural farmers with the idea of sharing experiences on different production systems. These farmers created the first Regional Consortium for Agricultural Experiments (CREA). Its main objective is to help its members to become economically and environmentally sustainable through the provision of technical assistance and knowledge sharing. Furthermore, it promotes testing and adoption of new technology among its members. Experimentation, capacity building and technology transfer are some of its main actions. It promotes exchanges and collaboration with national and international experts. Finally, it collects, processes and analyses information, and makes it available to its members. https://www.aacrea.org.ar/

Asociación Argentina de Girasol (ASAGIR). ASAGIR is a non-profit civil association to promote and develop sunflower production and its by-products, and to promote the sunflower business. The association was created in 2004 and it integrates more than 20 main actors of the value chain at the level of inputs, primary production, marketing and storage, industry and scientific-technological members. As a priority objective, the association develops actions to ensure the competitiveness of the sunflower production and its derivatives, through the organisation and promotion of research and development activities of sunflower and its by-products, as well as those related to its production, industrialisation, promotion and commercialisation. http://www.asagir.org.ar/

Asociación Argentina de Trigo (ARGENTRIGO). ARGENTRIGO represents agro-industrial wheat production. The association is formed by all actors of the wheat value chain, such as research and genetic institutes, agrochemicals, production, industry – manufacturing, storage, transport, export, and marketing services. Its main objective is the promotion and development of wheat production and its derivatives to enhance the profitability of the wheat value chain, in collaboration with government and private and public-private entities, through research, production, processing, commercialisation and marketing. It was created in 2004 and comprises 44 members (corporations, academic institutes, agroindustry, etc.). http://www.argentrigo.org.ar

Asociación de Cooperativas Argentinas (ACA). An organisation of co-operatives, ACA was created in 1922. ACA is made up of 150 agricultural co-operatives, equivalent to 50 000 producers, and represents a fundamental part of the Argentine agro-industrial value chain. The 150 co-operatives are present in 600 locations across the country in the provinces of Buenos Aires, Cordoba, Chaco, Entre Rios, La Pampa, Río Negro, Santa Fe and Santiago del Estero. ACA provides different services to its members, including commercialisation, input provision, credit, transportation and storage. http://www.acacoop.com.ar/

Asociación de la Cadena de la Soja Argentina (ACSOJA). ACSOJA is a non-profit civil association that was created in 2004 to represent soybean producers. It aims at improving the competitiveness of the soybean supply chain, by creating research and studies of key priorities of the chain. ACSOJA, promotes the scientific-technical research in production and industry areas, as well as commercialisation (by generating new external markets) of the high-quality by-products of soybean. ACSOJA, tries to develop new process and technologies and promotes the formation of ventures on the current and new uses of soybean. The organisation also interacts with public and private entities and organisations to encourage collective actions for a better social impact. http://www.acsoja.org.ar/

Asociación Argentina de Productores en Siembra Directa (AAPRESID). The association of no-till producers, AAPRESID is a non-profit, non-governmental organisation, integrated by a network of agricultural producers that, based on their interest in soil conservation, adopted and promoted the diffusion of the no-till production system. AAPRESID was created in 1989 and is a key player in the dissemination and adoption of No-Till in Argentina. Its main objective is to promote sustainable production systems of food, fibre and energy, through innovation, science and network knowledge management. AAPRESID promotes the exchange of knowledge, opens up its fields to producers to observe production systems, participates in technical trials, maintains strong international connections, and interacts with public and private organisations to achieve an integral development of the sector. Its actions respond to challenges of sustainable agricultural development such as environmental protection, more and better food systems, and new sources of renewable energy. By 2016 around 34 million hectares of the main grains in Argentina are under the no-till production system. http://www.aapresid.org.ar/

Asociación de Productores Exportadores Argentinos (APEA). APEA is a non-profit association of beef producers and exporters that was created in 2003, but its roots date back to the 1930s. Its main objective is to carry out any type of promotional, technical, scientific, research or administrative activity that supports the commercial activity of beef exports. Members include non-profit civil beef associations, beef co-operatives, breeders associations, and groups of beef producers. http://www.apea.org.ar/

Asociación Maíz Argentino (MAIZAR). MAIZAR brings together stakeholders of the scientific, productive, commercial, industrial, food and export chains of corn and sorghum. MAIZAR has over 120 plenary or adherent members (associations, chambers, organisations, stock exchange boards, universities, agro-industries, public institutions, etc.) promoting the production of maize and sorghum. Created in March 2004, MAIZAR's main objectives are to increase efficiency of the corn value chain by improving the competitiveness of the companies and institutions of the corn and sorghum chains; and to promote economic and social development in areas where the corn and sorghum value chains exist. http://www.maizar.org.ar/

Cámara de la Industria Argentina de Fertilizantes y Agroquímicos (CIAFA). CIAFA was created in 1990. Its main objective is to coordinate companies that manufacture, formulate, market and distribute fertilisers, phyto-sanitary products and their additives and/or components, as well as seeds, biological products and any other product related to sanitary issues or agricultural improvement. CIAFA is a main reference of the agrochemical industry in Argentina, grouping most of the companies that synthesise and formulate phyto-sanitary products and fertilisers in the country. http://www.ciafa.org.ar

Cámara de la Sanidad Agropecuaria y Fertilizantes (CASAFE). CASAFE is a business association that represents the Crop Science Industry and its partner companies. It is in charge of the requirements of the industry, within the national and international legal framework, on issues such as the promotion of good agricultural practices and responsible management of plant protection products. It also supports the sustainability of the phyto-sanitary products business based on three pillars: the environment, technology and institutional relations. http://www.casafe.org/

Centro de la Industria Lechera (CIL). CIL is a non-profit business association of a civil nature, which brings together small, medium and large dairy industries, wholesalers and milk producers. It was founded in 1919. The fundamental objectives pursued by CIL are: fostering the spirit of association among its members; contributing to the legislation related to the milk subsector that supports the economic progress of the agroindustry; improving scientific-technical capacity of all its members; disseminating scientific and technical knowledge; and boosting, channelling and advising the production and commercialisation of dairy products. At present, CIL associates the largest actors in the sector, who process between 65% and 70% of the industrialised milk in the country. www.cil.org.ar/

Comisión Nacional Asesora de Biotecnología Agropecuaria (CONABIA). Since 1991, Argentina regulates activities related to genetically modified organisms (GMOs) for agricultural use. To this end, the National Advisory Commission on Agricultural Biotechnology (CONABIA, Resolution 124/91) was created as an evaluation and consultation body within the remit of the Ministry of Agriculture, Livestock and Fisheries (SAGyP). At the beginning, CONABIA was in charge of the entire regulatory and evaluation process, with the administrative support of an area of the SAGyP called Technical Co-ordination of the CONABIA and then the Biotechnology Office. As these activities increased and became more demanding, CONABIA and the Biotechnology Office increased their roles. Both CONABIA and the Biotechnology Office aim to guarantee the biosecurity of the agroecosystem. For this, they follow-up, analyse and pre-evaluate the applications submitted to develop activities with GMOs. Based on scientific and technical information and quantitative data regarding the biosecurity of the GMO, they issue non-binding opinions jointly with the Secretariat of Agroindustry, the Application Authority, which authorises the requested activities. https://www.agroindustria.gob.ar/sitio/areas/biotecnologia/conabia/

Confederación Argentina de la Mediana Empresa (CAME). In July 1956, the Argentine Confederation of Medium-sized Enterprises (CAME) was created to discuss collective labour agreements in the commercial sector. CAME is a business association that represents 1 544 federations, chambers, centres and business unions. Through the sectors of Industry, Commerce, Regional Economies, SMEs-Young (CAME-*Jóven*), Women Entrepreneurs (*Mujeres Empresarias*), and Tourism programmes, they gather more than 600 thousand SMEs that employ around 4 200 000 registered workers. CAME's main objectives are: to channel the different problems linked to the primary productive sector in order to provide concrete solutions, and to formalise policies and concrete proposals through regional meetings and sectoral workshops to address the different demands of producers. http://redcame.org.ar/

Confederación Intercooperativa Agropecuaria Limitada (CONINAGRO). Founded on 18 September 1956, CONINAGRO is an organisation that brings together ten federations of co-operatives that, in turn, represent 120 000 agricultural farmers. The main objective of CONINAGRO is to have direct contact with the government on all issues relating to agricultural production co-operatives. Those co-operatives look after the economic interests of their members and provide different types of services, such as financial, extension, marketing services, and others. http://www.coninagro.org.ar/

Confederaciones Rurales Argentinas (CRA). CRA was founded in 1943. It is formed by 16 confederations and federations, which are, in turn, integrated by more than 300 rural societies throughout the country. In total, just over 109 000 agricultural producers (small, medium, and large scale) are represented through the actions of CRA. The main objective of CRA has been the protection of the interests of agricultural producers. It also promotes the development of agricultural production activities. Some of the federations and confederations that are part of the CRA are: Confederación de Asociaciones Rurales de Mendoza. Confederación de Asociaciones Rurales de Buenos Aires y La Pampa (CARBAP); Confederación de Asociaciones Rurales de la Provincia de Santa Fe (CARSFE); Confederación de Asociaciones Rurales de la Tercera Zona (CARTEZ); Confederación de Asociaciones Rurales de Tucumán. Confederación de Asociaciones Rurales de Chaco y Formosa; Federación de Sociedades Rurales del Chubut; Confederación Rural de San Luis. Asociación de Sociedades Rurales de Corrientes; Federación de Asociaciones Agropecuarias Santiagueñas; Federación de Asociaciones Rurales de Entre Ríos; Federación de Entidades Rurales de Salta; Federación Ruralista de Jujuy; Federación de Instituciones Agropecuarias de Santa Cruz; Federación de Sociedades Rurales de Río Negro. http://www.cra.org.ar/

Coordinadora de las Industrias de Productos Alimenticios (COPAL). COPAL was created in 1975 with the objective of incorporating the needs and voice of the food industry into the agroindustrial sector. Its central objectives are to foster and promote a strategic vision of the role and importance of the food and beverage industry as a fundamental vector for economic and social development. It aims to achieve a greater international insertion of Argentina, as well as to actively promote agro-industrial integration, both at the level of its economic activities and the entities it represents. Some of subsectors included in COPAL are: beef and derivatives; poultry meat and derivatives; fishing and by-products; dairy products; fresh and processed fruits and vegetables; sauces and preserves; infusions; milling products; bakery, pasta and cookies; candies and chocolates; margarines and hydrogenated products; drinks without alcohol; juices; wines; beers; spirits; sugar; spices, condiments, mayonnaises and dressings; ferments and colorants; starches and glucose; dietary foods; salt; ice creams; and dried vegetables. https://copal.org.ar/

Corporación Vitivinícola Argentina (COVIAR). COVIAR is a public-private body that manages and articulates actions to fulfil the objectives of the Strategic Viticulture Plan for Argentina 2020 (PEVI), through the organisation and integration of actors of the productive value chain and through the innovation of products and processes that increase value added of the sub-sector. The Plan PEVI was created in 2000 and established the actions to develop the wine sector in Argentina. http://coviar.com.ar/

Federación Agraria Argentina (FAA). FAA was created 15 August 1912 as an organisation dealing with the agrarian reform and land struggle, representing small-scale farmers, agricultural workers and landless people. Since its creation, FAA's main objectives have remained the provision of inputs, domestic and international commercialisation of products, access to land and land use, and the search for a sustainable and inclusive rural development for its members. Since its creation, FAA established a network of services for accessing land and extension services, and insurance and financial services, for accessing inputs, for marketing production domestic and internationally, as well for addressing problems of health in rural areas. http://www.faa.com.ar/Contenido/home.html

Fertilizar Asociación Civil (FERTILIZAR). FERTILIZAR promotes the rational use of fertilisers throughout the country and the conservation of the soil resource through the dissemination of technical-scientific information adapted to the local reality, which promotes the agronomic and economic advantages of the adequate balance of nutrients on crop and pasture productivity and on soil fertility, contributing to a sustainable agriculture. https://www.fertilizar.org.ar/

Instituto de Promoción de Carne Vacuna Argentina (IPCVA). IPCVA is a public non-governmental institution founded on December 2001, following the passage of the National Statute N°25.507 by agreement of all the beef chain representatives. The IPCVA is funded through the collection of levies paid by the country's producers and packers. The IPCVA improves and consolidates the image of Argentine beef products, taking into account the vast history and tradition of the country. The IPCVA is committed to increase the competitiveness of the entire beef chain by providing sectorial expertise and information for the decision-making process in business and also contributing to the creation of improved business environments, both in domestic and foreign markets. Its main activities include: to identify and create demand for Argentine beef products in domestic and foreign markets; to design and develop marketing strategies to improve the competitiveness of Argentine beef products overseas; to plan and develop promotion strategies to contribute to the improvement of domestic consumption levels; to work to consolidate Argentine beef quality and security, contributing to the efficiency of productive and industrial processes. http://www.ipcva.com.ar/

Sociedad Rural Argentina (SRA). SRA is part of the Nation's economic and political history. Founded in 1866, SRA is a civil association that has the following aims: to watch over the agricultural and livestock heritage of the country and encourage its development; to promote stability of people in the countryside by improving rural life in all its aspects; to contribute to the improvement of the techniques, methods and procedures applicable to rural tasks and the development and advancement of complementary and derived industries; and to defend agricultural interests. https://www.sra.org.ar/

Annex B. Argentina's main agricultural products

Cattle (beef): The main stock is found in the Province of Buenos Aires (35%), followed by Santa Fe (11.5%), Córdoba and Corrientes (9% each), Entre Ríos (8%), La Pampa (6%), and Chaco (5%). Thus, the central region covers more than 60% of the stock, with more than 33.5 million heads.

Citrus fruit: Citrus fruit accounts for about 50% of total fruit produced in the country. These fruits are mostly grown in the Northwest and Northeast, based on two different productive models. The Northwest is specialised in lemon (the main citrus produced in Argentina, accounting for 47% of the total), and Tucumán is the biggest producer (with more than 70%). Tucumán also grows grapefruit to a lesser extent (5% of citrus production). The Northeast is specialised in sweet citrus fruits, namely orange and tangerine (33% and 15%, respectively). The citrus-producing Northeast covers the provinces of Entre Ríos, Corrientes and Misiones (in the region between the Paraná and Uruguay rivers), which together grow 72% of oranges and 91% of tangerines in the country. Other areas growing sweet citrus fruit are found in Jujuy, Salta, Buenos Aires and Tucumán.

Corn: Córdoba is the main corn producer (with 30.1% of the seeded surface in the last campaign), followed by Buenos Aires (27.3%), Santa Fe (10.6%), Santiago del Estero (8.9%), La Pampa (5.6%), Entre Ríos (4.5%), San Luis (4.5%), Chaco (3.5%) and Salta (3.1%).

Cotton: The province of Chaco has historically represented the area of greatest cotton production, with its relative contribution ranging from 50% and 70% of the total. It is followed by Santiago del Estero, which in the 90s became the second biggest cotton producer in the country. Other producing provinces are Santa Fe, Salta, Formosa, San Luis, Entre Ríos, Corrientes and Córdoba. 89% of cotton plants are located in the primary production area, mainly in Chaco, Santiago del Estero and Santa Fe.

Dairy (milk): Production is concentrated in the Pampas region, in Santa Fe (35%), Córdoba (31%) and Buenos Aires (23%), and then followed by Entre Ríos (7%). These four provinces account for 96% of dairy farms and 96% of dairy livestock. The provinces of Santiago del Estero and La Pampa have a lower contribution.

Fishing: Sea fishing unloading is mostly concentrated in the ports of Mar del Plata (54.7% of the total – Province of Buenos Aires), where a significant fishing fleet operates, followed by Puerto Madryn (13.7% – Chubut), Puerto Deseado (8.2% – Santa Cruz) and Ushuaia (6.9% – Tierra del Fuego), where the freezing fleet operates almost exclusively.

Forestry: Six forestry regions can be identified in the Argentine territory: the forests of Parque Chaqueño, the jungle in Selva Misionera, the jungle in Selva Tucumano Boliviana, the Andean Patagonic forest in Bosque Andino Patagónico, the woodlands in Monte and the plains in Espinal. Extraction of tree trunks from the native forest: Chaco 56%, Formosa 13%, Salta 12%, Tierra del Fuego 7%, Santiago del Estero 4%, Misiones

4%. Extraction of tree trunks from the planted forest: Misiones 44%, Corrientes 31%, Entre Ríos 17%, Buenos Aires 3%, Córdoba 1%, Santa Fe 1%. More than half of the production of cellulose is conducted in Misiones (50.2%), followed by Santa Fe (18.8%), Buenos Aires (12.9%), Jujuy (12.8%) and Tucumán (4.5%).

Oil seeds (soybeans and sunflower): Buenos Aires, Córdoba and Santa Fe lead the production of soybeans, accounting for three quarters of the total surface where the crop is cultivated. The provinces of Santiago del Estero, Salta, Tucumán and Chaco incorporated or considerably increased the production of soy in the last decade. Sunflower growing is more concentrated: the province of Buenos Aires alone accounts for 51.8%, and the total area growing sunflower in La Pampa, Chaco and Santa Fe is over 94%.

Pears and apples: These account for about 30% of the total national fruit production, with a focus on the Northern Patagonian valleys (Río Negro and Neuquén), which represent around 90% of the total produced. Río Negro is the main producer (78%). Mendoza contributes to about 10% of the national production.

Pigmeat: More than 63% of the pig-meat production and 90% of the slaughter are found in the central region, mainly in Buenos Aires, Córdoba and Santa Fe. Breeding locations match the surfaces growing corn and the distribution of plants producing balanced feed, one of the main inputs for primary production.

Poultry: Feedlots for meat production are mostly found in the provinces of Entre Ríos (52%) and Buenos Aires (31%), especially near big urban centres. However, almost half the industrial plants are found in Buenos Aires (47%), and to a lesser extent in Entre Ríos (29%).

Rice: Corrientes represents 44% of the seeded surface in the last campaign, followed by Entre Ríos with 34.4%, Santa Fe with 15.5% and Formosa with 3.6%.

Stone fruit (plum and peach): Stone fruit accounts for 9.4% of total fruits produced in the country. Plum and peach stand out, with specific varieties for fresh and industrial use, with the latter being more relevant. Mendoza is the main producer (83%), due to its appropriate weather conditions. Other areas producing stone fruit are Buenos Aires, Río Negro, San Juan and Neuquén. Fresh fruit represents 26% of the growth of peach and plum in Mendoza, using 8 000 hectares. Fruit for industrial processing accounts for the remaining 74%. The surface seeded with peach and plum for industrial use amounts to 25.7 thousand hectares.

Tobacco: Jujuy is the province with the largest tobacco production, and with Salta they concentrate almost all the national production of Virginia (99%), almost 70% of the national tobacco production.

Wheat: Buenos Aires is the main wheat producer (with 33.4% of the seeded area in the last campaign), followed by Córdoba (24.2%), Santa Fe (16.3%), Santiago del Estero (7.4%), Entre Ríos (6.5%) and La Pampa (5.4%).

Wine: Mendoza and San Juan are the provinces with the broadest surface seeded with vines, thus concentrating the largest wine production and accounting for 76% and 18% thereof, respectively. Other provinces with outstanding production are Rioja, Salta, Catamarca, Neuquén and Río Negro.

Table A B.1. Main products produced in each province

Provinces	Agricultural product
Buenos Aires	Cattle, poultry, pigs and sheep, dairy, fishing, soybeans, corn, sunflower, wheat, barley, and onion
Catamarca	Walnut, olive, cattle and goats
Chaco	Cotton, forestry, soybeans, sunflower, and cattle
Chubut	Sheep and fishing
Córdoba	Cattle, pigs, dairy, corn, soybeans, wheat, sunflower, sorghum, peanut
Corrientes	Sheep, cattle, yerba mate, tea, sweet citrus fruits (orange and tangerine), forestry, rice and vegetables (tomato and pepper)
Entre Ríos	Rice, cattle, poultry, dairy, sweet citrus fruits (orange and tangerine), blueberries, chickpeas
Formosa	Fruits (banana, grapefruit, watermelon), vegetables (zucchini, squash, sweet potato, forestry, rice
Jujuy	Tobacco, sugar, legumes (beans)
La Pampa	Sunflower, corn, rye, oats, cattle, dairy
La Rioja	Walnut, olive, wine.
Mendoza	Wine, stone fruit (plum and peach), olive, garlic, goats
Misiones	Yerba mate, tea, forestry, sweet citrus fruits (tangerine; orange and grapefruit), tobacco
Neuquén	Pear, apple, goats
Río Negro	Pear, apple, sheep
Salta	Tobacco, legumes (bean and chickpeas), sugar, wine, citrus (grapefruit, orange, lemon), forestry, soybeans, goats
San Juan	Wine, olive, vegetables (garlic, onion, icicle tomato)
San Luis	Corn, sorghum, livestock
Santa Cruz	Sheep and fishing
Santa Fe	Cattle, pigs, dairy, soybeans, sunflower, corn, wheat legumes (lentil and chickpeas).
Santiago del Estero	Cotton, soybeans, corn, wheat, sorghum, beans, cattle, goats, forestry
Tierra del Fuego, Antarctica and Southern Atlantic Islands	Fishing and sheep
Tucumán	Lemon, sugar, vegetables, cotton, soybeans, blueberries, tobacco

Source: Background information by sector provided by the Ministry of Agroindustry for this OECD review.

Annex C. OECD indicators of support to agriculture

Indicators of Support for Producers

Producer Support Estimate (PSE): the annual monetary value of gross transfers from consumers and taxpayers to agricultural producers, measured at the farm gate level, arising from policy measures that support agriculture, regardless of their nature, objectives or impacts on farm production or income.

Percentage PSE (%PSE): PSE as a share of gross farm receipts (including support).

Producer Nominal Assistance Coefficient (producer NAC): the ratio between the value of gross farm receipts (including support) and gross farm receipts valued at border prices (measured at farm gate).

Producer Nominal Protection Coefficient (producer NPC): the ratio between the average price received by producers at farm gate (including payments per tonne of current output), and the border price (measured at farm gate). The NPC is also available by commodity.

Producer Single Commodity Transfers (producer SCT): the annual monetary value of gross transfers from consumers and taxpayers to agricultural producers, measured at the farm gate level, arising from policy measures directly linked to the production of a single commodity such that the producer must produce the designated commodity in order to receive the transfer.

Producer Percentage Single Commodity Transfers (producer %SCT): the commodity SCT as a share of gross farm receipts for the specific commodity.

Indicators of Support to Consumers

Consumer Support Estimate (CSE): the annual monetary value of gross transfers from (to) consumers of agricultural commodities, measured at the farm gate level, arising from policy measures that support agriculture, regardless of their nature, objectives or impacts on consumption of farm products.

Percentage CSE (%CSE): CSE as a share of consumption expenditure (measured at farm gate) net of taxpayer transfers to consumers.

Consumer Nominal Assistance Coefficient (consumer NAC): the ratio between the value of consumption expenditure on agricultural commodities (at farm gate) and that valued at border prices (measured at farm gate).

Consumer Nominal Protection Coefficient (consumer NPC): the ratio between the average price paid by consumers (at farm gate) and the border price (measured at farm gate).

Consumer Single Commodity Transfers (consumer SCT): the annual monetary value of gross transfers from (to) consumers of agricultural commodities, measured at the farm gate level, arising from policy measures directly linked to the production of a single commodity.

Indicators of Support to General Services for Agriculture

General Services Support Estimate (GSSE): the annual monetary value of gross transfers to general services provided to agricultural producers collectively (such as research, development, training, inspection, marketing and promotion), arising from policy measures that support agriculture, regardless of their nature, objectives and impacts on farm production, income, or consumption. The GSSE does not include any transfers to individual producers.

Percentage GSSE (%GSSE): GSSE as a share of Total Support Estimate (TSE).

Indicators of Total Support to Agriculture

Total Support Estimate (TSE): the annual monetary value of all gross transfers from taxpayers and consumers arising from policy measures that support agriculture, net of associated budgetary receipts, regardless of their objectives and impacts on farm production and income, or consumption of farm products.

Percentage TSE (%TSE): TSE as a share of GDP.

Annex D. Argentina: Estimates of support to agriculture

Table A D.1. Estimates of support to agriculture, ARS million

	1997-99	2015-17	2015	2016	2017
Total value of production (at farm gate)	**22 032**	**551 871**	**395 802**	**640 621**	**619 191**
of which: share of MPS commodities (%)	*76.5*	*85.6*	*82.7*	*86.2*	*87.9*
Total value of consumption (at farm gate)	**11 401**	**328 136**	**242 120**	**350 308**	**391 981**
Producer Support Estimate (PSE)	**94**	**-75 958**	**-105 484**	**-66 792**	**-55 599**
Support based on commodity output	36	-80 240	-108 782	-70 858	-61 080
Market Price Support[1]	7	-81 808	-110 121	-72 467	-62 836
Payments based on output	29	1 568	1 339	1 609	1 756
Payments based on input use	58	4 124	3 141	3 908	5 323
Based on variable input use	5	300	279	273	348
with input constraints	0	0	0	0	0
Based on fixed capital formation	38	2 809	2 107	2 687	3 632
with input constraints	0	0	0	0	0
Based on on-farm services	15	1 015	756	947	1 343
with input constraints	0	0	0	0	0
Payments based on current A/An/R/I, production required	0	158	156	158	159
Based on Receipts / Income	0	0	0	0	0
Based on Area planted / Animal numbers	0	158	156	158	159
with input constraints	0	158	156	158	159
Payments based on non-current A/An/R/I, production required	0	0	0	0	0
Payments based on non-current A/An/R/I, production not required	0	0	0	0	0
With variable payment rates	0	0	0	0	0
with commodity exceptions	0	0	0	0	0
With fixed payment rates	0	0	0	0	0
with commodity exceptions	0	0	0	0	0
Payments based on non-commodity criteria	0	0	0	0	0
Based on long-term resource retirement	0	0	0	0	0
Based on a specific non-commodity output	0	0	0	0	0
Based on other non-commodity criteria	0	0	0	0	0
Miscellaneous payments	0	0	0	0	0
Percentage PSE (%)	**0.4**	**-13.6**	**-26.3**	**-10.3**	**-8.9**
Producer NPC (coeff.)	**1.00**	**0.86**	**0.77**	**0.90**	**0.90**
Producer NAC (coeff.)	**1.00**	**0.88**	**0.79**	**0.91**	**0.92**
General Services Support Estimate (GSSE)	**174**	**8 292**	**6 934**	**7 902**	**10 039**
Agricultural knowledge and innovation	133	4 106	3 187	4 075	5 057
Inspection and control	23	2 170	1 846	1 835	2 829
Development and maintenance of infras	17	1 952	1 802	1 978	2 077
Marketing and promotion	0	63	100	13	76
Cost of public stockholding	0	0	0	0	0
Miscellaneous	0	0	0	0	0
Percentage GSSE (% of TSE)	**65.0**	**-12.3**	**-7.0**	**-13.4**	**-22.0**
Consumer Support Estimate (CSE)	**-82**	**23 523**	**35 191**	**15 285**	**20 094**
Transfers to producers from consumers	-65	29 453	44 623	18 934	24 801
Other transfers from consumers	-7	-56	-18	-50	-100
Transfers to consumers from taxpayers	0	0	0	0	0
Excess feed cost	-10	-5 873	-9 414	-3 599	-4 607
Percentage CSE (%)	**-0.7**	**7.2**	**14.5**	**4.4**	**5.1**
Consumer NPC (coeff.)	**1.01**	**0.92**	**0.84**	**0.95**	**0.94**
Consumer NAC (coeff.)	**1.01**	**0.93**	**0.87**	**0.96**	**0.95**
Total Support Estimate (TSE)	**267**	**-67 667**	**-98 551**	**-58 890**	**-45 559**
Transfers from consumers	72	-29 397	-44 605	-18 884	-24 701
Transfers from taxpayers	202	-38 214	-53 928	-39 956	-20 758
Budget revenues	-7	-56	-18	-50	-100
Percentage TSE (% of GDP)	**0.1**	**-0.8**	**-1.7**	**-0.7**	**-0.4**
GDP deflator 1997-99 = 100	**100**	**1 916**	**1 383**	**1 937**	**2 428**

Note: NPC: Nominal Protection Coefficient. NAC: Nominal Assistance Coefficient.
A=area planted), An=animal numbers, R=receipts, I=income.

1. MPS commodities for Argentina are: wheat, maize, soybean, sunflower, fruit and vegetables, milk, beef, pigmeat, poultry and eggs. MPS is net of producer levies and Excess Feed Cost.

Source: OECD (2018), "Producer and Consumer Estimates", OECD Agriculture Statistics Database.

ORGANISATION FOR ECONOMIC CO-OPERATION AND DEVELOPMENT

The OECD is a unique forum where governments work together to address the economic, social and environmental challenges of globalisation. The OECD is also at the forefront of efforts to understand and to help governments respond to new developments and concerns, such as corporate governance, the information economy and the challenges of an ageing population. The Organisation provides a setting where governments can compare policy experiences, seek answers to common problems, identify good practice and work to co-ordinate domestic and international policies.

The OECD member countries are: Australia, Austria, Belgium, Canada, Chile, the Czech Republic, Denmark, Estonia, Finland, France, Germany, Greece, Hungary, Iceland, Ireland, Israel, Italy, Japan, Korea, Latvia, Lithuania, Luxembourg, Mexico, the Netherlands, New Zealand, Norway, Poland, Portugal, the Slovak Republic, Slovenia, Spain, Sweden, Switzerland, Turkey, the United Kingdom and the United States. The European Union takes part in the work of the OECD.

OECD Publishing disseminates widely the results of the Organisation's statistics gathering and research on economic, social and environmental issues, as well as the conventions, guidelines and standards agreed by its members.

OECD PUBLISHING, 2, rue André-Pascal, 75775 PARIS CEDEX 16
(51 2019 01 1 P) ISBN 978-92-64-31168-8 – 2019

Printed by Libri Plureos GmbH in Hamburg,
Germany

9 789264 311688